YADAV

'An extraordinary tale of a difficult but ultimately happy collision between two very different worlds… Remarkable, honest, funny and frequently very moving'
William Dalrymple, author of *White Mughals*

'Told with honesty, this story is laced with details about the simple rural life, sights and sounds of places that the couple travel together. What's also remarkable is how Lowe makes Yadav come alive in the book…'
The Times of India

'Like the best kind of documentary film, it opens doors inside the walls of our own minds and hearts, showing us what we could all find if only we bothered to look'
The Pioneer, India

'The clash of civilisations becomes the clasp of civilisations… her sparse style gives this very personal journey of discovery a life and poignancy of its own… a story worth telling – and reading'
India Today

'a pleasurable, picaresque odyssey… Jill's attention to details while describing various Indian cities is superb'
The Tribune, India

'*Yadav* gives an impartial view of India and its people, with a love story running in the backdrop… The story highlights the differences between Jill and Yadav, their families and histories. At the same time it emphasizes the insurmountable power of love…'
Today, New Delhi

'a very real story, and very realistically written… It so happens that *Yadav* the book seems much like Yadav the man. Loving, but intrinsically down to earth'
The Statesman

'enchanting'
Friday magazine, *Gulf News*

'Jill Lowe's book will haunt you long after the ending… She finds the heart of India, and shows it, pulsating and alive, to the reader'
Harold Carlton, author of *Labels* and *The Handsomest Sons in the World*

YADAV: FINDING THE HEART OF INDIA

First published by Penguin Books India in 2003 as *Yadav: A Roadside Love Story*

This edition published in 2005 by Summersdale Publishers Ltd

Summersdale Publishers Ltd
46 West Street
Chichester
West Sussex
PO19 1RP
UK

www.summersdale.com

Printed and bound in Great Britain.

ISBN 1 84024 056 3

Acknowledgements

I started writing a diary the day I first landed in India. The diary grew and grew, but it wasn't until I went on a writing course in the depths of Devonshire, taught by William Dalrymple, that I began to think seriously about turning it into a book. 'Just write,' Willie said. 'Stop doing anything else and write.' So I did, and I must thank Willie first and foremost for his encouragement.

I would also like to thank my dear friend Paul Hoppe, advertising copywriter extraordinaire ('Put a tiger in your tank' was his), who sat with me hour after hour in his tiny flat in Bayswater editing my over-long sentences, double adjectives and clichés. It was Paul, more than anyone, who taught me how to write. Another dear friend and professional editor, Allison Selfridge, did a great deal of preliminary work as well.

Anne Morrow and her husband Gay Fenn Smith encouraged me at every turn and introduced me to Hilary Rubinstein, who in turn kept me going with his enthusiasm. My best writing friend has been Harold Carlton, who, despite being deep in the middle of writing his own book, found time to read and evaluate mine.

My school friend Genette Dagtoglu, having long ago helped me with Latin prep, also read and advised me on the manuscript; Genefer Jeffers kept pace with my constant revisions; Fred and Juliette Redding read, criticised and assisted; my brother John Lowe sent cryptic but apt comments from his farmhouse in France; Michael Boyle helped organise loose ends for me in England; and Prafula Mohanti and Derek More have shown continuing support and interest.

In India, my greatest thanks go to Yadav's and my best friends Annie and Martin Howard, who, apart from their ever-willing help and support, introduced us to Sunil Sethi, who I would like to thank for his help and encouragement, and to Manjula Padmanabhan, who became a good friend and instigated my meeting with Penguin India.

Many thanks to Christine Cipriani for her sympathetic editing after all of the above. In the face of my rantings and ravings about I'm not quite sure what, she often made order out of chaos.

Finally, of course, my thanks go mainly to my husband Yadav, without whom there wouldn't even have been a diary, let alone a book.

Yadav's Family

Krishan Singh	Father
Ma	Mother

Corrupt Brother — Eldest brother
Radha — Wife, and sister of Boss Brother's wife
Raja Singh — Son
Meena — Daughter-in-law
Anil — Grandson
Kamal — Grandson

Boss Brother — Second brother
Suman — Wife, and sister of Corrupt Brother's wife
Rama — Son
Nirmala — Daughter-in-law
Anu — Granddaughter
Vini — Grandson

Ramesh — Third brother
Shanti — Wife
Hanuman — Son
Hari Ram — Son
Bubli — Son

Yadav — Fourth brother; widowed
Sarita — Daughter
Manu — Son-in-law
Purdeep — Grandson
Sunita — Granddaughter
Meenakshi — Daughter
Rahul — Son-in-law
Chenamunia — Granddaughter
Puja — Daughter
Raja Ram — Son-in-law
Krishan — Grandson
Anita — Granddaughter
Ashok — Son

Sarti — Yadav's younger sister
Ravi — Son

Jagdish — Cousin; lawyer
Sunil — Shanti's nephew; policeman
Dinesh — Yadav's best friend; barber
Sushila — Dinesh's wife

*To my darling Yadav and his family
and in memory of my mother-in-law, Ma,
who died peacefully at her farm in 1998*

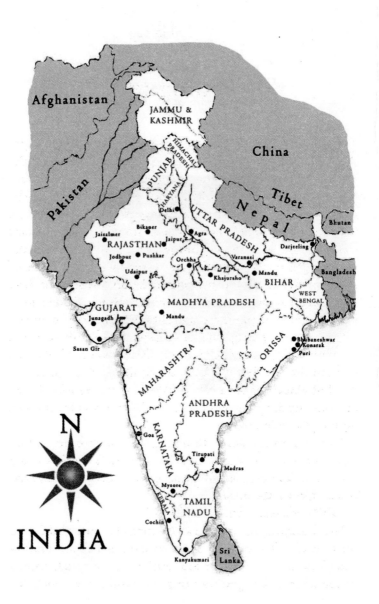

Prologue

The mustard sighs and sways, fighting to stay upright under the sudden onslaught of hot spring rain. It is 6.30 and the warm, damp-sweet air is darkening. As often happens around this time, the electricity fails. Crouching on the mud floor in the kitchen, we eat our subzi and chapatis by the light of the fire burning in the kitchen chula. Last year's dried mustard stalks crackle and shrivel up quickly. The light from the flickering flames is subsidised by a small wick in a bottle of kerosene. When we finish eating, Yadav and I stack our dirty metal plates under the mulberry tree outside the kitchen door. Men do not clean pots here, and although I have lived on and off the farm for a long time, in some ways I am still treated as an honoured guest, which is to say that I will not be allowed to clean them, either. We walk across the yard to our room. The buffaloes have already been taken in for the night. We lay out our bedding on two charpoys. With no light, there is nothing to do but sleep.

Thump... tump tump, thump... Ma's stick beats out an uneven rhythm on the veranda's concrete floor. The chain across our door clanks, but the door does not open. Yadav has locked it from the inside.

'Lala!' wails his mother. 'Lala!'

The thumping starts again as she drags her juti-clad feet to the far end of the veranda and tries the other door. It rattles and gives, and she shuffles into our room. Her stick clatters to the floor as her probing fingers feel for and touch the mound on the charpoy. She has found her Lala, her little boy. Yadav snorts and groans.

'Chup re, Ma... chalo!' He opens his eyes and reaches for his matches and bundle of bidis. His kurta-pyjamas are creased from two days' wear. He pushes back the dirty bedding and slides to the floor. I watch him from between my white cotton sheets printed all over with black elephants, purchased from a peddler on Kovalam Beach in Kerala. I sniff the scent of Coco Chanel, which I have sprinkled on my bedding to ward off the dusty smell of the sacks of mustard seed in the corner and the pile of bedding on the empty charpoy. Everyone uses quilts in the winter, but no one ever thinks of washing them when the nights grow warm and quilts are no longer needed. Sheets are unknown superfluities in Yadav's family, but his nephews like my Chanel, and occasionally come by for a squirt if they're going to a marriage party or just to meet their friends in the village.

Yadav throws a shawl over his shoulders and pushes Ma towards the door. I close my eyes again, thinking of the luxurious bath I will have tomorrow in the big, blue plastic bowl I bought in Delhi. Yadav thought it was a waste of money.

'We have good bucket. Why do you want such a thing? You are like buffalo, you needs too much water.' The bowl just fits into the concrete cell whose claim to the name 'bathroom' comes from a soak-away hole in one dark corner of the floor. With six buckets of water from the well, one of them heated on the fire, I can actually sit in my 'hot bath'. It's an improvement on the single-bucket-and-jug method.

Yadav comes back shivering. The strings of his charpoy creak under his weight. 'Now I will sleep again,' he says. 'Is early.'

The next morning we sit cross-legged, facing each other, on a charpoy in the middle of the farmyard. Balanced between us are a tin bowl of curd sprinkled with roasted cumin and a small dish of pickled red and green chillis. A pile of neatly stacked chapatis sits ready for dunking.

Yadav looks more like an Italian film director than a north Indian farmer. He is not very tall – only about two inches taller than I am – but he is thin and lithe, his features are finely sculpted, and the colour of his skin against a white T-shirt makes him look as though he spends much of his time sunbathing on the Mediterranean. Particularly handsome today in jeans and a dark-blue blazer, he tears off a corner of his chapati and scoops up a huge dollop of curd. With a loud slurping noise, he tosses it into his mouth.

Ma stands beside us, her right hand trembling on my hair in fumbled blessing. Her face – beneath the pile of clothes she always carries on her head for fear that someone might steal them – is wet with tears, turning her skin into that of a crinkly water chestnut. Nobody knows how old Ma is; the farm and village people do not bother, even now, to record birthdays, and hers was long ago. She wails again.

'Today she is not telling her usual story of how we steal her clothes,' Yadav tells me, translating Ma's Hindi. 'She is asking, Why you go back to your country? Why you do not stay at farm? She says now that Ashok, my son, is married you have a daughter-in-law to look after you. You shouldn't have to go.'

In deference to the family's conservatism I usually dress in a salwar-kamiz, but today, like Yadav, I am wearing Western clothes. In a few minutes Yadav will take me to the airport and I will fly back to London, to my other life as a breadwinning tour guide. It's more predictable than life in India, but, apart from the pleasure of seeing family and friends again, not something I look forward to.

The telephone will ring: 'Three panoramic tours plus the Changing of the Guard?' Certainly. 'London to Edinburgh and back in two days?' Well, they won't see much of Edinburgh...

We have no telephone at the farm in Haryana, or even in the village. The nearest STD office is twenty-five kilometres away.

And the weather in England – long, grey days when the wind blows umbrellas inside-out and the rain lashes the slippery pavements, soaking shoes and clothes with monotonous regularity.

And my children – how will our conversations go? What have I done and what have I failed to do in their eyes?

'Come.' Yadav climbs off the charpoy. 'I can see you are already flying in your thoughts. It is time to go.'

I bend to massage Ma's ankles, a gesture of respect to an older woman.

'Beti, beti,' she moans.

The family has come from the fields to say goodbye. They cluster round the jeep. I pick up the children one by one.

'Jill, ek kela, ek kela,' whines my favourite step-granddaughter, Chenamunia.

'No bananas today, I'm sorry,' I tell her, putting her down. Her cousin, two years older, drags her away.

I kiss Shanti, my sister-in-law. Normally we do not touch each other; we just press our hands together in namaste and bow our heads a little. Today she looks embarrassed and pleased, and says something I don't understand.

'Shanti, she says you must come back before six months. Is too long,' Yadav says. 'Now please say *Ram Ram* to my Boss Brother and come, or we will miss flight.'

Boss Brother, having skipped school as a child, is illiterate, but he runs the farm and everyone on it. I bend and touch his foot, as I know Yadav wants me to. Boss Brother usually ignores me, embarrassed by my unveiled face, but today he smiles.

The jeep bumps down the track between the bare fields. The harvest is almost over, the mustard seed ready to go to the oil extractor in the village. A flock of tiny birds, frightened by the roar of the engine, rises from the clump of long grasses. The family disappears from view.

We drive through the village, past the school. The children are outside for their mid-morning break. They have seen us a thousand times, yet their curiosity is never satisfied. Yadav slows the jeep almost to a standstill. He blows the horn, they scatter, and he drives carefully through the crowd.

'Chale, chale!' he shouts, but they are not afraid of him. They laugh and call after us. 'Angrezi, angrezi! Ram Ramji, Ram Ramji! Ram Ram, Ram Ram, Ram Ram!'

Three buffaloes, on the way to their morning wash in the village tank, slow us down again. They amble across the road chased by their owner, a small, veiled woman wielding a hefty stick. Now we are out of the village, on the road to the bus stand. We drive over the tenting man's carpets, laid across the road for airing and beating between marriage parties. Yadav waves. He knows everyone. Most people here are relatives or have close ties with our family. Letters have to be addressed to L.S. Yadav, son of Krishan Singh, so the postman can tell which of the L.S. Yadavs we are. Yadav is the name of almost everyone in the village.

'I hope you won't mind if I stop for one cup of chai,' Yadav says, stopping without waiting for an answer. He can never resist the tea stall at the bus stand. As soon as we arrive, his friends, most of whom will hang about drinking chai all day, crowd round us. Peering inquisitively into the jeep, they practise the few English sentences they learnt at the village school.

'England going? Very nice. Whisky you bring back? Party?'

Yadav finishes his chai, hands his glass to the stall owner and drives on to the main road. He stops in front of a pressing table, on which a big man is passing a monstrous, charcoal-filled iron backwards and forwards over shirts, trousers, saris and jackets. We know him well – he was once a batman in the army, and, having seen life outside the village, treats me a little less like a zoo animal than the other villagers do. Beaming, he irons our clothes. He even irons the money we hand him, putting each five-rupee note under his ironing sheet and giving it a good press.

'I think you will like to say goodbye to your friend?' asks Yadav. I walk over to the table and press my hands together.

'Ram Ramji,' we say, bowing our heads to one another. His wife, who would be pretty if she had not lost one eye, waves from inside the nearby open-front storeroom.

'Now we will leave your village, you have said goodbye to all the peoples. It is good.' Yadav accelerates and our wheels throw up a cloud of hot dust, hiding the village and the villagers.

'Do you like *Indian Autumn*?' I ask Paul, who has come to fetch me at Heathrow in his ancient Rolls-Royce. Paul is an old friend with whom I sometimes lodge when my London flat is let out.

'You know my feelings about the great Subcontinent,' he replies stiffly. 'No, I don't suppose I do.'

'Idiot. I meant as a title for my book. I always go to India in the autumn, and I suppose you could say I'm in the autumn of my life. It's got a double meaning.'

'Oh, oh! Yes, I see! Well, then it's splendid. Shall we take my shortcut and avoid the traffic on to the M4?'

1

I was two when the Second World War broke out. My father (fifty-seven), my mother (forty-one), my brother (away at prep school) and I moved from a small house behind Barkers, in Kensington, to a relatively bomb-free suburb in Surrey. Nine years later my mother died, leaving my father a sought-after but lonely widower. Although he despised suburbia, it suited him. Half an hour's train journey from London, surrounded by golf courses and bridge-playing friends from my father's tennis days, the house was comfortable and the rent was reasonable. After our temporary move had lasted sixteen years, my brother persuaded my father to return to London. He bought a house for the first time in his life, and we were back in Kensington.

My father's father had come from a family of Birmingham solicitors. After making a fortune building estates of back-to-back houses, he became the Tory MP for Edgbaston, a Birmingham suburb. The family moved to No. 2 Queens Gate, London, complete with horses, carriages and a mews to house them all. My grandfather's speeches grew longer with his years. He was offered a peerage, which would conveniently have removed him and his oratory to the House of Lords, but my grandmother, daughter of the mayor of Scarborough, decided they could not accept the title as they lacked a 'place' in the countryside. My grandfather took a baronetcy and stayed in the Commons.

My father, who had spent his time at and since Oxford on the tennis courts, had managed between love-alls and deuces to get a degree in law and qualify as a solicitor, but had given up his first job offer to travel the world with the British Davis Cup team. At the age of forty he met and married my mother. Her family owned a drapery store on the south coast, but 'trade' was a dirty word to her new mother-in-law – so, having always lived at home with a comfortable allowance, my father was cut off without a penny and forced to work. He became company secretary to a firm that owned theatres and variety halls.

Being the only daughter, I became my father's surrogate wife after my mother's death. I arranged his dinner parties, accompanied him to the theatre (for which, thanks to his job, we had free seats and permanent entrée backstage) and attended the Wimbledon fortnight and the players' dinners and parties that came with it. When not taking part in this social round, I rode my pony, looked after my dog, went to boarding school and grew up happy but lonely.

Victorian by birth, Edwardian by upbringing, my father did not approve of education for women. Through him and his indulgent charm, I inherited his old-fashioned ideas and my grandmother's insidious snobbery. I left school at seventeen with six O-levels, a mantra ('Gels do/do not do this at Friars Field') and a complete lack of any useful form of education. On the advice of Miss Picky, my art mistress (and by overruling the headmistress, who swore that Italian men had found even her spinsterish bottom irresistible for a quick pinch), I persuaded my father to send me to Italy. I learnt some Italian, fell in love with the country and its people and cried for weeks when, after twelve months, I was made to come home. Italy remained my greatest passion until years later, when India – like an overblown Italy in so many ways – supplanted my first foreign love.

Back in England I was presented at court, an occasion more important than baptism in my father's book. During my debutante summer, I met my future husband at the Boat Race.

He was an impoverished Catholic law student in the middle of his Bar finals. Against my family's advice, and totally unequipped for adult life in the late 1950s, I ditched a most suitable Old Etonian Royal Marine, married my law student, became a Catholic and had five children.

My father just had time to meet his first granddaughter before he died, three months after my twenty-first birthday.

Sixteen years later my husband went bankrupt and lost everything, including what was left of my share of my grandfather's back-to-back Birmingham houses. Our marriage ended.

I was thirty-seven. Our lives changed drastically, dramatically and permanently. Arrows of despair and hatred shattered my heart and flew through my veins, aiming their venom-coated heads at the world in general and my ex-husband in particular. He, through mismanagement rather than design, had brought about our difficulties. I and my five children, three of whom were at expensive boarding schools, were suddenly out on the street with nowhere to live, no money, and no possessions save those we had bundled into black plastic bags. Visits from bailiffs, nervous breakdowns and other adjuncts of bankruptcy gave me a new and constant fear of being penniless. During the first year of our troubles I often contemplated suicide, but was saved by not knowing precisely how many aspirin to take and being too tired to find out. Long, copious tears of despair eventually washed my mind clear. Finally, I battened down the hatches of memory and shut my earlier life behind them. I looked only at the present and towards the future.

I travelled to Somerset to tell my son's headmaster that I could no longer pay the school fees. When I arrived I was shown into his study, full of velvet chairs and portraits of illustrious

Old Boys. Father Dominic rose to greet me. He looked like Gregory Peck in the guise of a Benedictine monk.

'I'm afraid I'm going to cry,' I heard myself say. Embarrassing tears pricked my eyes.

'Well, which chair will you choose for it?' he asked. 'Pink, yellow or green?' Hearing that, I chose pink and didn't cry.

'You should stop worrying, you know.' A quizzical smile flickered across his face. 'I can see no reason why four hundred ninety-nine other boys cannot take care of the five-hundredth. Leave him with us.'

Later, my fifteen-year-old son told me that he and the headmaster had already talked. His future had been settled before our meeting.

My youngest daughter and I took refuge in my elder daughters' convent school. It was not easy for the girls to accept their new roles as everyone's poor relations, complete with a mother working in the school, nor was it a life I had ever imagined. I had not even attended a convent school. I had been brought up in the Church of England; my Catholicism had begun with my marriage.

When we arrived for the autumn term after a summer of homelessness, disoriented children and intermittent work conducting Italian tourists between London and Inverness, I was near collapse. My first job at the convent was to fetch a young nun from the local psychiatric hospital, where she had been recovering from a nervous breakdown. My second job was to sit in an isolated room at the top of a tower and make oven gloves on a sewing machine I did not know how to work. Mother David, a retired nun in whose care I had been placed, skipped up and down the stone steps keeping me company. She became my constant companion and the best friend I have ever had. Like the Cheshire cat's grin, her one-tooth-missing smile and gravelly voice still materialise in my mind when I expect them least and need them most.

'I'm so lucky at my age to have found a goddaughter, dear,' she told me. 'So good of the Third Person to send you. He'd look after you if only you'd let him, dear – do try it.' Through her kindness and love, I slowly began to thaw.

My children were embarrassed by my presence. 'Please, Mum, don't use so much scent on Sundays. The whole school smells you going up the aisle to Communion,' they said. 'And do you have to wear those awful red bell-bottoms?'

In spite of everything, I was happy there. The nuns were full of humour and enjoyed having an outsider in their midst. My friendship with them was an added thorn in my children's sides; to them, the teaching staff and community-at-large were the opposition. The very sight of a black-habited figure spelt disapproval and discipline. That their mother should be allied with the enemy was too shameful for words.

During my second week, the sacristan, a tiny, apple-cheeked Welsh woman, stopped me in a corridor. Blinking up at me through John Lennon spectacles, she felt around in the voluminous pocket in her habit, pulled out a medicine bottle and whispered, 'I thought you might need a cocktail before Sunday lunch. I know you worldly people do, so I've been saving the ends of the altar wine. In confidence, of course.' I had to stoop to take the bottle from her.

The nuns prayed daily, never giving the saints responsible for homeless families a rest until they had found us somewhere to live. After two years of convent work, with only five hundred pounds in the bank, a mortgage from a reluctant Westminster City Council and some help from my brother, I bought a broken-down house in Pimlico and began to believe in miracles. The nuns' prayers answered, Reverend Mother ordered me to London to earn a living, saying her community was quite capable of looking after my daughters.

On my last day at the convent I found an invitation to a farewell dinner lying on my bed. Reverend Mother, Mother

David and I dined by candlelight in the blue parlour. When Sister Patrick wheeled in a trolley from the kitchen across the corridor, Reverend Mother lifted a heavy silver cover. Three bone-eyed rashers of streaky bacon, sinking fast in a sea of baked beans to a soggy bed of buttered toast, stared up at us.

'Oh my goodness.' Reverend Mother's voice expressed gentle horror. 'I told Sister to prepare something special. What could have happened? I did find this old bottle in the cellar... do you think it will go with, er, baked beans and bacon?'

The vintage claret would have gone with anything.

'Well,' said Reverend Mother, sniffing the wine to make sure it was not corked, 'shall we say Grace?'

My tears the next day, as we crept for the last time down the long drive full of sleeping policemen and garlic-scented flowers, were unquenchable. The sisters prayed on. Mother David wrote to me, adding in a postscript that she was praying for a kind benefactor to pay for the many repairs our house badly needed.

My mother's sister, my last surviving blood relation from the older generation, died, leaving me just enough money to stop the house from falling down. Now there was no one left to turn to. My responsibilities towards my children, which I and certainly they felt I was not fulfilling, brought unbearable worry and self-flagellation.

Convinced that a man was the answer to my problems, I searched everywhere for the right one. I went to a marriage bureau, became a Friend of the Victoria & Albert Museum and tried lodgers as lovers and lovers as lodgers. None of it worked. I was lonely and distraught.

Finally, thanks to my job as a tour guide, help from friends during the holidays and their own persistent efforts, my children's education came to an end. My youngest daughter got her degree and started looking for a job. My responsibilities were, to some extent, over. After years of taking in paying guests, summers ferrying tourists from one overcrowded historic monument to another, and winters searching for menial jobs – which at best gave me chilblains and dusty fingers selling plaster casts in the British Museum, and at worst, varicose veins in Harrods' Christmas-card department – I was suddenly, for six months of the year, free. Faced with such unaccustomed liberty, I thought for a long time before I resolved to let my flat for the winter and go to India.

I chose India for all the wrong reasons. I knew almost nothing about it, but I had heard it was not too expensive, and I wanted to prove to myself and my ex-lover – who had left me for a house-sitting job in Notting Hill Gate – that I was just as capable of coping with life on the Subcontinent as he had apparently been. He immediately doubted my declaration, making me all the more determined to prove him wrong.

London lay shivering. The gleam from a single street lamp shone through the frozen mist of the January evening on to the floor of my room. It fell in a mute pool of light on to an empty suitcase and, beside it, a jumble of clothes, books, boxes and bottles. I shivered, not from cold – the radiators were on, and orange and blue flames leapt and danced from the fire in the grate – but from fear, fear of the unknown, of a flight to Madras and a three-month stay in India. I asked myself for the hundredth time, 'Why am I doing this?' But I knew the answer. I was fifty-two, and I needed a change.

2

'Madras'll be easier than Delhi. Leave the north for later.' Rosy, a travel agent who specialised in India, smiled across her desk. Comfortably round, with pink cheeks and frizzy hair, she was very British. 'You'll find the south less shocking.' She hesitated. 'Well, you know what I mean... the poverty, the smells and, well, you know.'

Rosy arranged a hotel for the first two nights, and recommended some guidebooks.

Terrified by the thought of going to India alone, I answered an advertisement in *The Times*. By return post, 'Travelling Partners' sent me two telephone numbers. The first belonged to a Scotsman who wanted a companion for a weekend in the Outer Hebrides. I tried the other.

'Tea next week would be quite convenient,' said a high-pitched female voice.

In the dark lobby of a hotel in Henley-on-Thames, a figure rose from the depths of a brown leather sofa. The highlights in her short, cropped hair looked like nicotine stains. Her designer sweater was stretched tight across her small breasts and down over her long-waisted body to meet short legs in black stretch trousers.

'I'm Brenda,' she said. 'I need a coffee – I've been waiting for you for hours.' She looked at her watch and yawned. I was five minutes late. Leaning across the varnished tabletop, she scrutinised me from behind enormous red-framed spectacles.

'I want to go to Africa to see the tigers. I like cats. I've got two at home – Siamese, actually. They're gorgeous.' She beckoned to the waitress. 'I'd like a pot of coffee for two, myself. You order what you like.'

I did.

While Brenda drank she told me about herself, pausing only to take delicate sips from her willow-pattern cup. After a disastrous marriage in Brazil, she had come back to England to look after her ailing mother, who eventually died of senile dementia. She was left with a house in Bournemouth, which she now ran as a prestigious bed-and-breakfast.

She stopped to drink and draw breath.

'I was thinking of going to India,' I said quickly, before she had a chance to start again.

'Well, I hope you realise what you're doing,' she said. 'Travelling in a Third World country, you won't be comfortable. I've had experience; I know.'

By the time we parted I had persuaded her, with promises of wildlife parks full of tigers, to spend three weeks with me in south India. What did I care if our ideas of holidays were worlds apart, our personalities completely incompatible? I had my travelling companion. For my first three weeks in India, I would not be alone.

Soon after meeting Brenda, I went to the Indian Tourist Office in Cork Street. The director read my letter of introduction from a mutual friend.

'I'd like to stay with an Indian family as a paying guest,' I said. The director summoned a colleague and a pretty Indian woman in a smart grey suit came in, filling the room with hot, sweet scent. The director introduced her as Nirmala Singh, and asked her if she could help me.

'You want to be a paying guest in Delhi?' she said. 'But of course you will not pay – my family will be delighted to be your hosts. They live in a lovely modern house. But I'm sure you'll want to see more of our wonderful country. Why don't you take my agency's beautiful tour, "The Grandeur of Rajasthan"?'

After twenty years of working as a tour guide, I had no wish to take a busman's holiday and pay for it. But I did want to stay with Nirmala's family, and I didn't see how I could accept one offer without the other.

'It sounds very nice,' I said, wondering where and what Rajasthan was. Nirmala handed me a glossy brochure. I glanced at the prices and felt sick. Grudgingly I wrote out and handed over a cheque – for more than I had meant to spend on my entire Indian journey.

'You'll love it!' Nirmala said. 'Will you be flying up to Delhi from Goa? Just give me the date and the flight number. A driver from our Delhi office will meet you at the airport. Enjoy your tour.' She smiled, and her long red fingernails beat out a rhythm on the tabletop.

At the thought of the money I had unnecessarily spent, a hot, nervous flush enveloped me. I tripped on the front step of the tourist office and fell headlong into the October sunshine. Brochures flew from my grasp and fluttered to the ground. There they lay, a brilliant collage of north India on the grey Mayfair pavement.

The doorbell rang. It was Brenda, wearing a sensible cotton dress under her mackintosh and carrying an almost empty suitcase. She looked at my overflowing bag with disapproval, yawned and picked up the guidebook I wanted to read on the plane. It was the first of many things that Brenda would need to 'borrow' during our three weeks together.

'I need space in my suitcase for shopping,' were the only words that my companion, engrossed as she was in my guidebook, uttered until our plane landed with a soft bump on the runway of Madras airport.

It was the seventeenth of January. Brenda and I were in India. Pushed, shoved and jostled, our noses assaulted by a mixture of aerosol room freshener, attar of roses, sweat and cigarette smoke, we emerged into the damp heat of mid-afternoon Madras.

Something touched my leg. A small boy stood beside me. He pointed to his mouth, rubbed his stomach and whined. Brenda found her voice.

'Now I suppose you see what it's like. I warned you,' she said.

I saw. And in those first few minutes I was hooked.

I could not stop looking. Through the tinted windows of the Ambassador, intriguing scenes unfolded. I suddenly wished my eyes were bigger, my brain better able to absorb the sights, smells and sounds that overwhelmed my senses. We plunged through crowds of half-naked, spindle-legged pedestrians, darted between motorcycles careering crazily from side to side of the dusty road, passed sweating cycle-rickshaw-wallahs pedalling stately matrons on shopping sprees and clutches of clean-cut children walking home from school for tea. Yellow and black three-wheelers buzzed about like bees, overflowing with families, cargo and fumes. Terrifying tinselled lorries bore down on us. 'Give side. Blow horn,' they blared in garish paint. 'Use dipper.' An elephant plodded ponderously, his tiny eyes alert in folds of flesh. Women in bright saris, like a swarm of frightened butterflies, scattered before our honking horn. Bullocks pulling mammoth loads, their blue- and scarlet-painted horns held low, strained against wooden yokes. Cows ruminated, chewed their cuds and munched on indigestible cardboard boxes.

Filled with elation, I looked at Brenda. She stared ahead, neat and tidy in her straw topi and cotton dress. I forgot her and gave myself up to India.

But it was hard to forget Brenda completely.

On our first full day in Madras, we went looking for Brenda's adopted Indian 'grandmother'. Brenda had discovered a charity called Adopt-a-Granny in a magazine, and was sure that her granny lived near a place called Tirupati. We took a tour that went via Tirupati (where we just had time for breakfast and a change of bus) to Tirumala, and found ourselves waiting three hours in a narrow wire-netted passage for darshan along with thousands of shaven-headed pilgrims.

'I'm not staying in here another minute. I might faint. Then what would you do?' demanded Brenda. 'I've told you I'm not interested in temples. Where do I get out? And what about my granny?' Her irrritation turned to hysteria. 'I never wanted to come here. It's a filthy, terrible place. I'm catching a plane back to London tomorrow. If we'd only gone to Africa...'

We never found the granny. Brenda calmed down.

At Mahabalipuram I swam in the Bay of Bengal, walked along the beach to look at the rock-cut temples and decided I had arrived in Paradise, or come as close to it as I was ever likely to get.

Brenda lay in a hammock under the pine trees. 'I never did like the sea; too many waves,' she said. 'Give me a swimming pool. And as I've told you at least twice, I'm not interested in temples, and I have a very delicate skin. Too much sun brings me out in a rash.'

We lunched on lobster – sizzling, golden-brown and tasting of salt water – and flew on to Cochin. Abu, a local fisherman, took us round the lagoon in his boat, and we stopped to see the Chinese fishing nets and the church where Vasco da Gama was buried. I chatted with Abu as he rowed us across the blue water, enjoying the ride, the company and the sunshine.

Brenda sat in stony silence. When we were again on dry land, her rosebud mouth pursed itself into a disapproving grimace, and spat out a sudden volley of fury that ricocheted across the water.

'Get rid of that man!' she barked at me, glaring at Abu. 'You shouldn't become friendly with the natives. Pay him half the fee he asks. He's a crook. And you! I got very bored with your chat, I can tell you.' She headed off in the wrong direction. I paid Abu and ran after her.

'And,' she went on, when at last we were sitting by the hotel swimming pool with a cool drink, 'we're seeing too much of each other. Why should we stick together like a pair of limpets? Unnecessary, I'd call it. I like my privacy. And another thing – I want my lunch and tea when I'm hungry. Do you think I can wait till eight o'clock at night for my tea? Well, I can't.' She yawned and lapsed into silence.

After that, we never spoke unless we had to.

A night at Periyar Wildlife Sanctuary failed to produce Brenda's tigers. We travelled by train from Cochin to Mettupalayam, and at dawn we transferred to the little blue-and-white steam train. It chugged upwards through the Nilgiri hills past tea gardens and eucalyptus forests, awe-inspiring scenes that would have left me speechless even if Brenda had wanted to hear my comments, which, of course, she did not. At 2,268 metres above sea level we came to Ootacamund, queen of the southern hill stations. Our hotel gave us an introduction to the Ooty Club, a relic of the Raj and of bygone 'Snooty Ooty'.

Brenda looked with disapproval at the disjointed members of the fox family that decorated the walls. Her hackles rose. 'Nasty barbarians, killing innocent little creatures. What's a "point-to-point", anyway?' she asked with a sniff, studying a notice on a board behind the desk. I explained that a point-to-point was an informal race meeting for hunt horses; the races cover about two kilometres, from one point to another, of someone's private land. We had a hurried gin and tonic in the company of a talkative man propping up the bar, who puffed smoke rings from his briar pipe while his wife sat at a table polishing her riding boots. Brenda sniffed and coughed.

We left Ooty and, after another abortive hunt for tigers at Mudumalai Wildlife Sanctuary, came to Mysore.

Mysore is a clean and spacious city with wide, tree-lined streets, a spectacular nineteenth-century maharaja's palace and a bazaar of enormous and colourful proportions. Brenda bought striped Mysore silk for pyjamas for her Middle Eastern boyfriend. I bought wild silk for my daughters and went sightseeing.

The end was in sight. We travelled northwards to Goa, where we spent our two days in a chauffeur-driven car looking for a hotel swimming pool for Brenda.

Finally we flew to Delhi. Our three weeks were over.

My love for India had grown in almost equal proportion to my antipathy to Brenda. I hoped I would never see her again, with her yawns, her blinking gaze, her disapproval and her nagging. I am sure my feelings were reciprocated.

'You want taxi?' My suitcases were whisked off a whirling carousel and on to a trolley. There was no time for more than a perfunctory goodbye. Brenda held out her hand. I shook it and dashed after my disappearing luggage.

Her querulous cry followed me out of the airport building. 'But where do I go? Can't you find out?'

'Ask someone else!' I yelled. 'Goodbye, Brenda!'

3

'JILL MADAME'

The placard stood out from a sea of waving signs, held high above the heads of the crowd outside Delhi's airport.

'Are you from Ravi Chhabra's travel agency?' I asked the thin man in the shiny grey shirt, referring to the name Nirmala had given me.

'Yes, Memsahib. And you is my tourist. Please come.'

'I want to go to the house of Mr and Mrs Singh.'

'I knows it. My boss, he already tell to me.'

Our conversation dried up.

I looked out of the taxi's purple-tinted windows. Delhi began to take shape. The traffic on the wide, tree-lined road was lighter than I would have expected on the highway into India's capital. Here, unlike the road into Madras, there were no bullock carts and no elephants – there were people dressed mostly in Western clothes, and groups of buildings interspersed with splashes of greenery. A line of shops selling furniture, a chai stall, a fruit market... I shut my eyes. Pictures of Brenda flashed across my mind. Why on earth had I stayed with her for three whole weeks? Probably, I thought, because of my tour-guiding job; I was used to putting up with impossible people and smiling. Anyway, with or without Brenda, south India had been magical. Now I wondered about the Singh family, and how they would feel about having a strange English woman to stay.

Men shouldering small sons and daughters sauntered along the road, shouting to each other above the noise of the traffic.

Women fluttered amongst buzzing auto-rickshaws and brake-screeching scooters. Bus conductors blew whistles, lorries honked horns. Pop music blared from a passing van. A cow, meditating quietly on a breakfast of cardboard, paused to raise her head and stare at the confusion.

The car roared to a sudden halt. I opened my eyes.

'Memsahib. Is house of Singhs.'

The driver got out and rang the bell. Melodious chimes summoned a dark-skinned girl in a salwar-kamiz and a stringy young man in a cheap Western suit. Beaming, they collected my luggage and stood aside to let me pass through the wrought-iron gates.

Everything about the Singhs' house was new, from the turreted roof and Moghul-style windows to the large Toyota in front. The family came from Amritsar. They lived in one of south Delhi's 'in' colonies.

Sujann Singh, in a carefully folded navy-blue turban and matching tie, stood politely in the hall beside a garlanded statue of the genial, pot-bellied Ganesh. The hall was filled with artificial flowers and demure glass and china figurines. A miniature Niagara Falls tumbled down the stairwell over a rocky jungle of potted plants to a drain in the white marble floor below.

Baby Singh floated down the stairs, one manicured hand extended in greeting and the other resting lightly on the gilded banister. Her heart-shaped face was framed in lustrous curls, her red lips lifted in a cupid's bow.

'Jill? We're pleased to meet you. How are Nirmala and family? On several occasions we have visited their house in Harrow. We enjoy shopping in your Marks & Spencer store. Please come – we will have snacks. I'm sure you're hungry.' Sujann excused himself.

'My husband is always working. It is so dull,' Baby said. Mary, the girl who had opened the gates to me, staggered in with a heavy silver platter of fried fish and ketchup. Baby helped herself.

'I'm on a diet. Do you think I'm a little bit overweight?' She popped another morsel into her mouth and wiped her fingers.

Sujann had made his money, and was still making it, as a land agent. Baby, his wife, was intent on climbing Delhi's social ladder. When not having her thick black locks teased into tight ringlets or her non-existent facial hair plucked, she divided her time between women's lunches in Delhi's five-star hotels, shopping sprees for saris and jewellery, and worries about the lazy behaviour of her servants and the marriage prospects of her two convent-school daughters.

'Shiv Singh! Shiv Singh!' she shouted. The man in cheap Western clothes ran in, grinning.

'Memsahib?'

'Take Madame's suitcase to her room,' she sighed. 'Such a good-for-nothing,' she said to me. 'Please go with him. Later we will drive to the market. Today is Sujann's birthday, so you will help me to buy him a present.'

My room was blue and icebox-cold. A giant photograph of a blue sea and blue sky was reflected in a wall-to-wall gilt-bordered mirror. A striped tiger glared at me from the centre of a blue blanket. The smell of Mary's curry seeped through the blue bathroom tiles.

Shiv Singh knocked on my door. 'Memsahib say shopping now,' he announced.

'Shit,' Baby said as someone slid into the only parking space at the market. 'People are so selfish.' She left the car in the middle of the road and walked over to where a fishmonger sat on a marble slab, ogled by fish of every shape, size and hue. With a huge curved knife which he clamped to the top of the slab with one foot, he sliced and gutted and chopped. Baby leant across to examine an extra-large, goggle-eyed sea serpent. I felt for my camera.

'Don't take my photo!' my hostess screamed. Apparently a photograph without the reassurance of a mirror, and with a fishmonger, of all people, was most unwelcome. 'Now,' she said, when she had calmed down, 'let us think of Sujann's birthday. He wants shoes.' We trudged from shop to shop, never leaving until every shoe box in each one had been opened.

'Poor quality. Your shop is stupid,' snapped Baby to one salesman, discarding a pair of green and black patent-leather brogues.

The next stop was Baby's dressmaker, a grand establishment behind an important-looking white door. We climbed sweeping white marble stairs to the first floor. Two security guards in white suits sat behind a white desk, nursing their revolvers. Inside, the shelves were lined with saris of every kind – silk, georgette, crêpe de Chine. We were met by Mina, the owner and manager, an effusive lady in early middle age. Her gorgeous pink chiffon suit, sewn with seed pearls, was draped in voluptuous folds over her portly body. We sat on a half-moon-shaped white leather sofa while a young man stood on a dais, unfurling sari after sari for our inspection. Baby chose six and ordered blouses to match.

Having exhausted the market and ourselves, we went home to find Baby's daughters, still in their grey-and-cherry school uniforms, at the kitchen table, eating pakoras and doing their homework. Rekha was sixteen. When not studying her books, she studied herself, pirouetting and rearranging her hair in front of the mirror. Sunita, her younger sister, overweight and untidy, was always smiling and cheerful.

'Say good afternoon to Aunty; she has come to stay.'

'Good afternoon, Aunty,' said the girls. Apart from the floor cleaner, who remained forever face-down on bended knees, and the mali, who came daily before anyone was up, I had now met the entire Singh household.

We celebrated Sujann's birthday with Johnnie Walker Black Label and French champagne. Many drinks and snacks later, we went into the kitchen for Chinese takeaway.

That night I tossed and turned under the tiger blanket, racked by stomach cramps that, at two in the morning, sent me rushing to the blue-tiled bathroom. Unable to stem the flow of my first attack of dysentery, I stayed till the first light of dawn. Weak and shivering, I crawled back under the unprotective tiger.

At nine o'clock Shiv Singh summoned me to breakfast in Baby's bedroom. Draped in a crimson chenille kaftan, she reclined on her king-size bed.

'I can't understand,' she said to me between telephone calls, 'why you are ill. We ate the same food, and we are perfectly well. Today I plan to visit my gurdwara – I hope you will come. It will be good for your illness, I'm sure.'

Baby took her religion seriously. Every day she spent half an hour in her puja room at the top of the house. We visited the gurdwara often, taking garlands of yellow and white flowers and bringing back lumps of halwa for those at home.

The telephone rang. It was Rajiv Gupta, a Delhi friend of an Indian friend of mine in London.

'Was that call for you? Please do not speak for long. I must keep the line clear for my friends.' Baby emerged from the bathroom in an unguent cloud, wearing a ravishing salwar-kamiz.

Rajiv came for me on Sunday in a very old car. He was younger than I was, and his wife had just had a baby.

'Do ask your friend to have a drink,' Baby cooed.

'No thanks – no time,' said Rajiv. 'We have a date with my uncle in the hotel he has just opened.'

Baby's smile was replaced by a look of amazed disdain at the sight of Rajiv's elderly, chauffeurless Fiat parked outside her gates.

'We have a new Japanese car and, of course, the Ambassador for our driver,' she informed him.

'I'm sure you have,' Rajiv replied. Adjusting the silk cravat tucked into the collar of his Newmarket checked shirt, he revved up the ancient engine and we drove away.

Twenty kilometres out of town, dwarfed by the ruins of Tughluqabad, we turned off the road into the manicured gardens of a brand-new five-star hotel, where we lunched in a private room with Rajiv's uncle.

Rajiv dropped me back at the Singhs'. We did not meet again; he had discharged his duty. His smart Delhi set had no room for middle-aged English women unable to drop a single name of interest to anyone.

Sujann wound his long red turban round and round his head, finishing it off with a high cusp in front. He smiled at his reflection in the mirror. His wife pulled, pushed, pleated and tucked herself into her silk sari, applied her makeup and arranged her hair. Standing back from the glass, she studied herself with critical admiration. 'Come, Jill. Let's go,' she said. We were going to visit Baby's brother, who had just returned from Amritsar with homemade sweets and pickles from their mother.

Baby's brother lived in a shabby apartment block on a narrow street in Old Delhi, where cooking fires exhaled smoke and sparks into the twilight heat. Inside, the smell of stale food lingered on the stairwell. In the flat, flies feasted on leftover crumbs on the tablecloth. A child in a pink satin frock was awakened and brought into the room kicking and screaming. Her chubby hand reached for a dish of sweets, and her mother stuffed one into her mouth. She choked, dribbling sticky spittle down her front.

'Chup, chup,' said the woman, giving her a violent pat on the back.

Baby collected her presents and, without waiting for the servant to pour tea from the silver teapot into flowered plastic cups, made her exit.

'Stupid,' she said, brushing imaginary dirt off her sari. 'Sujann, we will not go there again. They have no class.'

Relieved by a day's respite from the empty chatter of Baby's ladies' luncheons, I decided that another three weeks of beauty salons, dressmakers and dining out might be too much. I sat down in my blue bedroom and wrote myself an itinerary for a trip to east India.

The next morning I rang Raj Seth, another contact from a London friend, and was invited to the Gymkhana Club the following Sunday.

'Why do you want to go to that stupid old club? We can take you to lunch somewhere smart,' said Baby.

On Sunday, Raj Seth's driver dropped me at a long, white building with an armed guard at the door. Raj came down the steps to meet me.

'What a lovely house you have,' I began. He looked puzzled, and then burst out laughing.

'This is the Gymkhana Club. Come and meet my wife and daughter – they're in the garden.' Mrs Seth smiled and moved her white garden chair to make room for me. The sounds of tennis balls pinging on taut strings, splashes from the pool, the tinkling laughter of gentlewomen in chiffon saris and the polite guffaws of men in Nehru jackets reminded me, in an Indian way, of the London Hurlingham Club.

I told Raj I wanted to explore east India. 'Excellent!' he said. 'Come and see me in my office and we'll work out your route.'

Back at the Singhs', my travel plans upset Baby.

'Why should you go away?' she protested. 'And by train. You will be most uncomfortable.'

4

Raj Seth sat behind his desk in an office upholstered in green velvet. Our mutual London friends had not told me what he did for a living, only that he was a good friend and amusing raconteur.

'Please, sit. I have organised an itinerary based on your list: Varanasi, Darjeeling, Bhubaneshwar, Puri and Konarak. Since you are travelling alone I advise you to go second-class air-conditioned, what we call "2 A/C". You will share a compartment with several others. You can be quite private – they have curtains to divide the individual cubicles – but you will not be alone. I'll ring the station now, and warn them you'll be collecting your tickets.'

He reached for one of a battery of telephones and dialled. 'I'm sending an elderly lady,' he said (I didn't like that much). 'Please see that you look after her.' He scribbled a letter as he spoke. 'Ask for Mr Chopra – he's the boss – and give him this. And here's another letter to help you if necessary.' The letter stated that I was a London tour guide on a familiarisation trip; that everyone, everywhere, should help me in every way, except financially; and that I had the support and backing of Raj's office. The letter was signed and rubber-stamped by Raj himself. He had been very helpful.

Only when I arrived at New Delhi Railway Station, however, did I realise just how helpful. Pushing my way through the less fortunate, who did not have letters of introduction, I climbed the stairs to the international-tourist booking office. It was 4.20, the office was due to close at five o'clock and there were long queues at each counter. I waved my letter and was immediately conducted to Mr Chopra's office in a small, glassed-off corner of the room. All but one of the waiting chairs were occupied.

Mr Chopra read Raj's letter and handed me a booking form. Ignoring the waiting crowd, he ordered me a cup of coffee. The minutes ticked by. It was five to five.

'You've got to help me!' screamed a distraught Scotswoman, her face the colour of chalk. She rose to her feet. 'I've been waiting in this fucking place for five fucking hours. They say they won't take rupees – I've got nothing else. I'm leaving India in a few days, and it's all I've got, ALL I'VE GOT, can't anyone understand?' Mr Chopra sat ummoved, his chin peeping over the edge of his desktop. His eyelids flickered as if unaccustomed to bright light. When he spoke, his voice had no inflection.

'May I suggest that you take your rupees to the Indians' booking office downstairs. There you will encounter no difficulties.' Tears trickled down the woman's face. Mr Chopra, reiterating what he had said, added, with practised patience, that this was how the system worked. He could only suggest that she follow his advice. Speechless, she left, bumping into an equally irate Australian on her way out.

Breathing heavily, the Australian pulled himself up to his full brawny height. 'Three bloody hours I've been waiting for a ticket to bleeding Rajasthan. They told me it would be easier up here than downstairs. Well, it ain't.'

A lesser man than Mr Chopra might have been daunted by this onslaught. Not he; he sat swivelling comfortably in his swivel chair. 'Oh, but it is... without a shadow of doubt, it is,' he said passively. 'Please join the small queue at counter number four.'

'But it's fucking five o'clock! They're closing!' yelled the Australian.

'So they are,' said Mr Chopra, peering out through the glass. 'Now, Madam, your application forms?' I handed them over.

'You must get exhausted, dealing with the public all day.'

'Oh, no.' He looked surprised. 'I never get upset. You see, there is no point. It wouldn't make any difference and would only tire me.' He smiled. 'Now please go to counter number four to collect your tickets.' I took my place behind the Australian, but Mr Chopra had done his work well. Within minutes I was called to the front and issued everything I wanted.

'Wish I knew someone influential,' grumbled the Australian good-naturedly when I apologised for jumping the queue.

'God bless Raj Seth,' I thought. I climbed out of the station over a mass of grey blanketed forms.

A white-faced English boy with a pigtail helped me to find my name on the passenger list on the side of the train. The listing contained not only my name and seat number, but also my age and sex. Personal privacy seemed a rare privilege here. I boarded the train and sat back, relieved to be free.

My compartment was full of people, but before the train clattered out of the station, half of them got off. Grunting and groaning, the train gathered speed. Those left behind became blobs in the distance, and merged with other blobs until they became one big blob and finally disappeared. I had three companions: a couple who owned a tea plantation in Darjeeling and a young Swedish woman named Kristina, all travelling, like me, overnight to Varanasi.

The stench of sewage seeped through the windows as the train chugged passed a jhuggi village on the banks of a stagnant pond. The world turned brown – brown earth, brown huts, brown figures swaddled in brown blankets, busy with their daily defecation, oblivious to us and our flying machine. Porters on sinewy legs lurched under brown luggage on their scarlet-turbaned heads as they scampered along brown platforms; mountains of brown rubbish where urchins picked and scratched in search of... what? Vegetable peelings, broken bottles, torn tinfoil trays, yesterday's news, tomorrow's trash? Vultures hovered, lords of dirt and death. A sudden dive for a morsel of fetid flesh and they were airborne again, off to glide and guzzle.

'Ragpickers,' explained the tea planter. 'They won't live long. They catch diseases and die. It's inevitable...'

Slowly the browns changed to greens: sugar cane, bananas, cabbages, paddy. Stations came and went. New scenes unfolded as curtains rose and fell; new characters crossed from wing to wing. A monkey sauntered on to the platform, sat down and glanced from left to right, right to left... expecting a friend? Commuting? The tea planter leant out of the window and ordered chai from a chai-wallah. The man poured a stream of pale-brown liquid from his huge kettle into four clay bowls. The chai in the tiny, red-brown vessels was hot, sweet, spiced and refreshing. The train drew out of the station. I fidgeted with my empty cup.

'Just throw it away,' said the tea planter, tossing his out the window. I did as he said, but it seemed a pity: a throw-away mug of chai for only two rupees. I asked him about the igloo-shaped stacks made of dried cow pats. Dried dung is a cheap form of fuel, he told me.

'Veg. or non-veg.?' The attendant swayed on his feet, his pencil poised.

'He means dinner,' explained the tea planter's wife. At the next station, stacks of tinfoil thalis were loaded into our carriage and distributed. Peeling off the cover, I spooned up the curry and rice. The tea planter and his wife had brought their own dinner. They laid out their plentiful picnic on a newspaper on the lower bunk and sat, their legs neatly crossed, popping food into their mouths. They paused occasionally to offer me and the Swedish girl a taste of this and a mouthful of that.

Outside, it was dark. We made up our bunks with the bed rolls provided and slept.

Varanasi or Canaletto's Venice? The sacred Ganges or the Grand Canal? Varanasi's early-morning light, limpid as clarified butter, was as Venetian as it was Indian. The boatman dug in his oars. The sun rose slowly over the river. Tourists were out in droves: on the river, on the banks, clicking and clacking snap-happy pictures of crumbling palaces from another age. The sounds of a waking city rose, clamouring with the heat. A bell tolled; the Muslim call to prayer rang out. Vultures wheeled; dead men's garlands floated on the glassy surface; saris and bedsheets, side by side with saffron rags, lay drying on the ghats. Early bathers scrubbed satin skins; ash-smeared sadhus in skimpy lunghis and swinging beads practised yoga and stared into space; boys rubbed their heels on the stone steps; a white-wrapped body strapped to a stretcher was dipped in the god-sent waters once, twice, and once again; a wreath of smoke curled from a funeral pyre. A fleet of sand-dredgers chugged upstream; snow-white cranes ducked and bobbed for food, balancing on one leg; children with stinging, soap-filled eyes spluttered, squealed and splashed; a flashy drake swam by with his dowdy duck companion; dogs paddled frantically, snouts pointing upwards. The fort loomed at the water's edge. Cars clanked across a metal bridge. Dhobi-wallahs slapped and smacked their washing on the rocks.

Venice vanished, banished from my mind.

A few kilometres outside Varanasi, in the ruins of Sarnath, the third-century monastery where Buddha preached his first sermon, Kristina and I found a brief moment's peace from the frenzy of the sacred city. It did not last.

'Tunnel was built by one lady. With no luck to conceive in womb, she came to this place to meditate for many days, many months, even many years. At the end she succeeded. In state of high grace, miracle came to happen and she bear her child. Now couples with no good luck, they come to special ground near tunnel to make their love and pray for grace of lady. This story only I can tell you. Lucky you find me.' The guide clung to us.

'And now I will tell about yourselves. Yes. I will tell where all moles, all marks on bodies is mapped. Tonight please you check my statement true or false.' He grabbed my left hand and, gazing at my palm, told me that I would expire when I was seventy-two. My young companion was spared till eighty. 'And now I have told you all the things, you will give good baksheesh to poor Buddhist guide.' He took a hundred rupees without comment.

I bought two tiny stone elephants for the Singh daughters, and we took a rickshaw back to Varanasi.

With a couple of cows and a few passengers for company, I waited on platform three at Mughal Sarai station for the train to New Jalpaiguri, the stop for Darjeeling. In the waiting room, a rat snuffled its way through silk saris and trousered legs to the gloomy depths of the ladies' lavatory. The train raced in with a triumphant roar. I climbed on, found my bunk and slept.

A warm pressure on my leg woke me. I sprang up, scattering the scanty sheets.

'Do you mind?' asked a man's voice. 'I do not have place to sleep.' I told him that I did mind; I had paid for my bunk and did not wish to share it. Later I woke again to feel the same creeping warmth. I gave it a vicious kick and slept again, undisturbed until the lights came on at 5.30. The man in the bunk above mine bought me a cup of sweet, sticky coffee. I drank it and felt better.

The official at the registration desk in New Jalpaiguri station would not let me through. I hadn't realised I needed a permit. 'No permit, no Darjeeling,' he said with a satisfied smile.

I begged. I showed him my letter from Raj's office. I slipped a hundred-rupee note across the desk.

'Wait for officer of tourism,' he said, and relapsed into a silent trance. An hour later, when I had almost forgotten why I was there and was certain that he had, he came to life. Beckoning, he slid a grimy piece of paper across the desk.

'APPLY FOR REGISTRATION IN DARJEELING, SAY YOU CAME BY BUS.'

An overcrowded taxi threw me out into the darkness. I was in Darjeeling, in the Himalayas, thousands of kilometres from Snowdonia, the Dolomites or the Pyrenees, in mountains I had never dreamt of seeing. I took greedy gulps of the thin, breath-catching air.

The first cheap guest house on my list was boarded up. My courage failed. 'The Windamere Hotel,' I said to my two-legged luggage van.

The Windamere's brown Windsor soup, tipsy cake, lady pianist who tickled the ivories at teatime, roaring fires and romantic views of Kanchenjunga were worth every expensive rupee of my three-day stay. In the Ghoom monastery, a smiling monk and a small white dog with a curly tail took me to the prayer hall, where young and old monks bent their shaven heads in chanted worship. I walked to the Tibetan Refugee Self-Help Centre outside town, at the top end of a steep, narrow track. 'Twinkle, twinkle little star,' sang a small girl, accompanied by the clack-clacking of looms and the approving smiles of toothless weavers. I bought a carpet.

'When will it arrive in London?' I asked the clerk.

'Christmas.'

'But it's February already.'

'Christmas.' He meant the next one.

At dawn the next day, my alarm rang. The fire had gone out. The Windamere was silent, her guests asleep. I wondered if it was really worth getting up so early to see a Himalayan sunrise. People said that if it was cloudy, you saw nothing anyway.

It was still dark when my jeep driver stopped on Tiger Hill. The trees and bushes were shrouded in a blanket of mist. Huddled figures waited in frozen animation. A waning moon floated, a silver sliver in a cloud-smoked sky.

A murmur turned to a shout, the shout to a rasping intake of breath. Pinnacles of icing sugar, orange, pink and frosty white, broke the black emptiness and filled the sky. A hissing sigh rose from the crowd.

As suddenly as they had come, the peaks vanished, the curtains closed. From behind the faint outline of distant hills, a ball of burning fire pushed, shoved and wobbled its way up into a wakening sky. The ice caps reappeared, stark, virgin-white, stained with blood-red streaks.

Hot tears coursed down my cheeks. My body shuddered. My teeth chattered. A universal orgasm penetrated deep into my soul, and carried it upwards to fuse for a suspended moment with eternity.

A Cheshire-cat grin appeared through a gap in the closing curtains.

'Hello, dear,' said Mother David's gravelly voice. 'I hope you liked that. It was Him – He painted it for you.'

The curtains closed. The show was over.

A bowl of porridge, pony-wallahs in the square, uniformed schoolchildren, Buddhist monks, Grindlays bank, the clock tower... Darjeeling was behind me.

The little blue-and-white steam train puffed slowly down through the hills. I opened my Windamere lunch box and ate my prim and proper picnic – a hard-boiled egg with a paper screw of salt and pepper, a tomato sandwich and a slice of fruit cake – while the train wound its way down and down, round and round, past itinerant cows casually crossing the lines and villagers going about their daily chores.

Twenty-four hours later, in Calcutta, I had to wait six hours for the train to Bhubaneshwar. In Calcutta's botanical gardens, I visited a forest of trunks made by the two-hundred-year-old banyan tree and walked the gravel paths in a daze until it was time to catch a bus to the other train station.

Throughout the journey to Bhubaneshwar, my only companion, a middle-aged man from Calcutta, talked. After explaining that he was a Brahmin, he told me all about arranged marriages, the history of India and, when that was finished, world politics.

From Bhubaneshwar's station, I set off in the dark on a cycle-rickshaw to a hotel the Brahmin had recommended. 'We are full,' said the receptionist, waving his head in a noncommittal figure of eight.

'You must have a corner somewhere.'

'We have only one room in old part of hotel. I am thinking it will not be to your liking.'

'Oh yes, it will,' I said fervently.

I woke at five o'clock. Dark thoughts crowded my mind, filling me with anxiety. What was happening to my family? Was it right that I had left them to go looking for my own peace? I got up wearily. I didn't feel like doing anything. I didn't want to go on a tour of Bhubaneshwar's five hundred temples, I didn't want to walk around the town... I didn't even feel like having a shower. I wanted to give up.

Coffee, a free copy of the *Indian Express*, a shower and breakfast put me in a better mood. I bought a ticket for the tour of five hundred temples.

'Ten minutes,' said the guide as we galloped up the steps of the Udaygiri and Khandagiri Jain temples, tripping over the monkeys who had made the deserted cells their home. There was another quick stop at Lingaraj temple, dedicated to Tribhubaneshwar, the Lord of Three Worlds. It stood in an enclosure, dominating fifty smaller temples, and only Hindus were allowed inside. I was left outside to see as best I could from the platform built for Lord Curzon in the early twentieth century.

'Well, goodbye! It is so nice to meet you, and thank you for dressing properly,' said a middle-aged man from the tour group. 'Some of your Western friends look quite strange to us Indians.' His wife tucked her feet under her sari and pulled her pallu over her head. 'They do not cover themselves. Legs... arms...' He smiled and waggled his head in farewell.

'Puri, Puri!' The cry alternated with the piercing shriek of a whistle. I climbed aboard the waiting bus. At every stop people crowded on and in and up and out, squatting, sitting, standing, clinging. When there was no space left inside, they clambered onto the roof.

'Puri, Puri!' The whistle shrilled. Pop music blared. Garlands and tinsel danced a jig across the windscreen. A colourful patchwork flashed by – red and green fields, small thatched cottages, lakes covered with pink and mauve lotus flowers.

Decades had passed since Puri had been the Brighton of British East India, but somehow the South Eastern Railway Hotel had got left behind. Sitting on the veranda outside my room, on a cane chair at a cane table, I was joined for tea by Mr and Mrs K . Chatterji from Essex, on a sentimental journey to celebrate the fortieth anniversary of their honeymoon. We drank tea, ate slices of yellow railway cake and admired the view through the flower garden and a row of palm trees to the sea, where waves broke on a sandy shore.

After tea, walking across the gardens to the beach, I was met by an old man wearing a tall, conical hat. 'Memsahib, I am your own beach boy. I will look after you.'

'My beach boy?'

'Yes, Memsahib. I stop you drowning in big waves. Puri has waves like Himalaya.' He raised a hand above his head to indicate a great height.

'Oh, I see. Yes, drowning. Well, I wasn't going to swim just now.'

'Do not worry, Memsahib. I accompany with you anyways.' I could not get rid of this man. When I took off my sandals, he insisted on carrying them. When I sat on the sand, he sat, too, a discreet distance away. But he did not chase away the vendors and beggars who besieged me.

'Corals, beads from sea, you looking. I make special price. Look, look.' I looked up to see a man laying out a dozen necklaces on the sand. 'Sandalwood, you want smell? Very good wood. You like?'

'Coconut juice, I cut for Memsahib?'

'You have foreign coins?'

'You have pen?'

'You have chocolate?'

On the way back to the hotel, my beach boy began asking for his baksheesh and extracted a promise that if I swam, I would swim only with him. 'Please remember what I say. Your own beach boy. Special.'

I went to lunch.

'Memsahib, sorry. We have no single table. You sit with nice young gentleman from your country? He just arrive.' The waiter led me to a table where a very fair-haired young man was sitting. I did not mind, and hoped he would not. His name was Ralph. After leaving school, he had got a job in a bank in the City.

'A couple of months ago my mother died. I'd been in the rat race for seven years,' Ralph said. 'One day I decided to chuck up everything and... well... here I am. Don't really know what I'll do when I get back.'

The 1930s lunch menu left us both too bloated to even think of swimming. Through narrow streets lined with colour-washed cottages covered with delicate designs of fruit, flowers and animals, we walked to the Jagannath temple, home of the three gods of Puri: Lord Jagannath, his brother Balabhadra and his sister Subhadra. Outside the temple I bought a small, brightly painted picture of the gods for myself and a brass bowl engraved with their images for Baby.

Konarak was about twelve kilometres from Puri. The only space left on the bus was on the floor behind the driver's seat. I took it. A breeze blew in through the open window. The beautiful blue sea flashed at us coyly between passing palms while sugar-sweet Indian pop music seeped into our ears, hypnotising the squash of swaying passengers.

Konarak's temple crouches, a proud ruin of its former glory. It rises from a medley of chipped-stone chariot wheels, monumental animals and sculpted panels scattered on bland green lawns. The ancient grey-pink stones provide cover for blind beggars, beguiling guides and persistent postcard-sellers.

'Madam, I can see you are British,' said an old man, joining the group waiting for the Puri bus. 'I would like to inform you that our country has suffered since you left us. Things were better before.' I was surprised. Surely freedom at any price was better than colonisation?

Dinner was interrupted by the sounds of a wedding procession. Forgetting our food, we crowded into the garden to watch.

'Going to meet his bride,' said Mr Chatterji of the young man on the white nag, surrounded by generators and dancing youths.

After dinner, we sat on the veranda enjoying the peaceful sounds of crickets and waves breaking on the beach. More music-makers came slowly down the road.

'Funeral,' said Mr Chatterji. 'Music is indicating that body is old and very honourable.'

An occasional ripple, a brief cough, a sneeze – that was all I heard until, two hours out of Puri, the head of a middle-aged man poked through the curtains of the opposite cubicle in our luxury 2 A/C carriage. The curtains parted, and a body followed the head. It moved across the corridor and came to rest beside me. I waited for the standard opening lines, but they didn't come. This man asked only one question.

'Madam, I would like to ask you why you are travelling?' He didn't wait for my reply. 'What you are doing is unnecessary. I think you will be travelling to have peace and quiet, to leave worries behind you. Well, may I suggest, Madam, that you are able to achieve same, only by sitting in one corner of your own house, where you will shut your eyes and meditate. So doing, you do not have to make these effortful and exhausting journeys.'

'But I like travelling. I find other people and their ways and their countryside and their buildings very interesting and sometimes beautiful. If I stayed at home I wouldn't experience all this,' I said.

'Well, if you will excuse me for saying so, you are wrong. It will be better and altogether more sensible for you to make your own world as you want it, where you are.' I tried to explain that I didn't think I'd be able to; there were too many pressures and domestic preoccupations at home.

He retired behind his faded blue curtains, reappearing at intervals to take a rickety walk to the lavatory with a small plastic jug. He did not address me again.

I finished my book and turned towards the window. It was impossible to see through the double-glazed yellow-tinted glass. With my mind unoccupied, open to anything, my old fears and insecurities moved in. Perhaps the man was right. Perhaps I should have stayed in Pimlico.

My presents for the Singhs were a failure. The girls looked at the two little stone elephants from Sarnath in silence. Baby's brass bowl engraved with the gods of Puri was returned without thanks. 'Jill, please take this to England; there it will definitely be different,' she said. 'Here in India we have too many.'

The night before I was scheduled to leave Delhi for my tour of Rajasthan, Ravi Chhabra, the travel agent, rang to say that I would be the only traveller on the tour. My driver would pick me up at the Singhs' at nine o'clock the next morning.

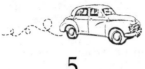

5

The wrought-iron gates clanged shut behind me. The same driver who had met me at Delhi's airport was standing beside the same white Ambassador. Ravi Chhabra had also come to see us off.

'Look after our client. Remember, she is VIP.'

'Yes, Sir. Do not worry, Sir.' The driver's smile took ten years off his age. It outshone his shiny shirt and ill-cut trousers. He was very good-looking.

As we headed southwest towards Rajasthan I studied the back of his head, the black hair carefully combed over a balding patch, and wondered what he was like. If there had been other passengers it would not have mattered, but now we had no escape from each other's company on the long roads ahead.

My mental gear box shifted to Britain, and to the bus drivers I had spent my summers with for the last fifteen years. Bobs and Johns, Eds and Bills, Joes and Kevs – I dined with the friendly ones night after night in a perfumed haze of Brut, Old Spice, roast beef, smoked mackerel and sherry trifle. Others were crabby, grasping and sulky. Bob, a Glaswegian alcoholic with a pock-marked face, had been one of the worst. His day began with a shot of vodka and progressed through bad tempers and foul language to unpleasant scenes with demanding but good-natured tourists.

My spirit stripped naked as Lady Godiva's body had been, I strode through the dripping streets of Coventry to her statue. Under a weeping sky, I told her story. We trudged on to shelter beneath the stretched concrete canopy that unites the modern

Coventry Cathedral with the original church, now an emotive ruin. Inside, the last notes of 'Onward Christian Soldiers' rose to the rafters.

That was the summer when my marriage disintegrated. We lived in three miserable rented rooms in Putney, where my husband, unemployed and filled with Valium, spent most of his time half-asleep on a heap of dirty bedding. As I climbed the narrow stairway every evening, tired from work, I could hear the hiss of frying hamburgers and smell the acrid smoke of burnt oil. Our youngest daughter, just eight years old, stood on tip-toe, tossing and turning the frozen discs. 'Supper's ready, Dad,' I heard her call.

A cow wandered across the highway. We slowed to let it pass.

'What did you say your name was?'

'I did not say, Memsahib. It is Yadav.'

'Yadav,' I repeated the name slowly. 'It's hard to pronounce.'

'Yes, Memsahib.'

Sometimes it's there and sometimes it's not: a magical, inexorable cord that draws two people together. I felt its tug now.

Alarm bells rang in my head. Red lights flashed: *You did not come to India for this. Keep yourself to yourself.* The message knocked and battered at my brain.

'Would you mind if I sat in front?' I asked. 'I think I'd see better, and it's difficult to talk to you from behind.' He seemed surprised. I later learnt that his Indian clients would not have dreamt of sitting with him, but for me, having shared much of my daily life with bus drivers, there was nothing strange about it.

'Of course. Please change your place.' He pulled over. The car behind us swerved, hooted and screeched past.

'Why did Mr Chhabra say I was a VIP?'

'I doesn't know, Memsahib. My boss, he says if you are not happy on tour, I am fired. No driver they wants to take you, so I must have to. It is my duty. I'm sorry, my English is poor.'

I said I thought it was very good, and sat wondering why I was so important and yet so unpopular with the drivers.

We drove through the suburbs of Delhi. Suddenly, without any warning, my driver swung off the highway into a driveway crammed with tour buses and taxis. Camera-clicking Koreans and overweight Westerners wandered about, bumping into one another and tripping over Indian families picnicking on dry grass verges. 'Here we will stop for your breakfast,' said Yadav. 'You will enjoy this place.'

'Would you mind if we went somewhere quieter?' I asked, explaining that I worked as a tour guide in England and was hoping, during my holiday, at least, to leave tourism behind me.

'I knew it already,' he said, heading back onto the road. 'And this is why other drivers, they doesn't want you. "She know her job very well," my boss, he tell us. "No commission, no tip." So they refuse. But, after all, I am happy. You are my respected tourist and I see you have very great mind. I thinks we will enjoy to each other. And now you will have your breakfast in dhaba. Is completely Indian place.'

The forecourt of the dhaba was filled with lorries, painted and tinselled in bright, clashing colours. Steaming silver cooking pots lined the counter outside an open-fronted shed. A sign swung from the corrugated iron roof.

YADAV HOTEL, BEST FOODS.

WELCOME.

'Look, it's got your name,' I said.

'Is because many peoples in this area has same name.'

Rough wooden tables and benches filled the dim interior. Outside, charpoys cradled drivers, some sleeping, others sitting cross-legged on the woven strings, scooping food onto triangles of chapati from tin plates and bowls. Two men stood by a tank of dirty water, sluicing their bodies with violent vigour. Limp loincloths clung to their skinny hips. Long, damp tresses of hair hung down their backs.

'These men are Sikh,' said Yadav, kicking off his chappals. He lay down on an empty charpoy and patted a corner invitingly. 'Sikh men, they mustn't cut their hairs in whole life, even from small baby. They doesn't follow caste system, but they do pray to all Hindu gods. And now is time we have our proper Indian food.' He tossed down a glass of chai and shouted for another.

Being one of the few people in the world who doesn't like tea – a terrible disadvantage in India, where it is offered on every occasion – I drank tepid Nescafé. We ate paranthas with lumpy curd.

'Now, my very dear friend and respected tourist,' said Yadav, 'we will enter my own state of Haryana and I think you will like to visit my farm and my family. My village is on road to Mandawa, where you will stay for your first night.'

'I would love to go to your farm,' I said. 'I'm sure it's more part of the real India than the places we're supposed to visit on the tour.'

Yadav looked mystified. 'Certainly it is real place. It is my home.'

Delhi's sprawling suburbs became industrial areas, and eventually met Haryana in a fever of construction sites – soon to be five-star hotels and so-called farmhouses, which were actually mansions in acres of acrylic gardens. Built by rich Delhiites with a yearning for country air, these monstrosities were mushrooming along the borders of the two states, along with golf courses and country clubs, just as Sunningdale, Wentworth and Solihull had mushroomed in England in the 1920s and '30s.

FINDING THE HEART OF INDIA

We struggled through the Gurgaon traffic and were suddenly in the country. Villages, sandwiched between fields of green and yellow wheat, barley and mustard, welcomed and waved us goodbye with well-disguised, stone-studded speed breakers guaranteed to snap any self-respecting suspension. The unemployed youth of Haryana stood by the roadside and stared at us.

Ebony buffaloes wallowed in village ponds, drinking deeply of their scummy soup. Cows, doe-eyed oxen and splay-footed camels ambled, oblivious to their cajoling barefoot masters – straight-backed, moustachioed men sheltered from the sun by turbans of psychedelic orange, pink and primrose-yellow. Chattering women peeped from the modest folds of their jewel-coloured silver- and gold-embroidered chunnis as they swung past us on provocative, heaving hips to hand-weed the fields.

We dawdled with the traffic, held up by flocks of goats and sheep controlled by flailing, shouting shepherds who had wandered hundreds of kilometres from their desert homes in Rajasthan to find grazing for their animals.

The capital of Yadav's district was a swirling cloud of dust. A jumble of wavering bicycles, cycle-rickshaws, rumbling tractors, unseeing pedestrians and animals, mixed with a smattering of camel carts, cars and jeeps, created a self-perpetuating horn of continuous, deafening noise. We stopped at the state-run tourist bungalow, the only hotel in town.

'For your coffee and your loo. At our village we doesn't have either, so please you take both here. This is our useful town – it has STD telephone. You can talk with Delhi, all India, and even whole world. In village we doesn't have telephone. But is only twenty-five kilometres away. And now, if you don't mind, I would like to buy fruits and sweets for childrens at my farm. I didn't see them for many days. Will you come in market with me?'

Hot, hard earth burned through the soles of my sandals. Brass- and copperware for kitchens and farms dangled in the shop doorways, performing a melting dance in the brazen rays of the sun. Tin thalis, ladles and lamps winked and blinked at the passing crowds. Barrow-wallahs bellowed. Bananas were ten rupees a kilo, oranges twenty; apples, grapes and unripe mangoes cost more. Yadav bought a huge hand of bananas. We turned into the cool of Punjabi Market, a dark little covered way, the local Burlington Arcade. It offered an assortment of sweets, knitting wools, women's clothing and children's shoes, the latter jockeying for position with plastic toys, glass bangles, hair clips and haberdashery.

'Childrens, they enjoy laddu too much.' Yadav bought a kilo of pale-brown balls from a sweet stall swarming with flies.

A blast of film music and political propaganda from the loudspeaker of a cycle-rickshaw pursued us between muddy puddles and neat piles of vegetables. Subzi-wallahs squatted on the ground, hand scales at the ready, surrounded by painters' pallettes of earthy potatoes, pink onions, carrots, creamy cauliflowers, emerald peas, deep-purple aubergines and red tomatoes. The smells of fresh garlic, ginger and coriander followed us into the fruit market and mixed with the scents of tangy oranges, red apples, yellow-green papayas, coffee-coloured chikus and bananas. Yadav stood politely to one side as a passing cow meandered through the throng, swinging her muck-covered haunches right and left. She was munching methodically through a plastic bag full of vegetables that she had filched from the back of a bicycle.

At the level crossing, vehicles, men and beasts jostled for prime position. 'Me first!' screamed horns and bicycle bells.

A train rushed through.

Engines revved for take-off. On the other side of the railway line, stallholders sold eggs: uncooked, hard- or soft-boiled or whipped into omelettes. Mechanics' workshops petered out, to be replaced by makers of furniture and clay water pots. The road divided at a roundabout that no one bothered to go round. We were in the country again.

We drove for twenty-five kilometres through sweet-smelling fields watered by sprinklers that sprayed their drops in circling cascades. We passed waving golden grasses with feathery silver fronds, next season's thatch, dividing the land into neat squares and oblongs. Yadav pointed to a group of clumsy deer grazing in a field of young wheat.

'They steals the farmers' crops, but is against law to shoot them. I think in your language you call them nilgai. Tall, thin chimney, is of brick kilns. In Haryana we makes many bricks, and we has slate quarries. Slate we exports worldwide. On your left is electricity company. Supply in Haryana is very poor; most often we have power cuts.'

We came to another level crossing. Here the gates were open, and the station master smiled and waved.

'See the carriage?' Yadav pointed to a rusting railway carriage lying halfway across the tracks. 'Almost two years it is here. No one they wants to move it. This is India.' He laughed, finding the inaction a joke.

Against a backdrop of hills, crowned by a tiny white temple, the dark silhouette of a camel ploughed up and down across the hard, brown earth. Intertwined branches, dark, cool and dank, roofed the road like a fairground tunnel of love, creating a grey-green camouflage of shadows shot through with the gold and silver shafts of early-evening sunlight.

'My bus stand.' Yadav's tone was proprietary. He waved to a group of men loitering round a tea stall. 'My friends.' We slowed to ride the rows of spiked speed breakers before lurching past open gates onto the railway tracks. Yadav stopped for a chat, right in the middle of the line. The red-turbaned signal man grinned.

'He ask me, "Who she is?"' Yadav said. 'I tell him my dear family friend and tourist.'

The potholed path skirted the paint factory's small round kiln, which baked stones that would be ground into the fine, powdered whitewash that was sloshed over walls for Diwali.

We wound past the tenting house. The proprietor, a pillar of society, was the magic man who, with yards of canvas and strips of red carpet, converted drab yards and alleys into fairy-tale glades for village marriages.

Wild peacocks ruled the road, strutting stupidly as if it were theirs. In a way, of course, it was.

Pye-dogs picked themselves out of the sand and chased us, barking and snapping at our tyres. Women and children hurried out onto flat roofs, pointing and screaming at us. Cars seldom passed their way, and even more seldom carried foreigners.

Lines of brick houses, some faced with mud and painted in pale colours, others as naked as the day their cement screeds dried, were separated by heaps of dried dung cakes. Through crumbling Moghul archways I caught glimpses of clean-swept yards, where children played hopscotch and busy women worked, washed, milked and cooked. Grander, free-standing houses with extravagant names hid behind wrought-iron gates tumbled with pink, red, white and purple bougainvillea. Little shops, half-hidden behind cave-like entrances, overflowed with vegetables, kitchenware, materials, candles, matches and bundles of bidis. Men squatted in the dust, hunched over playing cards. Yadav drove round every obstacle as if it were a roundabout in a well-ordered traffic plan.

'And this, you can say, is my birth house.' He stopped outside a ruined shack. 'Now we lives at farm, where we has our own tube well. Here in village is one well for all villagers. Even village well has electric motor. Womens can turn on tap and water comes. Square tank, that is for animals. It fills by itself.

Is all quite modern. Don't you think so? Only one problem is electricity. As I did tell you, quite often we do not have, then all must wait for water.'

A line of women waited their turn to fill their bulbous clay and brass water pots. The job completed, they hoisted their overflowing burdens effortlessly onto small embroidered circlets on their heads and left for home, posture-perfect, their hips swaying under coloured cotton skirts.

'Look!' Yadav pointed. 'My mum, she is coming.' The old woman's body curled round her wooden staff like a gnarled tree. Her pointed nose and button eyes were half hidden in a rough sea of wrinkled skin. She reached out a hungry hand, pulling her son's head down to her sagging breasts; her crooked fingers fondled his oiled hair in blessing. Unlike the villagers pressing round us, pop-eyed at the sight of me, she took me for granted, blessing me as she had blessed Yadav.

'Come, Ma, we will go to farm. Chalo!' he bellowed. 'She's deft,' he explained. 'She doesn't like to be at farm. Always, when she get the chance, she stay in village because she is used to home here.' Ma didn't move.

The village was behind us. The track, hemmed in by tall grasses, grew rougher and dustier. When we crested a hump at speed, our heads hit the roof.

'Is only tube from well. Farmers, they lay tubes under sand for irrigating crops. Is difficult to see, so I did miss it. Double sorry.' Yadav pulled up, hooting at a wooden camel cart with tyreless wooden wheels. The driver shook his fist in mock anger. 'My uncle's cousin, he is always joker. Why you do not take lift in his cart?'

I climbed up beside the uncle's cousin. The cart jolted forward. The camel, a natural dancer, lifted and dropped its huge hooves delicately on the uneven ground. The Ambassador followed, bucking and stalling. After a few metres, the uncle's cousin gave the rope reins a vicious tug, said something in Hindi and, with a sharp jerk, turned his beast's head to the fields. The camel stopped. My ride was over.

Yadav opened the car door for me. 'He must quickly have to go on with his ploughing; season is getting late. My own family, we hates camels. We has ox to pull our plough.'

Ahead of us, suspended between blue sky and yellow mustard, was a group of low white buildings – the farm. The roar of our engine brought three little children running down the path. Yadav opened his door and they tumbled in, nestling up to him like a litter of puppies. He steered with one hand and fondled them with the other.

An old man squatted in the dusty yard. He drew deeply on his hookah, wheezing and coughing, making it burble and bubble in the still air. Buffaloes shifted from hoof to hoof, tossing curly horned heads and rattling their short tethering chains. The old man's finely chiselled features, topped by a voluminous yellow turban, split into lines of pleasure. Bones creaking, he staggered to his feet. He wore a length of stained white cloth round his waist with the end drawn through his legs, creating something that resembled half a pair of Persian trousers. The tail dragged on the ground behind him.

'What is he wearing?' I asked. The camel-cart driver and most of the village men had been wearing the same garment.

'My father,' said Yadav, bending respectfully to touch his feet, 'is wearing dhoti. About that I can tell you funny story, I don't know it will make you laugh. British man was visiting Indian village. Only one villager he speak English. To make conversation, he takes hold of foreigner's necktie and asks him, "What is this?" British man tells him, "Is necktie." "Oh!" says Indian farmer. "And what is that?" asks English man, taking end of farmer's dhoti. "Is back tie," says farmer.'

I waited for him to finish the story.

'Is finish,' he said. 'Is very funny story. Yes?'

I said yes and laughed. I soon found that, no matter how hard I listened to Yadav's jokes, I often missed the punchline.

We were suddenly surrounded by relatives: veiled women in long, gathered skirts and short, loose blouses with bare midriffs, teenage girls in salwar-kamiz, shaven-headed children, and young men with two days' growth on their faces, their heads wound in colourful bath towels. Greetings over, we went through an open doorway, crossed two rooms-cum-stables, and came to an inner courtyard. One of the women brought bowls of curd and plates of roti glistening with melted ghee. They stood round while we ate, staring and giggling. I asked why they were laughing.

'They knows about Western peoples. Even before you come, I bring my tourists. But others, they do not enjoy to share our food. This is why they laugh. Please do not mind.'

Yadav's father, still smoking his hookah, handed his son a scrap of paper. Yadav looked at it and laughed.

'It say my father, he want I earn thirty thousand rupees to finish building second tube well. Someone, they write it for him. My father, he cannot read or write.'

I asked if Yadav had been to school. 'Of course I have, and all my childrens, now they does go. But in my generation only me and my brother who works in police, we went. All other family members of old generation is same like my father.'

'How can your father look after the farm? Accounts and things?'

'He does manage very well. In his head he makes sums too quickly. And money, he does recognise each note. And now, if you do need bathroom I will show you how you can manage. I am sorry, but I did tell you already we does not have latrine, so please you go in mustard field behind house. There you will not be disturbed, and mustard, it has very good smell.'

I returned from the mustard to find the entire family crowding into the car.

'Yes,' Yadav said, seeing my look of surprise. 'This car can hold twenty-five peoples. Once I tell to my tourist. She doesn't believe, so I stop and invite all villagers to come in. After she see with her own eyes, she must have to believe. Proof of all pudding is in eating. Now we has only fifteen peoples – nothing! Please get in and we will go to see new well.' I squeezed myself into the front seat beside five neatly folded adults.

A pair of oxen plodded towards us, their yokes straining on a rope whose end disappeared over the edge of the newly built well shaft. They took another step, the rope tightened and the head and shoulders of a young man popped over the rim. He climbed out and into Yadav's open arms.

'He is Rama, my Boss Brother's son. I love him too much.' He embraced the young man and, taking him by the arm, walked him off down the track, deep in conversation. Shorn of Yadav's protection, I was left to the mercy of the family. They posed for photographs, gabbling and laughing. They fingered my bangles, touched my earrings and pointed at my bare ankles. The hookah bubbled. The oxen drew load after load of earth from the well. Sweat trickled down my forehead and ran into my eyes. My head ached; my throat was full of dust. At last Yadav came back and after many a 'Ram Ram' we left, driving back through the village and on to the road to Rajasthan.

My thoughts were spinning with Yadav's brothers, sisters-in-law, nephews, nieces, uncles, aunts, cousins and children. 'Do they really all live together?' I asked.

'The most of them they does. Even we have relatives, or you can say close ties with all my villagers. We have been in village from hundreds and hundreds of years. We are relatives of Lord Krishna. He is god and I am too fond of him. In one of his lives after his birth in the prison, he is adopted by cowherd and brought up farmer, so he is Yadav caste like us. In villages we have strict caste laws – we cannot do work of other castes. Even we must marry in our own caste, but never in same village. Now in big cities they doesn't always follow caste laws, but of course in village we does.'

'Oh – I thought Yadav was your given name,' I said. 'Do you have another?'

'I am Lal Singh, meaning Red Lion. My good name is Kola, but never we use it. Did you enjoy to meet my family?'

'I did, very much. But there are too many! I could never remember who's who.'

'We are sixteen or more family members. Not too many for you to remember, I think? But that is only at farm. I should tell also about my whole family. We has relatives in village, in Haryana and even in Rajasthan.'

'Please don't. That's enough to keep straight for one day,' I said, laughing.

'Is good I can give you laugh. Now we will carry on.' He accelerated and we shot over the border into Rajasthan.

The lush greens and yellows turned into seas of arid sand, glaring and hot. Lonely camels reached their long necks into the branches of dry trees, nibbling at parched leaves.

'Why you are silent? What you are thinking? I am afraid you do not like to visit my family.' The furrows between his eyebrows deepened.

'No, I did, really, very much.'

'Good, is my pleasure. Then what?'

'I was thinking it's like going back in time. We don't have families like yours in England any more. On farms we use machines to do the work. The families are split up, living in separate units in cities. Many people live and die alone.'

6

Mandawa is a busy market town in the heart of Shekhavati. The maharaja's palace-cum-fort had been turned into a hotel.

Heralded by a roll of drums, we swept through an entrance guarded by costumed camel riders into the eighteenth-century forecourt. The drummers were not drumming for us; they were tuning up for an expected busload of tourists.

'Now you do your own work. Here is room voucher,' Yadav said. 'When you are ready, I will take you to guide for city sightseeing.'

The receptionist was far too busy preparing for his group to waste time on me. I sat and waited, fuming at finding myself caught in the clutches of Indian tourism. The drums rolled again and the coach drew up, disgorging its thirty-eight portly passengers. Bellboys bumped into each other and into their confused clients. The receptionist beamed and bowed. Bulging bottoms in tartan trews stood paralysed, waiting for their god, the guide, to direct their next step into the unknown terrors of a foreign land. Varanasi or Agra? Mandawa or Mysore? What did they care? The names were unpronounceable anyway. Big bodies with small heads sporting made-to-match golf caps helped themselves to Campa-Cola from trays carried by willing waiters, and distributed rupees to all and sundry.

'Where the hell is Liz, or is it Suze? I thought she was supposed to look after us. I'll sue if she doesn't do better than this.'

'Who?'

'Her. The company. The bus. What's it matter?'

'Doesn't this place belong to some kind of king... what did she call him, Maharaji or something?'

'Who?'

'Liz, or Suze, or was it Marj?'

'You mean the king man?'

'No. Yes. Hell – where is she?'

A middle-aged Indian man with greying hair and a slight paunch walked down the front steps. He was wearing a dark-blue blazer and dog-tooth checked trousers.

'That's him! That's the maharaja!' someone shouted. 'Evening, Mr Maharaja, Sir. How do you do?' The maharaja stopped and raised a hand in greeting.

Tired of sitting unnoticed, I walked over to him. He introduced himself and said he was on his way to the temple for his evening puja. He asked if I was being well looked after.

'Well, no, I'm not,' I said.

'I'm so sorry. Please come with me.' The results were immediate, including the sudden obsequious behaviour of the receptionist. I was shown to a round tower room with an enormous bed covered in heraldic drapes and bolsters. The old-fashioned bathtub was the size of a paddling pool. When I tried to take a shower, the top of the ancient shower head came off in my hand, followed by a scalding gush of steam. I gave up on washing and changed into a blue-and-gold salwar-kamiz made by Baby's dressmaker in Delhi, fancying myself an old India hand amongst the surrounding philistines.

I found Yadav talking to a guard at the gate. He looked me up and down with approval.

'Now you looks like real Indian princess,' he said. 'And before your dinner we has time to find local travel agent for guided tour.'

'Can we just go for a walk and look at one of the havelis by ourselves?'

'But you have paid for proper city guide.'

'Please?'

Reluctantly, he agreed.

Pursued by children and beggars, we found our haveli at the end of a rutted village street. The courtyard was filled with hanging laundry and grunting pigs and piglets. The once-grand rooms were occupied by families of squatters. Peeling frescoes recalled richer, happier times, before the British had disrupted the Marwaris' trade and effectively driven them out of Rajasthan. The house was a sad skeleton of its former glory.

Yadav walked me back to the castle gates. 'Where will you sleep?' I asked. He nodded towards the car.

'Do you have to?' I did not like to think of him folded on the back seat while I stayed in the castle, living it up with the maharaja and his tourists.

'I must have to,' he said. He drove away.

Not far out of Mandawa on the road to Bikaner, we took a detour to the village of Fatehpur to see what my guidebook called 'the most beautiful havelis in Shekhavati'. The beauty of the old mansions – like the face of a beautiful woman grown old – was still there, but had faded and worn with time and lack of maintenance. An overnight downpour had turned the streets into canals, and Yadav's immaculate white car emerged from the village streaked with brown mud. I thanked him for the detour. He replied dryly that it had been his pleasure.

'The road is not too bad, and traffic it is nothing. I think you would like to drive. Will you?' Yadav asked. 'Only please remember to use horn. In my country is most important thing.'

I sat behind the wheel feeling more like a traveller now, less like a helpless tourist. Yadav lolled in the passenger seat beside me. He asked about family and marriage and divorce in the West, and my own in particular.

'I have heard love is free in your country. Is it true?'

'Well, sort of.' I concentrated on the road. I did not want to be drawn into discussions of my unsatisfactory love life with a man I had known for one day. 'Yadav, I need a loo. Where can I go?'

'You have whole desert,' he said, waving his hand towards the shadowless sands and roaring with laughter. 'I tell like this to all my tourists – "You have all India!" It is good joke, isn't it?'

We stopped by the only hillock for miles around. Nothing and no one disturbed the whispering silence of the desert. A trio of vultures, crouching on a branch like Shakespeare's crones, waited patiently not for Banquo and Macbeth, but for a whiff of carnage to waft their way on the desultory desert breeze – a car crash, a camel carcass, a careless cur.

In Bikaner I followed a group of Italian tourists round the palace museum. Their leader translated into Italian from another guide who was translating into English from a Hindi guidebook. Impatient with the resulting nonsense, the Italians moved off in small groups to gaze at displays of guns, manuscripts and ancient black-and-white photographs in dusty glass cases beneath the glassy stares of snarling tigers and leaping leopards.

I have never liked eating alone in public places. I asked Yadav, who was becoming as much a friend as a driver, to dine with me in my hotel, the Lallgarh Palace.

In the gloom of the castle's dining room, twelve noisy tourists sat guzzling Kingfisher beer, their faces glowing like night lights. The food, insipid by a Haryana farmer's fiery standards, was served to us by a haughty waiter with hatred written on his face. He had not expected to see drivers ordering common dal in his dining room. He threw a plate in Yadav's direction and walked off to take a tray of hamburgers – respectable foreign food – to his more lucrative customers.

'Goodnight,' said Yadav stiffly as soon as we had finished eating. The evening had not been a success.

The next day, Yadav insisted on taking a tour of Bikaner with a local guide. The guide was a nice young man from a strictly vegetarian Brahmin family. 'We eat neither onions nor garlic nor meat of any kind. They are heaters of blood,' he explained as he led us through pavilion after pavilion and court after court of the royal palace and fort, telling stories of Raja Rai Singh. Faint with hunger and pre-summer heat, we eventually made our excuses and left for the bazaar, where Yadav insisted on buying me a Jaipur bedspread that I had stopped to admire. None of my protests could stem his excited generosity.

Day turned to evening. Beyond the fairy-lit gardens and the maharaja's obsolete railway carriage, Yadav sat in the car park, waiting to take me to dinner. An unopened quarter bottle of whisky lay on the seat beside him.

'Will you mind if I take drink?' he asked. Not waiting for a reply, he called to a passing gardener to bring some water. Unscrewing the cap, he sprinkled a few drops of alcohol on the ground.

'For my god,' he explained. He threw away half the water, filled the tumbler with whisky and tossed back his drink in one gulp.

The car inched through the traffic to the Amber Restaurant, listed as one of the best in Bikaner. A family party, encompassing everyone from silk-saried grannies to babies latched on to their mother's breasts, sat tucking into dishes as numerous and varied as themselves. The waiter led us to the only free table, hidden behind a pillar. Having left it to Yadav to order, I could hardly complain when nothing but curd and roti arrived.

'My favourite food,' he said, tucking in noisily. Afterwards, glad that we were hidden behind the pillar, I sat waiting while he cleaned his teeth with a forefinger.

A sudden downpour had flooded the streets with dirty water and disrupted the power supply. As we left the restaurant, a fat brown rat scurried in. Outside, we were plunged into damp darkness. London would have come to halt, but in Bikaner the crowds waded about their business as usual.

At three in the morning I woke, filled with the hopeless depression I had hoped to leave behind in London. Tears soaked my lumpy pillow. Furious thoughts of 'The Grandeur of Rajasthan' chased themselves round my head. The tour was nothing but an Indian milk run (as British tour guides called the standard eight-day tour from London to Inverness and back). My unhappy vigil lasted till the first light of dawn. I shut my eyes, trying to blot out the intrusive images crowding my brain. Suddenly, like unwanted guests, they left. With a faint click, the door that I had left ajar, shut. The bed was warm and comfortable. I fell asleep and dreamt of a grand camel-cart tour of Jaisalmer, tomorrow's destination. My guide was a maharaja who wore a dhoti and had a bald patch in his black hair. Someone was banging on the side of the cart. The camel snorted. The maharaja raised his whip and shouted.

'Memsahib, Memsahib – driver is waiting. He say you must leave by eight thirty on dot. Today you make very long drive.' A waiter stood in my doorway, slopping coffee from a cup on to a tray. I looked at my watch. It was nine o'clock.

We gave a lift to a Belgian couple following the same Rajasthan trail. They were on a pre-marriage honeymoon, a stop on the way home to Brussels after a veterinary seminar in Pakistan. Trying to explain to Yadav, who hardly knew what a honeymoon was, how it could happen before marriage relieved the boredom of the melting ribbon of carbuncled tarmac that led to Jaisalmer.

'These are your Western customs. I cannot help about them,' he said, shaking his head. 'In my country, only at marriage we meets our wife, and then we falls in love. You falls in love, gets married and after short time you get divorce. Is better our way, I think, and in village we doesn't afford honeymoon, neither before, neither after.'

A red light flickered on the dashboard, driving all thoughts of Western licence from his mind. 'Generator, it is not working well. This morning I am too worried when my memsahib she does not get up, and I forget to pray my god before I start engine.' Yadav's faith played a major part in his life, mixed with strong superstitions. If his first encounter of the day was with a sweeper, superstition dictated that he stop to give her five rupees. When passing a temple, he took both hands off the wheel and joined them together while bowing his head in silent prayer, endangering both car and passengers. A cat crossing his path required him to back the car up a few paces and sit still for three minutes. He never backed out of a parking space; rather, he started the engine and drove forward a bit, even if it meant risking a bump. Life must go ahead, never backwards.

Despite this morning's omission, Yadav's god was with us. Just as the needle on the dashboard touched boiling point, we found a mechanic. In the time it took to drink a glass of chai in a nearby tea stall, the man fixed the car.

The glimmering image of Jaisalmer's ninety turreted walls, red-gold in the dying sun, flickered into focus. The city and fort rose from a sea of sand that reached out in all directions to touch the horizon. Within the city's gateways, upper casements of carved houses nudged each other across the narrow uphill streets.

I glanced at Yadav, thinking of my dream. Concentrate on the splendours of Jaisalmer's architecture, I told myself.

We dropped the Belgians off and drove uphill. In a small café below the walls of the fort, we ordered two glasses of special lassi.

'Is good to cheer up,' said Yadav. 'Cheers!' He poured the creamy liquid down his throat the same way he had drunk his whisky, without drawing breath. If the gods have a favourite nectar, I decided, it must be Jaisalmer's lassi, the most delicious drink I have ever tasted. I felt extremely happy. We had a second glass and asked for the recipe.

'It is my secret, but I will tell you,' said the proprietor. 'Take curd of cow milk with little water, mix with special wooden tool, take few drops of rose water, then add cardamom, saffron and cream, and, last but most important, generous pinch of bhang. Of course is good. Western peoples come to drink again, again and again.'

I asked Yadav what bhang was. 'I thinks in your country you might make spelling p-o-t.'

Before the sun was up the next morning we drove from Jaisalmer to Khuri, on the edge of the sand dunes. The mud walls of the village cottages were decorated with delicate white patterns and topped with trim thatched roofs. At Mama's Guest House, a Fagin-like character in rags and bristling whiskers presided over a troupe of small boys and girls, sending them on endless errands for foreign camel riders (chai, Pepsi, camping equipment) and giving nothing but a cuff on the ear in return.

My guide, Girohari, was waiting. Raja and Ram, the camels, were harnessed and loaded. They sank to their leathery knee pads, their double-jointed legs folding like those of a loosely screwed toy. I clung to the camel driver's shoulders as Raja teetered unsteadily to his hoofs. Ram, loaded with luggage, took up the rear.

The desert sun rose slowly behind shadowless mountains. Mama's Guest House and Yadav disappeared behind range upon range of sand dunes. Our camels picked their dainty way through boulders and clumps of flowering cacti. Black goats with tinkling collar bells cropped the sandy land, guarded by statuesque herdsmen in outsized orange turbans. In a hamlet of mud huts crowned with perky thatched topknots, villagers peered out from dwarf-sized doorways. Girohari waved. He and his white-skinned giants had travelled this way before.

We stopped for the night in a rare dip in the ground, furnished with trees and bushes. The boys collected sticks and twigs to make a fire. Girohari squatted by the crackling flames, throwing small balls of batter-covered vegetables and paneer into a spitting pot of oil and spooning out golden nuggets. 'Pakora,' he said, grinning. For the second course we had curried aubergines, carrots and green tomatoes with dal and rice.

A pair of lovebirds chased each other round the bushes, descended on to my plate, pecked at the last grains of rice and, chirping and chattering, rose again. In a sort of ritual dance, they fluttered, rose again and fell, united at last, to the ground. The boys laid out mattresses for themselves and began struggling with a tent for me. I did not want it. They made me a bed on the ground, with soft pillows and starched white bedclothes. The scent of woodsmoke filled the air. Girohari sang a lilting song that echoed and died, swallowed in the silent sighs of the desert.

After that one romantic night and two days of crotch-shattering camel rides, I returned to find Yadav waiting outside Mama's Guest House, exactly where I had left him.

'It was so lovely! I wish you had come,' I said.

'Oho,' he replied, uninterested.

I was glad to have a hot shower and a large, soft bath towel. Afterwards I sat on the balcony enjoying the sun, nursing my aching muscles and writing postcards.

A high-pitched screech from below broke the peace. The hotel security guard was shouting at Yadav in English. 'You with paper bundle, YOU... YOU, driver. STOP! Drivers not permitted inside my hotel. Who you think you are?' he waved his lathi, salivating at the chance to show his importance.

I ran downstairs, wishing I could clout the man with his own stick. Instead, knowing that the parcel Yadav was holding contained my laundry, I grabbed it and took it up to my room.

'Bloody fool.' Yadav was not the least bit disconcerted. 'And now we will take our walk inside fort.'

From the stone-carved balconies above our heads, women called and chatted across the narrow street. We climbed to the summit of the fort, where, in the diminutive courtyard of the Jaisal Castle Hotel, we were served fresh orange juice by a princess of the royal house of Jaisalmer. I sipped my drink, Yadav gulped his, and we both admired the infinite views of the desert far below.

On our way down, tiny shop windows filled with mirrorwork and rich embroideries tempted me off the shadowy street. Yadav told the shopkeepers that I was his special guest and he was not seeking a commission. This embarrassed me so much that I bought nothing. I don't like begging, but being begged for was worse.

In the evening, Yadav dropped me off at a restaurant and went to meet a fellow driver. The restaurant owner had done his best to blend in with his Western customers. His hair was an unnatural shade of rusty red, and tight jeans bit into his loud floral shirt. Cole Porter competed with the clatter and chatter of the crowded room. 'If I had organised your camel safari,' the owner said, his hips swaying in time to the music, 'it would have been real cool – a proper bed, soap, loo paper, two four-course meals and plenty of good company. The works. So where's your friend?' I had been ashamed to tell him that Yadav was my driver. 'If he is Indian man, you must be careful. They are not reliable.'

An hour later, Yadav burst into the restaurant. 'Please take off Western music. I have bad headache, and I would like to tell you, if you do not mind, we are in India. We doesn't need stupid Western song.' Yadav sat down, cradling his head in his arms. He did not look at the menu, nor did he ask what I wanted. 'For me is dal fry and roti – they must be well cooked – and curd,' he ordered the waiter. 'And please bring quickly. I am hungry.'

'What's wrong?' I asked. 'Did you meet your friend?'

'Nothing is wrong. Nothing at all. Now please, you choose your food.' I ordered something, but I had lost my appetite. The owner, with a knowing smirk, went to turn off the music.

'I'm sorry,' I told him as we were leaving. 'I don't know what was wrong. Your restaurant is really very nice.'

'Don't you? He's been drinking, that's all.'

Why had Yadav behaved so badly? Why the hell did I care, anyway? I dreamt of the three blind mice. Instead of cutting off their tails with a carving knife, the farmer's wife lopped off their heads with a cutlass. I woke up screaming and dripping with blood. The scream was the horn of a lorry below my window. The blood was my own sweat. I telephoned my family in London just to make sure they were alive and well.

In Jodhpur, I stayed in another palace hotel and re-met the Belgian couple we had driven to Jaisalmer. After having tea together, we decided to go to the city.

Yadav was reluctant to take us. 'Fort will be closed; today is holiday. I will take you tomorrow, so where you want to go now?'

'To the bazaar,' we said. He was not keen, but we insisted.

'I hope you will not mind if first I will eat my food.' He bought some chilli pakoras from a roadside stall and insisted that we try them, too.

'But you have only three – you must eat them,' we protested. Yadav leapt out of the car and bought three more, pressing us to accept. The pakoras were immensely spicy; our eyes watered and our noses ran. Yadav drove on.

'Before bazaar I must have to pass hotel to confirm my own room booking.' He stopped the car outside a modern guest house in a dirty back street and went in, reappearing after a few minutes with the owner. 'This gentleman, he will be pleased you come in to take chai.' We declined as politely as we could. 'And he doesn't understand why you waste all your money in bloody expensive maharajas' palaces. Here is very clean, very cheap and very good.' He and the hotelier switched back to Hindi. The neighbourhood ragamuffins gathered and stood in a circle round the car, gaping at us and reaching through the windows to pull at our clothes. 'Pen, rupees, chocolate,' they whined.

'Yadav, please may we go now?'

'Very well, but city, you will not enjoy. I knows it.'

He was right. The shops were shut and there was no one about. Yadav drove back to the hotel like a rocket released from a launching pad.

'We would like to arrive alive,' I said, as casually as I could under the circumstances.

'Of course you will – I am driver.' He missed a bicyclist by centimetres and swerved into the hotel drive. Confronted by the raja's jeep on its way out, our Ambassador sat, refusing to give way. The raja got out and politely asked us to move.

'I will fetch you in morning for your tour. What time you want I come?' Yadav asked.

'Please come at eight forty-five. Thanks.' I hoped my voice sounded distant and dismissive.

'Nine thirty will be as good.'

'Eight forty-five,' I snapped.

He inclined his head.

'You should go and have a good rest,' the Belgians told him. 'Driving on these roads must be exhausting.'

I lay on my bed trying to read. Thoughts of Yadav crowded my mind. Did he resent my staying where he could not? Was I not being nice enough to him? Why had I landed up with such an emotional man? And above all, why did I care about his emotions anyway? It was the usual story – the hardest part of the tour was nursing the driver along. But this time I was not supposed to be working; I was on holiday. And it was not quite the usual story.

I did not want to admit, even to myself, that I cared quite a lot about Yadav. I wished I had stayed in the back of the car and kept my distance, but it was too late. We now seemed to be tied to each other by an invisible cord that had been tugging me towards Yadav since the beginning... and we had only known each other for seven days. There was dangerously little rope left, but with only five days still to go, I felt sure I could resist the final tug. If we could just get to Agra, we could say goodbye. I would give him his tip and we would go our separate ways.

The next morning there was so much to write in my diary that I forgot the time. At nine o'clock, fifteen minutes after the time I had given Yadav, there was a thunderous knocking. My eyeliner smudged, giving me a black eye. Cursing, I opened the door.

'Thanks God, you is all right.' Yadav's face brightened. He seemed to have forgotten yesterday. I had not.

'I'm not ready. I haven't had breakfast yet. And I just want to say one thing to you: if you ever drive like you did yesterday evening again, I'll get out of your car and catch the train back to Delhi. And you can go where the hell you like.'

His face contorted. The two vertical lines between his eyebrows deepened. He put his head in his hands. There were suddenly tears in his voice. 'Truly I am sorry, Ma'am.'

Later I found him standing at attention by the open car door. 'Where do you like to go this morning, Ma'am?' He had never, even at the beginning of the tour, spoken to me so politely.

I could not sustain such frigid dignity for long. Soon we were chatting as if nothing had happened. We shopped for a sari for one of Yadav's daughters and bought a tie-dyed salwar-kamiz for a friend of mine in London.

At Meherangarh Fort, the greatest and grandest in Rajasthan, we were forced to choose a guide from the battery barricading the gates. An hour later, bombarded with information on the armouries, palanquins, painted rooms, sumptuous saris and swings for idle young royals, we emerged from the cool gloom into broiling sunshine. We continued on the steep ascent to the topmost rampart, where, all but melting, we leant on the battlements, caught our breath and looked down over the old city, now a toy town. The clock tower, temple turrets and bazaar, teeming with armies of ant-like people, broke up the straight, narrow streets of back-to-back blue-painted houses. Dominating the hill opposite was the Umaid Bhavan Palace, home to the maharaja of Jodhpur and our afternoon stop for tea.

We were surprised by the utter emptiness of the huge reception hall. If there were guests, they were not in evidence. The bell on the reception desk produced nothing but an echo. The grand salon, its domed roof outshining that of Blenheim Palace, was devoid of life, more like a mausoleum than a drawing room. Through the French doors we could see no stroller strolling in the flower-scented gardens. Not a teacup tinkled on its saucer at the tables on the well-ordered terraces.

'Chalo,' said Yadav. 'We will take our tea in city. This is depressing place.' At a scruffy café in town, we shared a dish of puri served with spicy potatoes and kofta cooked in curd and curry. Scooping the last drops from our tin bowl, we ordered a second helping.

'I think you likes Indian food. It is my pleasure,' said Yadav. Getting up to clean his teeth at the public wash basin, he created a symphony of hawking, spitting and coughing.

The next morning steamed with expectant heat. Through the open door of my cottage, shafts of early-morning sunlight shot through the tangled branches of bougainvillea. The butter melted through my hot toast, mixing with the dark-red apple jam. The coffee smelt and tasted delicious. It was my last breakfast in Jodhpur.

We should have started early on the long journey to Udaipur, but I could not resist going on the raja's one-day jeep safari to some desert villages. Yadav, still making amends, promised that it would be his pleasure to drive through the evening, arriving in Udaipur at midnight or later.

At eight o'clock a small group of guests were ready and waiting in the courtyard. Our host arrived an hour late, with a cheerful 'Good morning' and an exhortation to hurry. This was India, I reminded myself. Did we not have a lifetime to spare?

Our whistle-stop tour was a kaleidoscope of village life and crafts, ending under a clump of trees beside a canal. Potters beat pot-bellied pots that smelled of damp earth. Painters decorated them with simple geometric designs. String weavers wove metres of twine for the ubiquitous charpoys. Sitting on a cottage floor, we shared plates of dal, beans and chapati, served by a hostess on whom jewellery – her dowry – hung like laundry on a line. With her hefty silver anklets, heavy earrings pulling her earlobes down to her shoulders, bangles from wrist to upper arm, nose rings and a nugget of gold dangling from a neck chain, she would never need a begging bowl.

'Last stop, vampire bats,' said His Highness, manoeuvring the jeep along a narrow tow path. A peacock, alarmed by the roar of the engine, took flight, resettling himself in the branches above our heads – the home of a family of weird, macabre, upside-down creatures. Someone threw a stone, and the giant bird-animals took off. Spreading their leathery wings they flapped upwards, monstrous black silhouettes that momentarily blotted out the sun as they flew straight into its blinding light. I wondered how they could see. Weren't bats supposed to be blind? But were they bats at all? Perhaps they were pterodactyls; anything seemed possible here.

'Gin-and-tonic time – the sun's going down. Everyone in the jeep.' The raja was brusque.

Back in Jodhpur, I paid my bill and ran out to the car, full of apologies for having made Yadav wait so long.

'Good evening, Ma'am. Your car is ready, Ma'am,' he said simply.

We drove through the darkening hills, catching hares, foxes and field mice in the beams of our headlamps and getting caught ourselves in the glare of the undimmed lights of oncoming lorries. It was midnight when Yadav left me at the jetty beside Udaipur's Lake Pichola. Miraculously, even at that hour, a ferry was waiting to take me to the Lake Palace Hotel.

I dreamt of Yadav. His arms and legs dangled helplessly as he was carried upwards, gripped in the beak of a vampire bat. (Or was it a pterodactyl? Bats didn't have beaks.) It soared upwards on giant, grey, varicose-veined wings until, no more than a black spot, it vanished with Yadav into the setting sun.

Sunlight streamed through a gap in the curtains, blinding my half-closed eyes and filling my mind with a sense of hopeless loss. Dreams are only dreams, but facts are facts. I had three days left in Yadav's company. After that it would be immaterial what kind of animal carried him away; I would never see him again. I forced myself out of bed, moved towards the window to draw back the heavy drapes and noticed my luxurious room for the first time.

And then I saw the view.

An early mist was rising from the lake. Small craft plied back and forth, slap, slapping quietly as they rose and fell on lacy little waves. Across the water, a mirror image shivered in the sapphire glass, a marble mirage of palaces, parks and temples touched with the colours of laundry drying on the ghats and bougainvillea running riot on the ancient city walls. I opened the window to let in the sweet, clean morning air. A stench of putrefying flesh drifted in on the breeze – below my window, where water lapped the grassy shore, four stiff, furry paws pointed skywards, the carcass of a dog and now the disputed breakfast of six hungry crows. Shutting the dog and its demise from my thoughts, I dressed in honour of the view in a bright-red dress patterned with yellow, green and white elephants. It was Rajasthani turban fabric, made into a Western dress by 'Fancy Tailors', a one-man band with a sewing machine and a large pair of shears in Jodhpur's bazaar.

The Lake Palace shrank to a sugar-icing cake as I stepped on to the whitewashed landing on the city side of the lake. There was no sign of Yadav.

He arrived at 10.30 and asked if I would mind waiting while he had a cup of tea. My fury left me speechless. Without a word I walked off, in what I hoped was the right direction for the City Palace. Before I had gone a hundred metres, the Ambassador drew up and the door opened.

'Double sorry, my respected tourist. Please forgive me.' Of course, I did.

To get into the palace we had to pass the usual posse of guides. Yadav looked apprehensive. 'They are saying I am your guide. They will not let me in – I am not official. Please you go by yourself.' Yadav was forever telling me that I was the only tourist he had ever visited anything with; he usually sat outside drinking chai and talking to other drivers. 'Is only because you are almost my family member, and you has job like my own. Otherwise I will never come in. Palaces and monuments, they are quite boring places for me.'

This time he came with me, looking uneasily over his shoulder. One of the guides followed us, and in the first room he edged up to Yadav and whispered in his ear.

'He say I must not speak single word until we leave this building.'

Unable to communicate, we soon lost each other. I imagine he hurried through the halls and courts, seeing nothing of the views of Udaipur through the delicate tracery of the arched windows, or the collection of miniature paintings of the palace, the city and its people. I found him, as I had expected, in the car park with a cup of chai.

Yadav could never see the point of walking when he could drive. For most of his life he had had to walk; he had never thought of doing it for pleasure. It took all my powers of persuasion to get him to climb the Moti Magri, or Pearl Mount. When we paused to rest halfway up, he opened a bag he had been carrying and took out a papaya the size of a rugby ball.

'Shall we eat?' he asked. We cut the fruit into slices, scooping out the ebony seeds. The flesh was juicy and bittersweet. Like India, I thought.

Below us, the car, parked on the banks of Fateh Sagar Lake, looked like a matchbox toy. Above us, the summit of the hill was topped by a statue of Maharana Pratap astride his horse, Chettak.

'He is my favourite hero,' Yadav said. 'And his horse is second.' He told me the story of how they had fought and beaten Akbar. 'And when we will come again in Udaipur I will take you to Haldi Valley, which is place where this story happen. Is called Haldi because rocks they are yellow colour.'

'But we'll never have another day together in Udaipur.'

'I will tell you very serious thing,' replied Yadav. 'No one can tell about the future. And now, one more garden I would like to take you. It was ladies' garden – name is Saheliyon ki Bari, meaning Garden of Maids of Honour.' It was a formal garden of lawns and pavilions with a small lake, from the edges of which stone elephants squirted fountains of water from their trunks. Groups of Udaipuris sauntered, eating ice creams and laughing as they squeezed into rented traditional costumes for romantic photos amongst the flowers.

We set off for Jaipur. I peeled an orange, passed half of it to Yadav and asked him if he could find a suitable pee stop. He drew up under a tree that was weighed down with blood-orange-coloured blossoms. The fresh air, however hot, was a relief after the stifling atmosphere of the car.

Coming back from behind the tree, I found Yadav halfway up it, picking a cluster of the gorgeous flowers. He slithered to the ground.

'Flame flower. Is for you. I want to change your mind. You seems me unhappy today.' He slid into his seat, took out a bidi, blew the dust through it and lit up. The smell of tobacco filled the car.

'Now I am telling you about myself. Please do not get bored. I have three daughters and one son. I hope you will not mind if I tell you about my wife. Our marriage is arranged by my parents when she is twelve and I am near about fourteen years old. Later I am working in Delhi and my wife, she live with me. Sometimes we laugh and enjoy to each other. One day, for joking, I dress in her sari and she wear my clothes and we go to cinema. But sometimes she get cross on me. She is pure veg, like all my family. One day I bring home my friend and he and I eats mutton curry. She refuse to wash plates. Instead she throw them outside. "Wash your own!" she shouts.

'At that time I work as conductor on Delhi buses. One of my daily passengers, she became my good friend, she is student. By my bad luck, it happen one day that my wife, she came on same journey and she see to me talking with my friend. She is so angry on me, she will not speak with me for one whole week. But most of the time we loves to each other too much.

'Once, in my village she call me lazy. I get angry, so I went from house for many hours. When I come back my mother and brothers is all round her and she pretend to cry. All family members, they is too fond of her. My Boss Brother – he is second eldest, and now my father is old he runs family and farm – he blame on me and beat me until I am blue and black. Same night my wife, she laugh at me too much, but then she smooth the bruises with her own hands and we laugh together.

'When she is twenty-seven and my son, he is eight weeks old, she die at my farm.'

'What did she die of?' I asked. And, because I was curious: 'If you got married when your wife was only twelve, did you stay together and start having children?'

'We doesn't know why she died. She fell sick for only one week and then she expire.' He looked at me sideways. 'You mean did we make love? Of course we didn't. She went back to her own village until she is fifteen. I must be then...' He counted on his fingers. 'Yes, almost about eighteen. At first was too difficult. She doesn't allow I even touch to her. She say if I do, she will scream for my mum. But after some days is all right.

'After she died, my father, he bought goat to give milk for my son. But is too difficult for me to look after him myself, so I take him to my sister. Her husband is in army. They had no children and he is like their own son. Even now he stays with my sister in her village. He is seventeen. Now she is widow with small boy of her own. It is turn of my son to look after them. My sister's husband, he die in crash on motorbike only four years before.

'Me now, I am lonely. My Boss Brother, he found me new wife, but I doesn't want. Perhaps she will not like to my children. So I leave my farm. Now two of my daughters is already married and third we will arrange for marriage soon. So all they are all right.'

'I think you should get married again,' I said. 'I'd like to, myself, if I could find the right person. It's not good to live alone.'

He stared at me in amazement.

'You would like to? I don't think so. And you are fifty-two years old?'

I shrugged. 'What difference does that make? My feelings are the same.'

'Well, if you are not too old, I, at, say, about thirty-nine, am certainly not.'

I agreed.

He asked me again, as he had several times before, if I had a 'friend' and how many 'friends' I had had since my divorce. I told him about my first boyfriend after the divorce and about the wonderful, funny and heartbreaking five years I had spent with him. 'You see, he was fifteen years younger than me, and in the end he went off with a girl his own age.'

'I see,' he said thoughtfully. 'And were there others?'

'Other what?'

'Other men?'

'Yes,' I said. 'One or two. Why are you so curious?'

'Tell me about the one or two.'

'Well, I can't remember.' I lied. I didn't want to tell him about what my eldest daughter called 'Mum's afternoon delights'... the ones who had lasted a few weeks or less. 'I lived with another man for four years quite recently. He left me a few months before I came to India.'

'Why?' Yadav insisted.

'I suppose we didn't get on very well together. He liked things I didn't, and I liked things he didn't.'

'What do you like?' he asked.

'Well, I suppose for one thing, I like hugging. He wasn't much of a hugger.'

'I see,' said Yadav thoughtfully. 'You do like hugging. But I have to say, Western peoples, they is very strange. They changes their husband or wife like we changes our underclothes. In India we cannot.'

The light was beginning to fade. Ahead of us, the gate closed on a level crossing. Cars and lorries hooted behind us.

'Would you like it if I hug you?' asked Yadav. He had switched off the engine.

'Yes. Thanks,' I said. He moved across the bench seat, put his arms round me and kissed me, a long, lingering kiss that left me limp and breathless. The invisible cord jerked and tightened.

The locomotive clanked through the crossing, trailing carriages, sleepers, freight and drums of Indian oil behind it. The gate rose slowly. Yadav drew away from me and, leaning out the window towards a barrow beside the road, bought milk-white mulli with bright-green leaves that dripped with water. He handed one to me in screw of newspaper.

Accelerating noisily, we bumped over the railway lines.

'Did you enjoy?' he asked.

'Yes... thank you.'

'And our sweet kiss?'

I nodded, wondering what chain of events we had set in motion.

'And now I want to ask you other question. Supposing I have chosen already who I should marry with, shall I tell you? Would you like to know?'

I was silent.

'Do you want to know?' he insisted. 'You can think it is joking. I want to give you laugh.'

'All right.'

'I want to get marry with you. I love you. You can live at my village and my family, they will love you. That is all. And now you must have to say what do you think?'

I didn't know what to say or think.

My ex-husband had proposed many times before eventually, unable to afford yet another proposal dinner in a Soho restaurant, he threatened to emigrate to the colonies if I refused one more time. I accepted.

Captain Albert F. was the only other man who had ever proposed to me. I had been lunching with a friend in a pub in Mayfair. We had almost finished our Cornish pasties and halves of bitter when a small American man in a raincoat sat down at our table. He told me that I was the most beautiful thing he had ever set eyes on, and asked me to marry him. I gasped. At the time I was homeless and desperately searching for eleven thousand pounds, the shortfall on the mortgage I had been offered on the house in Pimlico. I decided to try the same kind of shock tactic.

'No,' I said. 'But will you lend me eleven thousand pounds?'

His answer stunned me even more than his proposal. 'Yes.'

He took me to dinner at San Lorenzo. The restaurant was full, but Captain Albert did not take no for an answer. He waved a fifty-pound note at the head waiter and a table miraculously appeared. Albert leant across the white cloth and offered me the keys to his kingdom – a house in California, a yacht in the Caribbean, a fleet of oil tankers somewhere off the coast of Ireland. His little eyes, sunk beneath folded lids, had an acquisitive gleam. His grey, pudgy hand crept across the table. I felt sick.

My children were upset. 'But Mum, we could have had our house, gone skiing like everyone else, bought a music system, had a party. Why didn't you marry him?'

'Thanks very much,' I said. 'I'd have had to live with him.'

I wondered what they would say if I married a penniless Indian driver and went to live on a farm in the middle of the mustard fields. They would certainly be less enthusiastic than they had been about Captain Albert.

'Soon we will be in Jaipur city and I must have to leave you in hotel.' Yadav looked sideways at me, the two worry lines deeply etched between his eyebrows. 'Why you do not answer my question? Did you mind it?'

I said no, I didn't mind at all. It was a compliment. I had not imagined I would get a proposal of marriage in India. But there were so many reasons why I could not accept.

'Now you say you cannot, but as I have told you before, no one can tell about the future. See what will happen. And now, my respected tourist, carry on!' Overcome by the intensity of our conversation, not to mention our kiss, I felt incapable of 'carrying on'.

'You drive now. I... I can't.' We changed places.

The bellboy took my bags and ushered me into the lift. I went to sleep in solitary opulence in Jaipur's Rambagh Palace, wishing I was folded up with my driver on the back seat of his Ambassador.

The next morning, sitting beside Yadav on my way to meet the maharaja, I thanked God that our evening had ended when it had. There could be no future for us. There were only two more days, and then 'The Grandeur of Rajasthan' and all that had come with it would be over. Only two days...

Yadav drew up in the forecourt of Jaipur's other palace hotel, the Jai Mahal, where the maharaja had his office. He leant across me and opened my door.

'I'm sorry... I'm sure I won't be long... he might not even see me,' I said. 'Do you mind... I mean... waiting outside?'

'Why should I mind?' He looked puzzled. 'Now please you have your nice time with maharaja. I will be here.'

I handed my travel-worn letter of introduction to a secretary. He looked at it with distaste.

'His Highness is unavailable, and may be for the foreseeable future.'

I said I would be grateful if someone could take the letter, as I had promised His Highness's friend in London that I would deliver it safely. The secretary took the letter and returned almost immediately, surprise written all over his face. 'His Highness will see you now.'

I followed him down an endless passage. He opened a door and ushered me into a long room lined with bookshelves and signed photographs of people playing, having played or about to play polo. The maharaja was sitting at the far end behind a desk piled with papers. He half rose from his chair and reached across a heap of files to shake hands.

'What a pity you were not here yesterday. You could have come to watch the polo. Well, perhaps tomorrow.'

I said that, sadly, I was leaving Jaipur that day.

A servant brought in two glasses of orange squash on a silver tray. Conversation was sticky. I took a sip of my drink and almost choked on an ice cube as I remembered that ice was taboo for weak Western stomachs. I had managed to avoid it so far. I took one more sip for politeness' sake.

It was time to go. We shook hands again. At every step of the long carpet leading to the door, a photograph winked at me: Prince Charles... the maharaja with Prince Philip... the Mountbattens... I opened the door with a sigh of relief. I had delivered my last letter of introduction.

We spent the rest of the morning in the dark little alleys of the jewellery bazaar, lit by the glitter of silver and gold and the glints of precious and semi-precious stones. Yadav insisted on buying me a pair of silver-filigree earrings. 'Sorry I doesn't have rupees to buy gold,' he said. I assured him that I preferred silver.

'On our way out of Jaipur, we will visit Amber Fort. You can ride up hill on elephant, is all include,' said Yadav, anxious that I get my money's worth up to the last minute of my tour. I left the elephants to others, having had enough of such gimmicks in my years of guiding, and rode up to the fort by car.

Yadav had not mentioned last night's stop at the level crossing. I hoped that he, too, wanted to maintain the status quo, so that tomorrow our goodbye would be less painful. I was wrong.

In a small, forgotten room at Amber, full of rubbish and cobwebs, far from the grand salons and courts, Yadav pulled me towards him and gave me a huge bear hug, breaking all twenty-four of the bangles I had been wearing since I'd received them at a Delhi wedding.

A middle-aged Indian couple, attracted by the tinkling glass, peered into the room. They registered the broken bangles, my Indian escort and my dishevelled appearance and, with a look of mild surprise, withdrew. Our invisible rope was now knotted.

That night, in a cold, green room in a modern hotel in Agra, I was violently ill. Morning broke on my sleepless night. It was my last day with Yadav. That evening, he would return to Delhi and I would continue by train to Madhya Pradesh.

I cursed the maharaja's ice and rang downstairs for a doctor.

Dr Gupta picked me up and drove me to his clinic. A youth was swishing a mop backwards and forwards across the floor, leaving a trail of dirty water and an overpowering smell of disinfectant. The doctor told me to climb up and lie down on a narrow bench that stood six feet off the ground on rickety legs. His assistant attached a plastic bottle to a wooden pole and the doctor pricked a vein in my arm, attaching a piece of rubber tubing from the bottle to the vein. An agonising pain shot up my arm.

'Sorry. Wrong vein,' he said cheerfully. 'If at first you don't succeed, try, try again.' I braced myself.

'Good, that is very nice – see, the drip has started. After three hours you will feel fine.'

The minutes dragged slowly by. Dr Gupta dealt with his other patients in quick succession: a pregnant woman, a man who had recently lost a foot, two children with fever and a boy with a septic ulcer. Most of them were given an injection and sent away with a little screw of newspaper filled with multicoloured tablets. At last the clinic shut for the morning. It was then the turn of the travelling salesmen, dapper in over-pressed suits and clipped moustaches: a case full of ginseng; a new kind of liquid aspirin, elasticated leg supports, suppositories and contraceptives. Their droning voices sent me to sleep.

I was awakened by Dr Gupta's assistant, who was detaching the plastic tubing from my arm while the doctor recited a long list of things I should not eat – chillis, spices, sweet tea, chapatis. I asked him what was left.

'If you would like truly health-giving food prepared in the proper way, you are welcome to have lunch in my house,' he offered.

Before I had time to answer, the door opened and a distraught Yadav rushed in. His uncombed hair was a bird's nest. His clothes were crumpled. I wanted to kiss him. But this was India; women did not kiss men in front of the doctor, and certainly not if the man in question was their driver.

'Thanks God I find you. I went to hotel for city sightseeing. Agent, he tell me you had gone to hospital. And now, here you are.' He began massaging my head violently, as if it were a lump of chapati dough.

'Yadav, I'm fine, but I feel a bit weak. Would you ring Mr Chhabra and ask if I can keep you and the car to go to Madhya Pradesh? I don't think I can deal with transport bookings on my own today.'

Was it true, or was my illness just an excuse not to say goodbye?

The doctor's living room doubled up as the Gupta family's portrait gallery. Grim faces in faded black and white looked down from garlanded frames, the tops of which met the ceiling. Tipping my head backwards, I recognised in the face of a young girl staring intensely from a frame the same face I now saw on the old woman coming through the door with a tray full of dishes. 'My mother on her marriage day,' explained Dr Gupta. 'My school cricket team; I was captain that year. My father; he is now expired. My graduation day. My eldest son when a baby; of course, he is now B.A.'

Dr Gupta's mother put down her tray and began serving the food. There was dal (cooked without chillis), curd, chapatis, papads and a salad of raw carrot and cucumber washed with boiled water.

Yadav came back. Dr Gupta gave me his bill and at least five kinds of pills, each in their own screw of newspaper. 'Please take as directed,' he said, handing me half an old envelope covered with illegible scribbles. 'And please keep in touch. I have made many good friends through traveller's dysentery. If you are in doubt, I have letters to prove it.'

'So!' said Yadav. 'I done everything. Mr Chhabra, he say, "Fine, keep car and go with Madam." So here I am. And now may I suggest you that before leaving Agra we will visit Taj Mahal and marble factory?'

The path leading to the pink stone entrance arch was filled with guides and beggars. I shook off an urchin who had attached himself to my skirt, and pushed away a sheath of postcards that was repeatedly shoved under my nose.

Suddenly none of it mattered. The Taj Mahal was in front of us, filling our eyes. As millions had before us, we stood looking at the most beautiful building in the world, a flawless virgin, perfectly proportioned, unassuming in her marble whiteness. The elongated reflection beckoned us forwards along the marble canals. No photograph or picture could ever do justice to Shah Jahan's tribute to his most adored wife, nor could any number of tourists and touts tarnish its beauty. We walked beside the dancing mirror image to the white marble steps and left our chappals on a pile of discarded shoes. The marble was cool and smooth on the soles of my feet. For two rupees I bought a rose to lay on Mumtaz's tomb.

'Take guide with torch or you see nothing. This old man, I knows him very well,' Yadav advised me. Blinded by the dim interior after the glaring afternoon light, I was glad to have the torch and the man's guiding hand on my arm. The pinprick of light travelled over the walls, illuminating delicate flowers and foliage inlaid with lapis lazuli, coral, malachite and a thousand other stones. In the lower chamber, we filed round the tombs. An overpowering scent of attar of roses filled the air. Natural scent had never smelt so sweet.

'Same families still making inlay in marble as in time of Shah Jahan,' said the salesman at the marble factory. I believed him and went out to the car. I didn't want marble tables, ashtrays or even boxes. Yadav came out a few minutes later, clutching a package wrapped in newspaper.

'This is for you,' he said when we were both inside the car. 'Please open now.' He leant across, impatient for me to tear off the paper. It was an alabaster miniature of the Taj Mahal. There were small holes for windows. 'See, if you put torch inside, it will be very bright in the night. Do you like it?'

'Of course. I like it very much. I'll keep it always, and if I have grandchildren, they'll ask me about it and I'll tell them about you and my tour of Rajasthan.'

'Thank you,' he said. 'Thank you very much. And now we will carry on. We must reach Gwalior in Madhya Pradesh by dark. Is dangerous country.'

When I got back to London I put the Taj Mahal in a glass-fronted cabinet amongst a collection of antique cups and saucers.

'Mum, what's that ghastly piece of plastic tourist trash?' asked one of my daughters, peering into the case.

'It's not ghastly,' I said indignantly. 'It's marble and it's the Taj Mahal...'

7

The package tour was over. We were on our own with the Ambassador and a couple of guidebooks.

The country was desolate: ridge upon ridge of miniature sand dunes that looked like a relief map of the Scottish Highlands. 'Is full of dacoits,' Yadav explained. 'They loot the peoples and kills them, even they shoots them. One woman, Phoolan Devi, she is chief dacoit. Her father is poor man, she also marry poor man. Dacoits, they murdered him and they take Phoolan Devi and about four or five, they raped with her. She decide to become dacoit herself. She fall in love with dacoit chief; he is very handsome.'

'Like you?' I asked.

'Now I think you are pulling my foot. She join his band. But dacoit from other group, he become jealous and he kill to this man. So she make herself leader. She take her men to murderer's village, and herself, she shoot many men, say at least eighteen. Now she is in the prison. She try to be politician woman, and she will success, because she is famous in all India. Even they are making film about her.'

We stayed at the Regal, which was regal in name only. At night I lay awake, attacked by huge mosquitoes whose bites kept me scratching for days. The next day Yadav showed me his room, essentially a broom cupboard. Seeing my comparatively luxurious quarters, he offered to share them with me.

'Like that we can save our fifty rupees each night,' he said. I shook my head. He left without argument, picking his way through the potted plants and rubbish.

'See you at breakfast!' I called after him.

But the next morning he was not among the crowd of chattering men who stood, squatted and sat round the restaurant's television set. The volume was turned up to its maximum. There was a sigh of pleased anticipation followed by silence as, for the next half hour, every eye was focused on the small, flickering screen showing the *Mahabharat*. Breakfast was out of the question; there was no one to serve it. When the episode ended, the TV was switched off, the crowd dispersed and the waiter resumed his duties.

Yadav joined me at the table. 'I miss my favourite story. I shouldn't have to sleep so late,' he said.

Gwalior's fifteenth-century Chit Mandir was the most beautiful and interesting palace I had yet seen, perhaps because it was not written into an obligatory itinerary. With no guide to tell me what I should and should not see, I wandered at will amongst the half-ruined buildings, around whose blue-, green- and gold-tiled friezes ducks waddled, swans swam, peacocks pranced and elephants paraded. Below the crest from which the massive fort presided over the plains were two ornate temples known as the Saas-Bahu. Built in the ninth century, they were now a favourite tiffin-picnic spot for parents visiting their teenage sons at Gwalior's boarding school.

Later, Yadav took me to sit on the grass beside a pink gazebo in a beautiful garden. Boys and girls played ball games while young men posed hand in hand for film-style photos. The formal beds were crammed with flowers: narcissi and forget-me-nots, cynerarias, foxgloves, begonias and giant French marigolds. It was a garden of dreams, a perfect place to rest until twilight fell, bringing a thick cloud of mosquitoes. They buzzed and dived, dived and buzzed until we could bear them no longer. Yadav got to his feet, pulling me after him, and reluctantly we left.

A strong smell of garlic and spices enveloped the Regal. The terrace tables were filling with early diners. From the privacy of curtained alcoves in the bar, curious faces peered at us. My guidebook reported that guests at this hotel had occasionally discovered peepholes in the their bathrooms.

'No one can understand your taste,' said Yadav when I told him I was glad we had not stayed at the Usha Kiran Palace Hotel across town. 'That is lovely place. Regal, it is dirty and not good. Why you like it?' I did not know myself, except that I felt I was seeing real life here, rather than a tourist's dream of it.

The next day, driving towards Orchha, Yadav picked up my left hand from my lap and held it.

'May I hope you are happy. But I can read your face – I know that you are. And now I will give you challenge. Before you go back to your country I will put stamp on your heart. It will stay always with you.'

I must have looked doubtful

'Yes, is true. I am not liar.'

We came to the small medieval town of Orchha as the sun was sinking from a pink and grey sky shot with golden threads. The only hotel was the half-ruined seventeenth-century Sheesh Mahal Palace, and it had only one vacant room. I hesitated. If Yadav and I took it, we would move even further down the path to God-knew-what destination. Yadav was too busy lighting a bidi to notice my questioning glance.

'Yes... please... we'll take it for two nights,' I said. I had tried hard not to fall in love with Yadav, but I had failed. And I felt that I had not only failed myself, but I had failed India – I had come as a serious traveller, not to look for a lover. Sharing a room with my driver had not been part of my plan.

'Passport.' The receptionist gave Yadav a look of disdain.

The room had a vaulted ceiling, two beds and a wash basin. The plain below the small arched window was alight with flame trees, and dotted with small white chattris pointing skywards like upturned bells. Yadav disappeared on an errand, reminding me that I was not to go to the village by myself. 'Dacoits,' he said darkly, and he was gone.

Outside the hotel, a grassy bank led down to a stone bridge that forded a fast-flowing river. A photogenic group of cows sloshed through the shallows. The last rays of sun broke through overhanging branches, dappling the gurgling water and warming me through my T-shirt. The air was fragrant with blossoms and the muddy smell of the river. For a moment I wished we could stay in Orchha forever.

That night, as I had known would happen when I took the room, the last bit of slack in the rope that had bound Yadav and me – loosely at first, but more and more tightly as the days had passed – was lost forever. We slept in one of the two narrow beds in our vaulted castle room.

Yadav kissed me. 'Please you tell me what you like we do together in our bed?'

'Well I, um, I don't... I *can't*.'

'But you have too many lover in your life. You must have to know.'

'Well, I don't.' The teachings of my boarding school were indelible. One just didn't talk about this sort of thing.

My incapacity to communicate did not spoil the night.

Lying close to Yadav, my leg felt the contrast between his smooth skin and his rough cotton underpants. 'Why do you wear them in bed?' I asked.

'I must have to. It is my favourite clothing and I do not take it off never. Only after bath I can change for clean one under towel.'

'Well, that's like me not being able to tell you how I want to make love. It's called an inhibition.'

'Now you are talking your high, stupid, bloody English again. But you should not worry, yaar. I knows very well what you and me, we both wants to do.'

I woke early and watched Orchha come alive beneath our window. A tractor lurched into noisy movement. A shepherd, whooping and hollering, coaxed his jingling flock across the plain. A pair of creamy oxen, yoked to a loaded cart, made their ponderous way towards the village. Sari-clad women swayed towards a well in the distance, balancing two, three and four glinting brass water pots on their head. The birds, their morning chorus over, flitted from branch to branch of the flame trees, chirping and calling at random. It was breakfast time, and I was hungry. Leaving Yadav asleep I ran down the stone stairs, two at a time, my heart leaping and bounding, my head singing.

Sun spilled through the open doors and windows into a long, pillared room filled with white wicker tables and chairs and fleshy, green potted plants. It had the air of an Edwardian palm court in a sea-front hotel in Sussex. At one end, two long, Formica-covered tables served as the dining room; at the other, the receptionist sat writing in his ledgers behind an old school desk. Sniffing the coffee and toast, I was wondering whether to have an omelette or fried egg when the receptionist summoned me.

'Please you settle now your dinner and room bill. I have to tell you, there are no rooms available tonight.' He gave me a disapproving look. Disappointment dredged through me. 'Any corner would do,' I pleaded. 'We're not fussy.'

He softened. 'Very well. Wait till later in day and I will inform you if room is available.' At least there was hope. Later in the day he told us we could stay where we were.

99

'This night we will be quiet,' said Yadav. 'Yesterday we enjoy our sweet night too much. Didn't you hear to us? I thinks waiters, they listen on outside stairs.'

A hot flush rushed from the top of my head to the soles of my feet. 'Oh God, how awful,' I said to no one in particular.

A small man who had introduced himself as a guide on our arrival now came to offer his services. I was too traumatised by the emotional ups and downs of both night and morning to refuse. I followed him through the cobweb-infested ruins of the palace to a dark attic, where bats whirred round my head and wings brushed and batted my face and body. But it was not a bat whose arm slid round me, feeling for and squeezing my left breast. Shuddering with disgust, but still too shaken by the morning debacle to make a scene, I pushed the offending hand away, backed out of the darkness and followed the guide down the crumbling steps and across the courtyard to a series of frescoed rooms, sadly cracked and peeling from damp, disuse and neglect. After an exhaustive explanation of the paintings, including the births, deaths and marriages of what seemed like every god in the Hindu pantheon, we drove to the Laxmi temple in the village to see more frescoes. This time the explanations were embellished by Yadav, who preferred to recount, rather than listen to, a good god story.

With an expectant gleam in his eye, the guide asked us for five hundred rupees. Yadav gave him fifty. Looking at the note in disgust he handed it back, shaking his head.

'Give him a bit more and let's get rid of him,' I pleaded. Reluctantly Yadav doubled the amount. The guide pocketed it and turned away, muttering.

We picnicked beside the river. Yadav ate six apples and four bananas in quick succession and, stretching out on his lunghi, slept. I took out my sketchbook, trying to re-create three little children wading through the upside-down reflections of the chattris in the rippling shadows, but the scene lost its magic under my amateur hand. I gave up and took a photograph.

It was siesta time. Nothing, not even the song of the birds, disturbed the hot, somnolent air. The sploshing and laughter of the three children as they waded into the shallows clashed happily with the silence and Yadav's gentle snores.

Just outside the village, where the road became a bridge over the river, we found a small mud hut tucked amongst the trees. 'Let us take chai,' said Yadav.

Inside the dark, windowless hovel, a shadowy figure squatted by a chula of smouldering logs. Yadav shouted his order and the chai-wallah set his saucepan on the fire. He blew through a metal tube till the flames leapt and danced, bringing the chai once, twice, three times, frothing and foaming, to the boil. He strained the liquid into small glasses and handed one to Yadav.

'I think you have lonely life here. Where is family?' Yadav asked the man. He could not bear the thought of anyone being alone.

The man told us that he and his wife had lived happily, farming their land, until five years ago he had taken ill with cancer. While he was in hospital, his wife had sold everything – house, land and gold – to pay for his treatment, all to no avail. The doctors told her there was no hope; he would surely die. Unable to face life without her husband, the woman jumped from the bridge when the river was full and killed herself. Then, miraculously, the man recovered. He came home to find neither wife nor land.

'But she left me one son,' he said. 'We built this hut. We make chai. We are happy.' His gentle grin showed three remaining teeth in otherwise gap-filled gums.

Bending to avoid the thatch, two men entered. One carried a shotgun. The second, who had bright-blue eyes, had a bottle tucked under his arm. They settled down on the bench beside us and called for chai. Supping and blowing, they drained their glasses, threw them to the ground and, after a gusty bout of coughing and spitting, turned to Yadav. Unscrewing the cap from the bottle, they explained that it was filled with a wonderful wine, distilled from vegetables. Their neighbours had discovered that by adding fertiliser, they could achieve the perfect drink, so strong that two of them had already died from it.

'But they are stupid – they use a cheap brand of fertiliser. Me, I only use the best. My wine is most perfect.'

The fumes from the raw alcohol stung my eyes. Yadav accepted a generous helping in his cupped hands. Before they rode away on their bicycles, the men persuaded Yadav to buy the remains of the bottle. When he wasn't looking, I stole it and poured it down a nearby drain.

On our last morning at the Sheesh Mahal Palace, while Yadav was still sleeping, I breakfasted with a white-haired Englishman and his Indian friend. I enjoyed our talk, thinking with pleasure of being back in London, surrounded by English-speaking people – until I remembered the crowds at the Changing of the Guard, and the long queues waiting to see the crown jewels on a wet Sunday afternoon at the Tower of London. I decided that I would probably miss India and Yadav far more than I now missed the occasional English chat.

Twenty kilometres outside Orchha on the road to Khajuraho, I realised that I had left my pyjamas in our vaulted bathroom.

'Would you like we go back?' asked Yadav.

'No, thanks,' I said, thinking of the poker-faced receptionist who had nearly chucked us out.

We were on the point of finishing the lengthy business of registering at the tourist bungalow in Khajuraho when three men burst in, shouting and gesticulating. We ran out just in time to see our car rolling down the slope.

I had once asked Yadav why he never used the handbrake. 'Because,' he said, 'car doesn't have one. For what it should? Handbrakes are not useful in my country.'

This time he had forgotten to leave the car in gear. It careered down the slope towards a young couple from Lancashire, who were busy erecting a tent. They stopped hammering and retreated rapidly. Twenty metres from the tent, where the land rose in a gentle ridge, the car came to rest.

'Good luck,' Yadav said, breathless. He patted the bonnet and noticed the British couple for the first time. Instead of apologising, he asked what they were doing. They explained that they planned to sleep in their tent that night.

Yadav shook his head in bewilderment. 'But here is good hotel. I thinks you are not too poor to rent room. Why you sleep like poor man on the ground? Indian peoples, they will not live like this unless they has to. Never in whole life they will choose such a house.'

'You should try it sometime. It's fun,' said the girl.

'Fun! I don't think so it is.' Yadav shook his head.

Apart from the shopkeepers, who descended on us like a plague of locusts in the village square, and the occasional roar of a plane overhead – shattering the peace of the twilight fields, where Yadav gave me a lesson in the art of cutting tufts of golden barley with a sickle borrowed on the spur of the moment from a bemused farmer – Khajuraho was a quiet and peaceful place.

The riotous sexual joy of the sculpted figures rampaging in ecstasy across the temple walls, so alien to the modesty of much of present-day India, failed to tempt Yadav into further sightseeing. Some say these images helped devotees to clear their minds of worldly thoughts before entering the temples. Certainly by the time I had climbed the last step of the last temple, I was too hot, sticky and thirsty to lust after anything more than a cold drink. I found Yadav sitting under a notice, holding a huge bunch of marigolds.

'ON NO ACCOUNT PICK THESE FLOWERS,' I read.

'I would like to give you these,' said Yadav. Embarrassed, I tried to hide the tell-tale bouquet. Yadav looked disappointed.

'Don't you like them?' he asked. I pointed to the notice. 'Please, yaar, we should not read stupid British writing,' he said, shaking his head.

After a quick lunch of samosas and cashews, Yadav suggested that we go to see a nearby waterfall. 'I have seen it only once; was in rainy season. Then there was much water. Now I am not sure we will find.' He reached down beside his seat, and his hand reappeared holding a quarter bottle of whisky. 'Do you mind?' he asked. 'I feels like whisky.' He poured the contents of the bottle down his throat. The car leapt forwards over the boulder-strewn road, just missing a mother sow who was foraging in the gutter for her offspring.

'I would like to drive.'

'Is because you think I am drunk.' But without further argument, he pulled over and we changed places.

When we next left the car, we followed the riverbed over giant boulders rubbed smooth by a million years of monsoon floods. Under the March sun, they felt hot and dry beneath our feet. We came to a deep pool fed by a trickle of water, all that was left of the river until the rains came again. A channel of water cut its way through the rocks on the far side of the pool and fell two hundred feet to the floor of the valley below. Two small dolls – a Western couple, dwarfed by scenery and solitude – stood naked, showering themselves under the waterfall. Their laughing cries echoed across the valley.

'Thanks God waterfall is still here, but in monsoon is very big.'

I wished I could be in India when the rains came, forcing the swollen river to overflow and fall, shouting and screaming, in a sumptuous stream of blue-green water and dancing soap suds through deep ridges of the rocky ravine. I contented myself with the gentle springtime drip.

'Pool, it is made by millions and millions of years of whirlpools cutting into rock.' Yadav took my hand, helping me over a boulder. 'Do you like to swim? Water is very clean and clear and in centre is very deep, say fifty feet.' Stripping off his clothes, he stood on the edge in his Indian underpants, boxer shorts with a drawstring designed to fit a waist of any size. With a loud splash, his body hit the water and disappeared. I waited, praying that he could swim. He came up, gasping and spitting, and dog-paddled to the side, inviting me to join him.

'But I haven't brought my bathing things.'

'Doesn't matter, yaar, nobody is here. You can keep undergarments like me.'

'Certainly not,' I said prudishly.

But the water looked so tempting that I stripped off my clothes and jumped in, more worried about freshwater worms getting under my skin than about my Marks & Spencer underclothes. Five strokes took me to the other edge of the pool. I lay on my back in the water, looking up at the sun and the blue sky through the tall rocks. Yadav rolled over as well, but he panicked and sank.

'I like too much. How you can do it?' I tried to help him to float, but he could not relax his body and was more often under the water than on it.

The sun and the hot rocks dried us quickly. Yadav insisted that I turn my back when he took off his underpants to wash and dry them.

'Why are you washing them?' I asked. 'They've just been in the water with you.'

'Is different thing.'

Back on the road a Western boy, wearily pushing a bike up a steep hill, refused Yadav's offer of a lift. 'But we wouldn't have got his bike into the car,' I objected when the boy had gone.

'Doesn't matter. First we must find space in our heart to lift him. After, bicycle will certainly find proper place.' Perhaps he was right.

'Roads are very bad. Three hundred and fifty kilometres will take minimum ten hours.' When Yadav described a road as 'bad', he meant it. Rusty and not-so-rusty carcasses of buses and lorries littered the verges, reminders of those who had inadvertently taken their eyes and minds off the job for a second too long. I stared at the lotus blossoms painted on the lorry in front of us and wished the trip would take a lifetime. We were going to Sanchi, our last stop, or so I thought, before our return journey to Delhi and the future.

Surely nothing much could happen on these quiet country roads. For once I could forget my evening chore of scribbling the day's events into an Indian exercise book.

'What you are thinking?' asked Yadav. 'Where you are? I think you are flying very far. Are you in the London?'

'No, I was thinking about a brochure I picked up in Orchha. It described a place called Mandu. It looked very pretty.'

'I knows about it, but I never been there. Is too far, and we must have to go back to Delhi for your flight to London. You do not have so many days.'

'I know.' I went back to thinking about the coloured photograph of a blue pool surrounded by white arches, and the descriptions of the ruins of the long-deserted 'City of Joy' on a high plateau.

I was wrong, of course, about nothing much happening. For two hours the road was blocked by heavy traffic, dissipating the time we had hoped to gain by getting up early. At last it cleared, and we shot forward. A man dawdled down the middle of the road, holding a small child by the hand. Yadav hooted, keeping his hand on the horn, and the man turned to give us a vacant stare. He made no attempt to move aside. The child, panicked by the blasting horn, slipped free and darted towards us. Yadav slammed on the brakes, missing the small body by inches. The child got up from where it had fallen and scuttled away, screaming but unhurt.

Yadav yelled a stream of abuse through the open window. The man sauntered slowly across the road and stopped in front of the car, gazing at us, still blankly, and muttering.

'What did you say?' I asked.

'Is not what I say. Is what he say. He say it is my fault if I run over child. Bloody fool.'

We drew up at a level crossing next to an ox cart loaded with lengths of cane. 'Is sugar cane. You want to try?' Yadav jumped out, leaving the car in the middle of the road.

The train rushed through the crossing and the gates re-opened. Yadav returned with an armful of sticks. Irate horns screamed at us. Unmoved, he selected a cane, snapped it in half and passed a piece to me. I watched him worry at his, like a dog with a bone, until he had stripped off the outer bark and was left with a glistening, fibrous stick. We moved off at a decorous pace with a line of furious drivers behind us.

Yadav chewed and spat, spat and chewed. I tried to imitate him. He took the cane from me, peeled it and handed it back, clean and white. 'Now, bite with back teeth,' he instructed. A delicious syrup filled my mouth and trickled down my throat. I leant out of the window and spat out a mouthful of fibre. We drove along chewing and spitting until all the canes were finished and I was covered from head to foot in liquid sugar.

'Don't worry, my dear family friend, I will show you how we will take off.' We pulled up in front of a chai stall. Watched by a group of gaping villagers, Yadav borrowed a rusty tin from the chai-wallah, filled it with water and threw it all over me. I looked down at my dripping clothes. At least the sticky feeling had gone, and by the time Yadav had drunk his chai, my clothes were dry.

Sitting on a charpoy, on either side of a wooden board, we ate spinach and potato curry, spooning it into our mouths with bits of chapati.

'Clean your mouth,' said Yadav, handing me a handkerchief.

'Don't give me orders. I don't belong to you,' I said, suddenly feeling a need to show my independence. But, noticing my green fingers, I did as he suggested.

Our afternoon drive continued at a snail's pace behind a train of ox carts piled high with orange, green and brown lentils. 'From these we make dal,' Yadav said. 'You have eaten many times.' He stopped beside a field of feathery green plants and bent down to pull up a large bunch. Angry shouts from the next field brought him hurrying back to the car.

He handed me a fistful of wet branches covered with small pods. 'Now you can learn to eat fresh grams.' He popped a pod, putting the peas into my mouth. 'Good. Now you are really Indian woman – you knows how to eat sugar cane and grams. I like it too much.'

At Sanchi's tourist bungalow I asked for a double room. 'But where is second lady, your friend?' questioned the receptionist. 'I need also her passport details.'

'I, er...' Yadav was standing behind me. 'This is my friend.' From the sudden heat that suffused my face, I knew it had turned bright scarlet.

'But he is driver, he will sleep with car. Your friend, I am asking you. Where she is?' he insisted.

'We will share room together. No one else is here,' Yadav said. The man's mask of respect dropped.

'Boy, he will show you room.' He looked straight through Yadav to stare at me in disbelief.

His reaction, unpleasant and intrusive as it was, caused me some serious soul-searching that night. Why, I asked myself, was I lying in bed beside this man, who a few days ago had been nothing more to me than my driver? He was at least twelve years my junior, a peasant farmer from an Indian state I'd never even heard of until I'd met him. Had I really fallen in love with him, and he with me? In three weeks I would be back in England. Would his name join the list of 'afternoon delights', or were we really linked together, part of the inescapable sequence of past, present and future?

For Yadav, karma decided the paths we would take. I thought of other 'unsuitable' situations I had been in – had karma led me to my first kiss at the age of twelve? A fishy experience aboard a pilchard trawler that plied nightly between the Cornish villages of Mousehole and Newlyn? Coming up out of the stuffy little cabin below deck, I was grabbed and pinioned to the mast by the ship's captain. His bristling chin and beery breath sent me reeling to the side of the vessel, where I was violently sick into the choppy waters of the Atlantic.

Had karma plunged me, after sixteen years of marriage, into a passionate romance with another trainee during a tour-guiding course in London? The consummation of our affair was no more than a quick kiss in a taxi on the way to visit Karl Marx in Highgate Cemetery, but it almost led to divorce for both of us. When his wife, tipped off by a fellow trainee guide, stepped out from behind a parked car and whacked him smartly over the head with her brolley, our half-baked affair was over. He realised that he did not want to leave his wife, and I, that his duo-tone platform shoes would quickly have dulled my passion.

Had karma led me to India and to Yadav?

To hell with everything, I thought, especially uppity hotel receptionists. I would leave it all to karma and to India. They would do what they liked anyway, so why worry?

'Jill, wake up! Wake up! We are in hurry.' Yadav, who rarely used my name, patted my cheek and shook my shoulders.

'Why? We've got all day, and Sanchi's not very big.'

'You are wrong. Now I have change all programme. I am going to give you very lovely surprise. Now please you get up and pack.'

I did.

'Now I must hope you will be very pleased, yaar. We will go to Mandu because I knows you want to see it too much. This is new programme. First I will leave you at ruins. After I must take my shave.' Yadav had never learnt to shave himself. A visit to the barber and his cut-throat razor, whether in a shop or a seat under a tree, was as essential a part of his daily ritual as his first bidi of the day and his 'inner cleansing', a terrifying five minutes of coughing, hawking and spitting. 'I will drink one cup chai because in hotel is very poor, pick luggage, pay bill and meet with you on hill. At exactly midday we will leave this place.'

He dropped me at the foot of the hill and disappeared in a cloud of exhaust fumes. The warm air was alive with humming insects. Hot and short of breath, I climbed to the main stupa, each of its four entrances carved with scenes representing the life of the Buddha – his mother's dream of an elephant before his birth (shown by a lotus), the tree under which he achieved enlightenment, the wheel of his teaching, and the footprint and throne of his presence.

The ruins of the monastery were filled with an air of peace and pleasure. Ashoka must have been delighted to find such a remote sanctuary for his Buddhist monuments, high above a plain lit by the candles of orange-flowered flame trees. Sad to leave, I hurried down the nearest set of twisting stone steps and found myself in a farmyard of clucking hens. Three cackling women struggled up the adjacent hill, bent beneath bundles of firewood twice their size. They pointed me towards the village.

We did not make Mandu that day. We spent the night in Indore, an industrial city covered with a cloud of pollution.

'You must be very tired from driving all this way,' I said to Yadav. 'I'm sorry.'

'Tired is not question. You must have to go to Mandu and I must have to bear it. It will be my pleasure. And please you do not say, "Thank you." "Thank you" means something, it is finish. All life I want to live for your pleasure. And please do not think I am after your money. All I want is your love.'

'I didn't think...'

He held up his hand, stopping me in mid-sentence. I wanted to say that money had never crossed my mind. I had been too busy trying not to fall in love with him to think of such mundane things as money.

'And now you please smile,' he said. I obediently turned up the corners of my mouth. 'Thank you very much,' he said, forgetting what he had just told me.

Exhorted by huge placards to admire the view and save a tree for India, we wound our way up a steep-sided, tree-clad valley and passed through the arched stone gateway to Mandu, a kingdom founded in the tenth century by Raja Bhoj. Now deserted, its stately buildings were crumbling into romantic ruins haunted by ghosts and memories.

'Please you take room here. Tomorrow chief minister for Madhya Pradesh will visit in Mandu. Is only room free in all village,' said the manager at the Travellers Lodge. Relieved that he asked no questions, I signed the register. From the flower-garden terrace outside our room, we looked down over the sweeping valley. With such a view, it did not matter that the room was basic and the 'attached bath' a cubbyhole with a rusty tap sticking out of the wall.

Impatient to see whether Mandu lived up to its brochures, I went out, leaving Yadav asleep. The narrow road between the fields was deserted. I enjoyed my own company, the sunshine and the freedom to stop whenever I wanted. I clambered over piles of masonry, sat amongst the ruins and imagined them as the houses, bazaars and offices of a bustling community, ruled from the Jawaz Mahal of Sultan Ghiyas Shah. The palace seemed to float between the lakes that flanked it on either side. Standing at one end of the Hindola Mahal and looking down its length, I had the sensation of swaying backwards and forwards, as if on a waterborne vessel. It was a builders' joke, an optical illusion created by the inward slant of the walls. Downstairs, a series of Moghul arches led to the small swimming pool whose photograph, sparkling with blue-green water, had seduced me into coming here. Now, apart from a few plastic bags and bottles, it was empty.

Below the palace walls, however, the great tank reflected and elongated the shimmering domes and minarets. Wavering pinnacles reached out to touch the opposite shore, where buffaloes grazed in the shade of the sun-dappled trees. It was better than the brochures.

'Please, we would like to take photo with you.' A smiling Indian family grouped itself round me. The father, hidden behind a camera and a drooping moustache, took our photograph. 'Now, please, you take one of us.' I posed again with a couple on their honeymoon and a group of art students, out from Indore for a day of sketching.

I longed for a drink, but there were no shops or stalls along the road that led to the great mosque and tomb of Hoshang Shah. Goats and sheep bleated, searching in vain for an edible mouthful in the dry scrub. Birds swooped from tree to tree.

The sound of my own feet, crunching through the stony dust, rang in my ears.

Beyond the domed tomb I was drawn to the shade of a long, open-fronted colonnade. Within the cool forest of columns I felt, rather than saw, a presence. Looking around, I caught sight of a shadowy figure that stopped when I stopped, moved when I moved. I hurried out into the open and across the grass to the steps of the tomb. My shadow, who I now saw was a boy of about fifteen, followed me. In the vast interior of the mausoleum it was almost dark. Now the boy's voice was beside me.

'One rupee, one rupee.' The muttered echo rang round the dome, dislodging a flurry of bats. I ran out into the sunlight and walked briskly, trying not to look back, but the boy's voice stayed right behind me. I glanced over my shoulder and found myself staring straight into his eyes. He smiled and made an extremely lewd gesture that I had never seen before.

The open door of a small restaurant at the village crossroads was a welcome sight. I hurried in. The boy did not follow me. I drank two bottles of Limca in quick succession. Prolonging my departure, I stopped to talk to the pot-bellied proprietor and to study the jars filled with every sort of namkin, biscuit and sweet.

Finding no more excuses to linger, I braved the village street once more. Children and babies were rushed out of their cottages to see the gori pass. Little boys, their small round bottoms bared to the sun below their shirts, small girls in frilly dresses and older girls in sober school uniforms ogled me with enormous eyes outlined in kohl.

'Ta-ta,' they called. 'Bye-bye. Have you pen? One rupee? Chocolate!' Even the youngest knew the words. The cottages petered out, and I was alone. Suddenly, from nowhere, the boy was with me again, keeping abreast of me on the other side of the road. I stopped. He stopped.

'What do you want?' I asked.

'One rupee.' He reached out to touch me, and I stepped back. He shrugged and shook his head. I walked on, and he walked beside me. Passing a ruin, he stopped and made signs for me to follow him off the road.

'Ram Ram.' I hoped my very limited Hindi would make him understand that I wanted to be left alone.

'Ram Ram,' he replied, and he stretched out his hand. My bag was in my left hand, so I put out my right to meet his, thinking this was a goodbye shake. Quick as a flash, he reached forward and felt my entire body up and down, then retreated.

Trembling, but making a great effort not to run, I turned and walked away. I could hear the boy throwing pebbles down the road after me. Rounding a corner, I came to the Travellers Lodge. Yadav was in the forecourt polishing the Ambassador.

'If I will meet with this boy, he will be too sorry,' Yadav promised.

Later, in the twilight, we walked back down the village street to buy beer and Yadav's quarter bottle of whisky at the 'English Wine Shop,' which, despite its name, sold no wine and nothing English. An ox cart rumbled past us, filled with women and children jogging home from the fields, the women's chunnis turned to jewels in the dusk. Oil lamps shone like glow worms, and the flicker and sound of television came from almost every cottage.

The next day we went to the post office so that Yadav could telephone his office in Delhi. 'No Admission,' read a notice above the door. Business was conducted through a small barred window cut into the wall at twice the height of eye level. Yadav stood on tiptoe on the far side of the ditch that separated us from the window, trying to attract someone's attention. A passerby stopped and stared at us. 'Post office opens at nine thirty,' he said. It was ten o'clock. 'But bus of postmaster does not arrive before ten thirty.' He walked on.

At 10.45 a bus arrived and the postmaster got off. He invited us to step over the ditch and under the 'No Admission' sign. He shared his office with several birds, which flew in and out and used the facilities as it suited them. Oblivious to the sparrow perched on his inkwell, the postmaster asked how he could help us. We sat down to wait while he booked a call to Delhi. Twenty minutes passed, then thirty. After an hour I asked how things were going. He put the telephone to his ear, shook his head and explained patiently that this was not easy, as Delhi was many kilometres away.

Then a look of excitement crossed his face. 'One minute only.' We waited.

'Ah! Line is engaged,' he said with satisfaction.

We sat back in our chairs. Half an hour went by. I decided we should leave the call till mid-afternoon, when it would be too hot for sightseeing. Yadav and the postmaster looked upset. They explained that the cost of a call to Delhi would double after lunch.

'Worth it,' I said. 'Cancel the call.'

The sunlight made us blink. The car seats were almost too hot to sit on. We were about to drive off when we saw the postmaster waving and shouting. 'The call, the call – it has come through!' Yadav leapt out of the car and dashed across the road.

'This is India,' he said when he came back. 'And now we can carry on.' We drove through deserted countryside to the Rewa Kund buildings on the edge of the lonely plateau. From the battlements of Rupmati's Pavilion, we could see the Narmada threading its way through the plain. It was this very view that tempted the beautiful Hindu singer Rupmati to leave her village on the plains and come to live with Bahadur in this pavilion, which he had built just for her. Akbar, inspired by stories of Rupmati's beauty, attacked Mandu and Bahadur fled, leaving Rupmati behind. She poisoned herself and died.

A teenage boy had been hovering near us for some time before I recognised him as yesterday's tormentor. Yadav grabbed him by the collar and spoke sharply. Wriggling free, he ran off.

'I tell him I will chase him if he doesn't get lost. He become very frightened and say he is afraid of police. I think we will not see him again.'

It was our last evening in Mandu. Yadav stopped the car and walked over to a tea stall to ask directions to a restaurant. Then I saw him reach into his pocket and bring out the whisky. Throwing back his head, he glugged down the entire quarter bottle. I slid into the driving seat, fury welling up in me.

'I'm driving back,' I announced.

'I am not drunk, so please move back in your seat,' he said, raising his voice to match mine.

I did not want to drive down the narrow village street in the dark. The risks seemed greater than giving the wheel to my slightly inebriated friend. I did as he said.

Our first stop the next day was for a cow. She stood in the middle of the road, staring at us. Yadav slowed down. 'Good morning, my mother,' he called. 'Please move quickly, we are in hurry.' All cows were Yadav's mothers, all oxen his fathers and all buffaloes his aunties.

We passed a donkey trotting down the road in a determined way. 'See, he is in hurry. Is his day off, he is going to meet his sweet girlfriend. Good morning, my friend. You are not working today? Very good.' I pictured a pretty girl donkey with a jaunty straw hat perched between her ears, hurrying to meet her young man. We skirted round a herd of black goats.

'What relation are *they* to you?' I asked.

'My wife's younger brothers and sisters. Can you remember when I tell you about my father? He bought goat to give milk to my son after my wife died.'

At about five o'clock in the evening, exactly four weeks from the day we had left, we drove into Yadav's village, a place I had never expected to see again.

I found that I was looking forward to seeing the family. I wondered if they would notice the change in our relationship, and what they would think of it. I knew that many Indians thought Westerners were obsessed with sex, and indulged in it as, when and with whom they chose. I hoped that Yadav's relations would not judge our love affair in quite those terms.

I need not have worried, as Yadav on his farm was a very different man from Yadav off it. He was the youngest son in the family, and he obeyed the rules of his elders meticulously – no meat, and certainly no cohabitation. So, as it was difficult to find any private space on the farm, no sex. On reflection, I realised that Yadav's mother and father had never heard of Western sexual practices. His brothers were too busy dealing with the farm to be curious about their youngest brother, and the nephews and nieces and sons and daughters would not have presumed to think such thoughts about their elders, even if they had had such thoughts to think, which was doubtful.

The sky was heavy with rain, the air almost cold. Before arriving at the farm, we had gone to a tiny shop filled with bolts of cheap fabric. There was not much choice; we bought two metres of green synthetic cloth with yellow flowers on it.

'It is custom. My mother should have to give her respected guest a gift. After, you will also give gift to her of only five rupees. Is not too much, I think?' The material would be her present to me.

Ma heard the car's engine before anyone else did. She hobbled out to meet us, pleased to see Yadav and even more delighted that I had come back. She led me through a doorway, ordering two of the nephews to lay a red quilt on the charpoy and another round my shoulders. Cross-legged, we sat opposite each other trying to make conversation. Her eyes, as sharp as flint stones, were glued to my face. Her voice rose to a high-pitched crescendo and dropped to a whisper, and with it, her mood changed from joyful elation to tearful sadness. She picked up the corner of her red-and-yellow cotton chunni and wiped her watering eyes.

'Take no notice of my mum – she always play the drama,' Yadav said as he came in with the green material and gave it to his mother. Ceremoniously, she passed it to me.

'Thank you.' I bowed my head, fishing in my bag for five rupees. She seemed overcome by the small note. When I refused to take it back, she cradled it to her cheek, muttering and crying. I could hear the *ping, ping* of milk hitting a galvanised bucket. Someone was milking a buffalo.

'Come! We will go to peoples at next farm. They wants to look you.' Not sure what Yadav meant, I followed his nephew's wavering torch across the muddy field. Yadav told me which crops we were walking through: grams, onions, spinach and wheat. The rain clouds, which had been growing blacker by the minute, opened, and a deluge of water soaked us to the skin. We hurried across the last field and into a room similar to the one we had just left. The whitewashed brick walls were decorated with bright posters of Hanuman, Ganesh, and Shiva and Parvati holding hands. Old clothes were slung over wooden pegs, and farm implements hung from the walls. The only light came from a fire burning in the open hearth, where a veiled woman squatted as she cooked chapatis. Another, her face also covered, lit a kerosene lamp and passed around small cups of chai.

After our chai, the men left the room. The rest of the farm women then trooped in to 'look me'. It was a very unpleasant experience. As soon as the last man had gone, all the women lifted their veils in unison and stared, not with kind or friendly curiosity, but with an intrusive look that left me cold and alone.

I thought of the times I had stared at animals in the zoo. If I ever went to the zoo again, I thought, I would wave, smile, perhaps make some polite conversation with the animals – anything but stare.

The moment the men came back, the spell was broken. The veils were pulled forward, and the faceless women drifted from the room.

I was glad to return to Ma's cosseting. Seeing my damp, unhappy state, she called for more quilts to wrap round my shoulders.

A family debate was being held. 'They are thinking where you will sleep,' Yadav said. 'At first they decide for you in this room in middle of my father and my mum, but she thinks they disturb you with snores. Now they decide for next room, between me, my nephew and small baby. Will be all right for you, I think?'

I said that I would rather sleep with him alone, as we had been doing in Madhya Pradesh. He looked aghast. 'I'm sorry. At farm we cannot,' he said.

While we ate subzi, dal and roti, Yadav's favourite nephew sat in a corner and watched us. A sad expression darkened his face.

'Why does he look so unhappy?' I asked.

'You are wrong,' said Yadav. 'He is only frightened in case you does not like his food.'

'His food?'

'Yes, he cook it only for us, especially you.' I tried to look as though I was enjoying the extremely spicy food immensely.

There was no possibility of undressing. Everyone climbed on to their charpoys fully clothed, pulled the covers over their heads and went to sleep.

I lay awake, working out the geography of the farm. The main building, divided into windowless rooms and stables with beaten-earth floors, centred on a square yard. Three sides of the square had flat roofs; the fourth was thatched. The women's cell-like bathroom, distinguished by its soak-away drain, was next to the kitchen, and both rooms had cracked concrete flooring. The outer doorway to the front room, our sleeping quarters, was covered with a piece of sacking. All the rooms opening on to the central yard had big, wooden doors except those in the thatched section, which was used for the buffaloes on cold nights. Along one wall were stone troughs for buffalo feed. Under a mulberry tree in the middle of the yard, the women did the washing-up with a bucket of water and handfuls of earth for scouring. Apart from wooden pegs (for clothes and farm implements) and charpoys, there was no furniture. When not sitting or lying on a charpoy, the family squatted on the ground.

To the left of the main building was the engine house for the tube well. Yadav told me that the water table was a hundred feet below ground and sinking yearly because of poor monsoons. The well fed water to three tanks: the first for drinking water, the second for the buffaloes' drinking water and for the men, children and buffaloes to bathe in, and the third (in which there lived a giant, white-bellied frog) for washing clothes and anything else that needed soap or detergent. The water from the third tank drained into a ditch running alongside the garden, a small area where Ramesh's son Hari Ram grew carrots and garlic under the shade of papaya, guava and lemon trees.

At the far end of the building, Corrupt Brother and his family lived in a separate lean-to, taking their share of the produce and profits. Across the front yard, planted with wooden buffalo stakes and shady trees, Rama, Boss Brother's son, had built his family and buffaloes a thatched hut. There were a couple of thatched sheds where farm equipment (such as the animal-feed chopper) and extra charpoys for visitors were kept, and the foundations of a new room that, Yadav said, would be finished in two months.

The alarm clock rang loudly. We needed to get up early to beat the rush-hour traffic into Delhi. I had left some of my things at the Singhs', so I would spend my last two days in India with them, and Yadav and I would only see each other once more – when he took me to the airport for my flight back to London. He reached across my charpoy and turned off the alarm, grunting that we needn't get up for another half hour. The light grew stronger in the open doorway as the birds' morning chorus turned to twittering chatter. Yadav's niece looked in.

'She say your hot water is ready for bath – chalo!' He jumped off his charpoy as if he had never slept. We walked through the room where Yadav's brother, who shared his sleeping quarters with the oxen, lay rolled in his bedding. The animals gazed at us incuriously as we passed.

The only light in the 'bathroom' came from cracks in the door. Yadav added a little cold water to the two buckets that the girl had left, and went out. I shut the door, put the wooden bar across it and washed myself in darkness.

Dressed in clean clothes and feeling better, I walked back across the yard. The women were hurrying about their work. They swept dust from one place to another with brushes made of twigs. They loaded pats of fresh dung on to round metal dishes with their naked hands, lifted the dishes on to their heads and carried them away to be dried and used as fuel. They fetched water from the well in pot-bellied brick-red water pots. Bapu, Yadav's father, squatted on the ground examining a farm implement and inhaling the first puff of the morning on his hookah. Only Ma slept. Yadav said she had been awake all night, making continual visits to our room to assure herself that I was asleep and well.

Now the family stood together in front of the whitewashed buildings, waving goodbye as the sun rose slowly behind the hill beyond the mustard fields.

Summer had come to Delhi. Crowds sauntered on the lawns at India Gate. Everyone was out buying ice creams and balloons, or just sitting in the shade of the flower-filled trees.

Back at the Singhs' house, it was becoming more and more difficult to distinguish dreams from reality. One side of me longed to be back in London with my family and friends and a life I understood, or thought I did. The other side dreaded leaving India and, now that I was in Delhi and so close to him, ached with a terrible longing to see Yadav. Baby's dulcet tones would have turned to a screech of horror had she known about him. With numbed feelings and a heart as heavy as a ton of sticky toffee, I followed her on her rounds to the dressmaker, the beauty salon, and coffee and snacks at fashionable ladies' 'housi housi' parties.

The Singhs had a new Mercedes. We bought it a garland of red and white flowers and took it to the gurdwara to be blessed. The priest, cross-legged before the *Guru Granth Sahib*, not only blessed the car but handed Rekha an extra garland.

'Aunty, he has given this for you,' she explained, hanging the flowers around my neck. 'It is so unusual to see a foreign lady in our temple.'

Palm Sunday at the Catholic church down the road made me feel more certain of who and what I was. Listening to the Mass, even though half of it was in Hindi, gave me a feeling of solidarity and security that I had rarely felt in the last three months. It was a comfort to think of people saying the same words and chanting the same chants halfway across the world – at Brompton Oratory, at my children's convent school in Dorset, at the Holy Apostles in Pimlico. And the Bunch of Grapes and the Cross Keys would still be pulling pints for thirsty communicants. But, I reminded myself, in reality most of my Sundays were spent weaving my way round overcrowded Windsor Castle or singing the praises of the white cliffs of Dover. Listening to the organ at the Oratory and drinking a glass of wine at the pub afterwards were rare treats.

The red-hot orb of the setting sun sank over Delhi, pulling my heart down with it.

The Singhs' manservant opened the door as the last note of the chiming doorbell died away. 'Memsahib, driver is waiting with car.' Baby and Sujann stood in the street waving us off.

At last we turned the corner. Yadav and I were on our own.

'Before we go to airport I would like to show you something,' he said.

'What is it?

'Wait and you will know.' He stopped the car on a grass verge. 'Now, please, you follow me.'

We were in a no-man's-land of rough scrub and building sites. Yadav took my hand and we dodged through a stream of belching lorries. A hot wind blew sand through the air, filtering the sun's rays until the polluted light was as grey as fog. An ugly complex of concrete blocks towered before us.

'Come.' Yadav led me through a malodorous entrance into a building knee-deep in rubbish. 'It is on ground floor,' he said with modest pride. Unable to guess what he wanted to show me, I followed him down a long, cement-floored corridor. He stopped in front of one of the many chipped, peeling doors and flung it open, standing aside to let me pass.

'Do you like it?' he asked anxiously. 'I am renting it so next time you comes, but I do not think I can hope that you will, you can stay here.'

I looked round the dark, ill-painted room. A bucket in one corner caught the drips from a leaking tap. A single charpoy stood against the wall. One dim light bulb hung from the ceiling. A small window, set high in the wall, half hidden in dust and dirt, let in little or no light.

'Well, yes. It's lovely,' I lied.

'Thank you. Thank you very much. Now please you lie down on cot.'

'But Yadav, we've got to go to the airport.'

'Please you lie there, only for one minute. Then I can have the impression of your figure in my eyes. You will be here in my heart, even if you are in the London. Please! It is last request. We have plenty time for your flight.'

I lay down on the charpoy. He stood quite still, looking at me.

'Thank you very much. Now we will go to airport. Carry on.'

'Carry on,' I repeated.

At the airport Yadav ordered the porter not to overcharge me. I couldn't say goodbye or look back; I did not want to leave him.

Inside the terminal I took one last look at him, smiling and waving his square hands, rubbed hard and smooth by a lifetime of work.

I thought I heard his voice.

'Carry on!' he said.

8

After three months on the Subcontinent it was wonderful to be back in London. My old friend Paul, holding the most enormous bunch of flowers I had ever seen, and my youngest daughter, Mary Jane, met me at the airport. I could hardly wait to get home to open my suitcase full of presents. There were cushion covers from Jaisalmer, bedspreads from Jaipur, miniature paintings from Udaipur, spices from Kerala and tea from Darjeeling. For my four daughters there were the wild-silk dresses from Mysore – so right in India, yet entirely inappropriate, I now realised, against the grey skies and biting winds of London. My daughters rushed round to see me, and my son rang twice from his office to ask me out to dinner. I made long and blissful telephone calls to my friends. I ate platefuls of salad with oceans of olive oil and piles of toast and Marmite while I arranged to meet everyone and go everywhere.

But life was not really like that. A packet of letters arrived from my solicitor, and the bills were back. They glared up at me. 'Ignore us if you dare,' they seemed to say. I moved out of my bedroom on to a sofa-bed, put an ad in *Loot* and had a houseful of lodgers a few days later. Pimlico was popular.

I rang round the tour operators. Before long I was up at 6.30 every morning and returning at eight in the evening, too tired and mindless to see anyone or do anything.

India became my lifeline. At bus stops, in the Underground and in hotel lobbies where I waited for my tourists, I lived India vicariously, burying myself in memories, reading books, looking at photographs and even chatting up Indians on buses. I bored my best friends with endless talk of India. I may or may not have been suffering from *mal d'amour* – I still was not sure about my feelings for Yadav or his for me – but my *mal de l'Inde* was very real.

My world had been turned upside-down and inside-out. In India I had lived so many lives, had discovered alien emotions and senses that had rocked my foundations. I no longer knew who I was or where I belonged. Conventional values seemed irrelevant. I could not take my country, my religion or anything else very seriously. The mores and foibles that held Western society together now appeared idols of self-importance and prejudice. Perhaps I did not know India well enough, or perhaps I had forgotten that whatever country we choose to inhabit, rules are unavoidable – no matter how hard we might try to evade and ignore a society's judgments and however ludicrous we might find them, a change of scenery will only bring a change of rules. Wrapped in my Indian dream, willingly blinded by its enmeshing web, I imagined I had found freedom. I thought I knew the answers. But no one does, no one can, till time and Fate dictate the future and it suddenly becomes the present.

Yadav wrote often. Flimsy aerogrammes, falling apart before I could open them, dropped on to the doormat every other day. Reading the uneven capital letters, I could hear his voice.

My very dear sweetheart Jill. Now it is too hot at your farm. My family members is all very well, thanks God! We are badly waiting for monsoon. As I have told you many times and you knows very well, I love you and love you and love you a lot. Excuse my poor English. I am very tired from writing in your stupid British language. Please send letter soon. Yadav.

'I hear you're having an affair with an Indian taxi driver,' my ninety-year-old aunt said gleefully as we sat eating sardine sandwiches and drinking Nescafé in her untidy little drawing room.

'A farmer,' I said defensively.

Deciding I should keep my options open, I rang the marriage bureau. A voice that I did not recognise answered.

'My name is Sarah,' it explained. 'I'm part-time.'

I told her I had just come back from India.

'I expect you're feeling rather disoriented,' she said. 'I lived there many years ago. I still have friends from those days and I still miss it. Once you've been there, you're never quite free of its magnetism. It's almost like a disease, but quite a nice one.' We talked about India for half an hour before I remembered my real reason for ringing.

'I rang you about a husband,' I said at the end of our conversation. 'But I'm not really sure that I want one. I think I've fallen in love with India. All I want to do is to go back.'

'I do understand,' said Sarah. 'Why don't we have lunch?'

I had unwittingly joined a club. Anyone who has fallen under India's spell becomes a life member.

I was determined to return in the autumn, but not as a tourist. Sarah gave me the address of Vinobaniketan, an ashram and home for poor children near Trivandrum. I wrote to Sister Paravrajika, the head of the ashram, and arranged to go to Kerala for three months.

I was back in India by December, celebrating Christmas away from my family for the first time. It was as austere and simple as Western Christmases are commercial and elaborate.

I had imagined that the ashram would be something like my daughters' convent school: polished floors smelling of beeswax, nuns in whispering habits and fresh-faced school girls in neat uniforms. I could not have been more mistaken. Both the convent and the ashram had been founded on a spiritual basis, but there the resemblance ended. Sister Paravrajika was a Hindu by birth and a follower of Gandhian principles. She was sixty-five, but with her cropped black hair and sweet smile she could have passed for forty. She dressed in the traditional saffron garments of a sanyasi. The children went barefoot and slept on the floor of a huge wooden barn. Their daily diet was a mound of rice flavoured with a tiny spoonful of chutney, made from jackfruit or tapioca.

Yadav and I wrote to each other often. We could not talk, as neither his farm nor the ashram had a working telephone. He suggested making the three-day journey to Kerala but I discouraged him, unsure of both his reception by Sister Paravrajika, who came from a strictly orthodox family of high-caste doctors, and his tolerance for the ashram. We agreed that I would fly to Delhi at the end of my three months in south India.

In February I left Vinobaniketan, taking with me a deep affection for it and its inmates. I interrupted my journey from Kerala to Delhi with a stay in Bombay, partly because I was feeling insecure about meeting Yadav again and partly because I was curious about all of India's major cities. I spent a few days with a friend of Sarah's named Carlo, an old and crusty but eccentrically hospitable man. Italian by birth, he had come to Bombay at the age of seventeen and stayed on to become a film director and photographer. Together we tripped and trudged round the streets of Bombay, his hometown for fifty years.

My few days with Carlo brought me back to reality and gave me time to think about seeing Yadav again. I didn't talk about him, as I felt sure that Carlo would disapprove. He had lived in India for too long to be able to imagine having a relationship with one's driver. I became more and more unsure about what I was doing. Shouldn't my life be spent with people like Carlo, Westerners who understood and thought about the same things, who ate the same food and had the same values, even if they didn't always stick to them?

In some ways I could not wait to be with Yadav, but our time together had been so short... after our long separation, I wondered what we were to each other and what we might become.

He was waiting behind the barrier at the airport, smiling and waving. I wondered how I could ever have doubted the rightness of coming back.

His face was as I remembered it, very thin with two deep, vertical furrows of stress that split his brow in half. A stray piece of black hair flopped over one eye.

'Wait. Please wait,' he said as I was about to get into the familiar white Ambassador. Seconds later he was beside me, arranging an enormous garland of orange, white and yellow flowers round my neck.

'Now you please get in.' He waited until I was seated before passing me a newspaper packet. Inside was a rough, hand-woven purse with a cotton strap. I hung it over my shoulder and thanked him. 'No, no. Please open – I think you will like very much. Anyway, I can hope.' He leant over, watching me pull another newspaper parcel out of the bag. 'Open, open,' he said impatiently.

Inside was a pair of silver anklets and a small heart-shaped locket on a silver chain. Yadav took the locket, fastened it round my neck and, bending down, latched a chain round each of my ankles. He sat back admiring his handiwork. 'Now you are almost nearly my wife,' he said.

Yadav had given up the rented room. We spent three nights together in a run-down tower-block hotel, getting to know each other again and discussing plans for the rest of my stay.

'You will spend some days with your friend Mrs Baby Singh. After I will pick you from her house and you and me, we will go to my farm for Holi festival. Then we will have our holiday in the Gujarat state,' Yadav decided. 'I will tell to my boss that you are my good friend Mr Purdeep Kumar. Actually is name of my own grandson. This way my boss he will make cheap price for car rent. I think to save money will be good for you?'

I had written to Baby but had not heard from her. I rang to say that I was in Delhi. Out of guilty gratitude for their hospitality, I felt I should stay with the Singhs once more.

'I thought you were coming a week ago,' she cooed. 'I've been waiting for you.'

I lunched with Ranji, a distinguished elderly friend of Sarah's, in the cool green garden of the Imperial Hotel. His impeccable English and gracious manners belonged to an India I had barely met. We sat under a striped umbrella and chatted about Sarah and her family in England. I asked him some questions I had been longing to ask about India, but I did not talk about Yadav; again, I felt that my new friend would not understand our relationship. Sitting there, enjoying the flowers, the food and the conversation, I was not sure I understood it myself.

Nothing had changed at the Singhs'. The driver was dusting the cars. Shiv Singh, with Mary at his heels, let me in at the first chime of the bell. Through the open door I saw Baby drifting down the stairs in a yellow and green sequin-spangled salwar-kamiz.

The family was as kind and hospitable as ever, except Baby, who seemed to have got a little bored with playing hostess to her 'English friend'. I reminded her that I would be leaving in a few days, on the twenty-eighth. 'I've hired a car,' I said. 'I'm going to Gujarat,'

'But you can't!' Baby squealed. 'It's Holi and I'm giving a party especially for you. You will tell the driver to come later, any day. It doesn't matter.'

'But I can't get in touch with the driver – he doesn't have a telephone.'

'Well, when he comes, send him away,' she said impatiently. 'Tell him to come back in two days. It's easy.' She tossed her head. 'So you will come to my party. That is fixed.'

She began talking about her new farmhouse. 'Today Sujann will take us for a picnic at our farm, and you will have an opportunity to see how beautiful it will be when finished. Sunita, stop that fucking computer game at once and tell Rekha to send her tutor home. It's almost time to go.'

'Jingle Bells', the reverse-signal music of all Gypsy jeeps, came on as Sujann backed the third of the family cars out through the gate. Baby sat beside him. The girls sat together on the middle seat.

We passed tall brick walls pierced by massive wrought-iron gates, some enclosing mansions, others enclosing mansions in the throes of being built. All occupied land that had once belonged to real farmers like Yadav's family.

The Singhs' three-acre plot was in the early stages of development. The great gates already set in the brick wall would have suited the grandest of Scottish castles. An army of workmen crawled backwards and forwards over an artificial hill built of earth and boulders. Pipes stuck out in all directions, making it look like an angry porcupine. The men were adding concrete logs to a picturesque concrete pagoda on the edge of a deep ditch. The architect was waving papers and shouting in an unnecessary display of power.

Seeing Sujann, his arrogance evaporated. He slithered up to us, his bearing now obsequious. 'All pipes hidden by next week, Sahib.' Sujann stared at him coldly, not bothering to reply.

A family of peasants came out of a little brick shed at the far side of the plot and hurried towards us. The man began speaking, but Sujann cut him short. Pointing to our basket of tiffins, he barked out an order. The family scurried round, setting up a table and chairs and laying out our picnic in the shade of an enormous, green plastic plant house where wilting potted plants stood in regimental rows. Baby screamed at the man to bring water.

'Servants are so lazy. It's never-ending, the work I must do. Come, I will show you around.' We walked across the parched, uneven ground while Baby told me her dreams of how, when all the work was finished, she and Sujann would rest peacefully in their pagoda beside the waterfall, watching the stream cascade down its artificial hill into a lotus-covered moat.

'Such sweet sights and scents,' she sighed, her voice a mixture of pride and self-sacrifice. 'I have designed it myself, every inch of it. So beautiful, don't you think?'

I nodded. All I could think about was Yadav and the twenty-eighth.

She looked again at the wasteland surrounded by raw red walls and the pile of rocks in the corner. 'My mother is sending us a dear little cow from Amritsar, and I am having a house built specially for her. She's a Jersey. Her house will have running water and electricity laid on. I will have to teach those stupid servants to give her a bath night and morning and look after her properly. I am so fond of animals.'

The small, wiry guard dog, freed from its chain outside the servants' hovel, bounded up to us. Baby gave a small scream and yelled for someone to remove the beast.

I had been asked to dinner by Ranji, who gallantly came to collect me even though he lived just round the corner from the Singhs. I gave him a bottle of Johnnie Walker Red Label that I had bought at the airport. He thanked me politely, put it to one side and offered me a glass of Chivas Regal.

The flat was filled with books and silver-framed photographs of members and ex-members of the government. Ranji's wife Rosemary, a Catholic, talked nostalgically of the days of the Raj.

'It was sometimes a little difficult,' she admitted. 'I remember once going on a long train journey. I'd just put my luggage on the rack when an English officer came into the compartment. There was another seat vacant, but for some reason he wanted mine. I had to sit on a box in the corridor for two hours.' She warmed to her memories as she told me me about her father, who had been a judge, and her visit to the Vatican some years ago.

'What did you drink at your friend's house?' Baby wanted to know when I returned.

'Whisky.'

'What sort?'

'Scotch.'

She nodded and said she supposed it was Black Label – that was what everyone drank. She slotted Ranji and Rosemary into their rightful place in Delhi society. If my answer had been 'Indian,' they would have fitted into a different pigeonhole.

Yadav rang and said that his office wanted 'Mr Purdeep Kumar's' payment for the car in advance. I caught up with Baby at the front door.

'That was my driver. I really must go on the twenty-eighth.'

She shrugged. 'Oh, go if you must.' It was as easy as that. But from then on our friendship, if there had ever been one, went from bad to worse.

Thankful for my lucky escape, I got into the Ambassador, happier to be with Yadav again than I could possibly have imagined. On our way to the farm, we visited relations. Our first stop was the factory where Ramesh, Yadav's one-eyed policeman brother, was employed as a security guard. At our next stop, Yadav bought a crate of mineral water, refused my offer of payment and, picking up my hand, began to sing.

'Is very sweet song about my gods. And now we will carry on. We must have to see my sister Sarti, the one who is widow and look after my son.' The moment the car stopped outside

Sarti's house it was surrounded by the women and children of the village, all agog to see the white woman. I felt like the fat lady at the fair.

'Come.' Yadav pushed through the crowd. 'Here is my sister.' With a delighted smile, Sarti joined her hands in greeting. She was thin, lined and minus most of her teeth, but I could see that she had once been beautiful and was probably ten years younger than I was.

'And these,' said Yadav nodding towards a teenage girl and a youth with the shadow of a moustache on his upper lip, 'are my son Ashok and my naughty daughter Puja.' He caught her by the waist and hugged her. 'Ravi, my sister's son, is at school.' The children dragged a charpoy into the middle of the yard.

'Please sit,' Puja said in shy English. We stayed long enough for them to light a fire and brew a cup of chai for Yadav. A dozen faces peeped at me through the half-open gateway.

Next on the list were Yadav's eldest daughter, Sarita, and her family, who lived in another village about twenty kilometres away. They were all out working in the fields, so we went to see another friend, a grey-haired schoolteacher dressed in whiter-than-white kurta-pyjamas. He embraced Yadav and led us into a whitewashed room in his spotless village house, inviting us to sit on a charpoy covered with a freshly laundered white quilt.

'He is trying to help my son-in-law, who is brilliant teacher of mathematics but without job,' Yadav told me. 'In my country is too difficult. To find work you must have to pay too many rupees under the table. Brilliance does not help.'

Suddenly, without warning, Yadav produced a bag of bright-pink powder and emptied it over my head, rubbing it into my cheeks and scalp. 'Now you can say Holi has begun,' he said with satisfaction. I looked at the mess on the bedcover. 'Please don't worry,' Yadav said as he flicked ash from his bidi on to the well-swept floor. 'My friend, he is very happy we play Holi in his house.' A smile spread across his friend's clean-shaven face.

The family returned from their work. Sarita led us into a tiny room filled with a double bed, tin trunk and makeshift shelves filled with battered books and piles of papers. Yadav introduced me to the children. He picked up a thin, elongated child with big feet.

'He is Purdeep, my eldest grandson, and this is Sunita, my granddaughter. She is still baby.' Black eyes stared up at me. Then the face crumpled, and Sunita began to cry. Her mother scooped her up, lifted her own top, squatted on the floor and fed her. Yadav and his son-in-law sat on the bed downing half a bottle of whisky and puffing bidi smoke into the already dense atmosphere.

It had started to drizzle. Yellow and orange sparks flew like fireflies, hissing softly, enraged by rapidly falling raindrops that interrupted their road to a storm-ravaged sky. Our noses tingled with the scent of wet woodsmoke. Villagers crowded round the fitful firelight of the huge bonfire as flames flickered through the damp twigs. There were cheers and shouts – a boy had climbed a bamboo ladder. From high above our heads he hurled canfuls of kerosene on to the sodden stack, where it flared and spat and roared and sent him slithering down to safety. More cheers. Purdeep jumped off my knee and ran from the car, fascinated by the fire and the fiend-like figures hopping, skipping and poking their long poles, tipped with sheaves of wheat, into the kerosene-crazy flames. Women and children fed the fire with small circlets of dried buffalo dung, strung like giant necklaces on lengths of string. Holi had begun.

Pinpricks of light from cottage windows, the smell of damp fields, a howling dog tugging at its chain. Yadav's family were still up. It was late for them. They greeted us and melted away.

'Weren't they surprised to see me again?'

'Why they should be? You are as our own family member. Whisky?' Yadav settled down on a charpoy, gesturing to me to do the same. I was cold and tired. With one sip, a rosy glow suffused my body. A second mouthful put me to sleep.

'Wake up, wake up! Your dinner is waiting you.' I opened my eyes to see Ramesh's one eye squinting down at me. 'I got my leave today and so I have come to cook your dinner. I hope you like my dish.' I was too tired to eat more than a mouthful. Yadav put the thali down on the floor near the empty whisky bottle. Boss Brother came in followed by Meenakshi, Yadav's middle daughter, carrying a hookah. She set it carefully on the floor and, picking up my discarded plate but not touching the bottle, left us.

'She cannot see whisky, because at farm we doesn't drink, same we doesn't eat meat. So for her is nothing there,' Yadav explained. The three men squatted round the hookah, taking turns to draw greedily until the smoke rose through the water with a thick bubbling sound and the smell of tobacco filled the room. Yadav's voice rose and fell in emotional crescendos. Boss Brother and Ramesh were earnest, but stayed calm. Suddenly all three rose from the ground. The meeting was over. I later learnt that they had been talking about finding a husband for Yadav's youngest daughter.

Yadav picked up a heavy blanket and wrapped it round me. 'Chalo,' he said.

'Where are we going?' I felt too tired to walk another step.

'We will sleep at new well.'

I followed the beam of his torch. Wading through dripping crops, we came to a small brick hut. Cloggy soil squelched between my toes, my teeth chattered in the damp air. Yadav pushed open the door and turned on the naked light bulb that swung on a stringy wire from the rafters. The tiny, clean-swept room was warm and dry and smelt of new twine, like the potting sheds of my childhood. There were two charpoys piled with heavy bedding. The walls were decorated with a haphazard assortment of hoes, wooden ploughs and water pipes. Yadav laid out the bedding.

'And now we are completely by ourselves. We will have our sweet night,' he said. 'Come. Let's enjoy.' He turned off the light. The charpoys creaked and squeaked in protest as we climbed onto them. I put out my hand and felt the wooden frame of his cot, the plaited string and Yadav's brown velvet body.

'I'm sorry, but you mind it or not, I will come in your bed,' he said. The strings sagged under our double weight, rolling us into a dip in the middle. I was not dreaming. We were at the farm, and after our 'sweet night' the morning would come, and we would celebrate Holi together.

At 8.30 the women and children – including me – climbed into the Ambassador armed with lethal bags of Holi-coloured powders and liquids. Yadav tipped a bagful of colour over his grandson. Purdeep looked down at his small hands and his special going-away clothes, stained green and red, and started to howl, taking cover behind a buffalo. He flatly refused the return ammunition of purple powder that Yadav held out to him. We drove away leaving the little boy in the arms of his great-aunt Shanti, blinded by his own bitter tears. Next year, when Purdeep was older, he too would enjoy Holi.

Traffic was building up along the track leading to the main road. Every temple had its own Holi fair, and everyone was going to visit as many fairs as they could. Loads of chattering women, decked out in clean blouses, scarlet and gold chunnis from their marriage chests and rainbow-coloured embroidered petticoats, joggled and bumped behind and before us, overflowing from tractor-pulled trailers and ox and camel carts. Amongst the few privileged car owners, we drove to a temple in a remote valley, where, Yadav told me, lived a very rich saint.

'Temple is built on body of old-time saint. He buried himself and stay alive. Now many pilgrims come and bring much money.' To judge from the present-day saint's fleshy body and pot belly, part of the pilgrims' money went towards his culinary pleasures. He sat under an elaborate tinselled awning, enjoying the adulation of his admirers as they swarmed round him, pushing and pressing to get near enough to touch his foot or his saffron lunghi. Seeing me, the only white face in the crowd, he beckoned with a pudgy hand. I smiled and waved.

Back in our own village we were surrounded by Holi players, eager to embrace and plaster us with colours that had already turned most of the villagers into grinning devils. Yadav's mother watched from a doorway. Nobody troubled her; she had played many Holis, and her time was past.

'Ah, beti, meri beti,' she wailed, rubbing the top of my head as I bent to touch her feet.

The sounds of drumbeats, singing and music drew nearer. A bright-red tractor roared round the corner, spewing up the dust. Between two loudspeakers, which tannoyed music village-wide, sat our priest, receiving homage and rupees from his flock. His eyes twinkled in his black-bearded face as he accepted a thick wad of notes from Yadav and stashed it away in the folds of his saffron robes. Yadav's family hoped the gift would encourage the gods to give them many blessings.

I was standing beside Yadav, and then I wasn't. With shouts of laughter the crowd lifted me and set me down on the tractor with the priest on one side and a statue of the saint, out for his Holi airing, on the other. We were pulling a trailer that overflowed with people singing, waving and throwing fistfuls of colour, making spectacles of each other and the passersby. A man with pink and green eyes winked at me while another with vermilion hair, a blue face and yellow, mauve-tipped hands gave me 'Ram Ram.' His pearl-white teeth leered like a detached set of dentures in his pale-green jaw. A girl with large red spots, like coloured kisses, on her cheeks, her black hair streaked yellow and green, followed her brother, who had been transformed by different dyes into a grinning goblin.

Our cavalcade moved on through narrow streets to the temple. We took off our chappals. Inside it was dim, quiet and cool. A fat priest sat beside the space soon to be reoccupied by the gadabout god. He filled our hands with sweet prasad. Not being very fond of sugar, I tipped most of mine back into the big brass dish.

'You shouldn't have to do that,' Yadav reproved me. 'Keep them to give to all family. They are gods' sweets.'

Behind the temple, people thronged the stalls of sweets, paper hats, streamers, plastic baubles and bangles. Sellers of bobbing balloons hung tightly to their strings, struggling through sweltering seas of feet and faces. Packed tightly between the rows of parked cars and jeeps, families sat eating.

'Look at all the people picnicking,' I said.

'They have come from other villages to celebrate Holi,' Yadav told me severely. 'You are completely wrong to think they are having picnic. They are eating their lunch. Only rich people have picnics.'

In the evening, when the grey-streaked sky had turned a velvety pink and yellow and I had scrubbed most of the colour off my face and body with the last of my Floris soap and a bucket of cold well water, we went for a walk through the fields. When we were far enough away from the farm, we threw away my red-dyed underclothes. Rubbish was difficult to dispose of, wherever it was thrown, as one or another family member always hurried to inspect it lest anything useful be discarded. My Holi-stained salwar-kamiz had already been put away in a tin trunk amongst Yadav's late wife's clothes, ready for next year's festivities.

Before we left for Gujarat, Yadav had to find a bridegroom for his youngest daughter. He announced that I was going to help him decide this important matter. Together with Ramesh, looking official in his uniform, and Boss Brother, tall and thin in a dhoti and blue-and-white checked turban, we set off to a nearby village to meet the family of a prospective husband for Puja. The old men of the boy's family were seated on their veranda, waiting for us. They passed the hookah from one to another and sipped their chai.

'Come, we will go for walk,' said Yadav. 'Is the job of my elder brothers. They and boy's family must decide between them.'

'Will we meet the boy?' I asked.

'The father does have to give his permission. Let us see.'

When we came back, Ramesh said something to Yadav and he nodded. 'We will not see the boy. His father wishes his son will marry with girl from richer family.'

Pushkar, a small town of white temples and houses, was built around a lake. The ghats were filled with pilgrims scattering pink and red rose petals on the translucent waters, which swarmed with overfed sacred fish. Brahmin priests oversaw, and pocketed rupees from, pilgrims chanting pujas. The main street was busy day and night with Western travellers buying loo paper, mineral water, Indianised Western clothes and costume jewellery. For Hindus there were garlands, mementoes of Lord Brahma, talismans, cassettes and pamphlets, sacred and profane, catering to pilgrims and tourists alike.

Pushkar is entirely vegetarian and dry. Influenced by thousands of foreign visitors, especially during the camel fair, the restaurants offer Western, Indian and Chinese foods, homogenised into tasteless dishes with Eastern names. To Yadav's relief, we found one authentic Indian restaurant at the far end of town.

In our hotel, Yadav disappeared into the bathroom to wash himself and our clothes. It was useless to protest or offer assistance, as he told me I did not know the proper Indian dhobi-wallah's way.

Yadav had a set bathroom routine. It began with a cigarette, followed by a vigorous tooth cleaning, after which came the violent throat-clearing and coughing sounds of the 'inner cleansing'. Squatting on the floor in his underpants, he then scrubbed his body till it and the soap were almost rubbed away. Next came bucketfuls of cold water. Finally, shaking himself like a dog, he carefully changed beneath his towel into a pair of dry underpants. Then, on his haunches once more, he did our laundry. With vicious slaps, bangs, rinses and a final wringing, he sat back on his heels. He had finished his 'daily duty'. Then it was my turn – I hung the clothes out to dry.

From our balcony, we looked across the lake to two conical hills that rose like giant sandcastles out of the flat plain, crowned by temples dedicated to Brahma's wives Savitri and Gayatri. Husbands who go to Savitri's temple for darshan believe that they will not die before their wives. Yadav reluctantly agreed to climb the hill to Savitri's temple.

I had heard that Brahmin boys up to the age of twenty-five had to promise to remain celibate. I asked Yadav if this was true. He said we should ask the temple priest, and that was how we met Beni Gopal, sitting cross-legged beside the image of the goddess. The sacred thread hung diagonally from his shoulder across his naked torso. His answer to Yadav's question was considered, his voice compelling and musical.

'The time for study is from extreme youth to the age of twenty-five. Study should not be disturbed by other thoughts and preoccupations. After study it is time for marriage and family. But...' He paused to think. 'Nowadays, with television and modern media, people no longer follow these old laws. This does not matter. Who can say exactly what is right and what is wrong?' He stopped again and looked at us. 'I must admit that for myself, I am happier away from all the new-fangled things.' He glanced around, his face luminous, as though he were counting the wealth of the world in the shape of the goddess and the bare little courtyard of his lonely hilltop home.

Halfway down the hillside, we stopped and looked down in silence on a miniature Pushkar. The town was cut in half by the silver thread of the sacred lake. Picking up my hand, Yadav asked in a serious voice. 'You knows that I love you and I want to marry with you?' Pause. 'And you do not say if you will marry me. I love you a hundred and one per cent. How much do you love me?'

How could I say that I would marry him? Even if we had been of the same nationality, our backgrounds and education were worlds apart. Perhaps that would not matter so much in England, but Indian society would never accept us. And in ten years I would be an old woman; he was only just entering middle age. Everything was wrong.

'I love you ninety-five and a half per cent,' I said.

'Thank you. Thanks a lot. Now I feel better.' He got to his feet, pulling me up after him. 'And now we will take anklets to jeweller to make shorter, and then you will wear them and be real Indian wife.'

Pushkar had vanished, lost in the rocky landscape. Only my shortened anklets and a few photographs proved that we had been there.

Mount Abu, Rajasthan's only hill station, had become a holiday resort for Gujarati honeymooners.

'Yadav, would you mind if I bought you some kurta-pyjamas?' I had an idea that new and different clothes might reduce the scorn with which hotel receptionists, waiters and doormen treated him. I guessed that people could be easily fooled by a good piece of silk or a politician's waistcoat.

'Why should I mind? It is very kind suggestion of you.'

In a single-lane street in the busy bazaar we stopped at a shop full of Rajasthani saris and fabrics in eye-catching designs and colours. We asked the owner to suggest a place selling more sober materials. The man gestured vaguely, pointing neither to right, left nor centre. Yadav chose the centre. Behind a couple of cows busily sorting through a pile of boxes, we found the right shop. Roll after roll of white, cream and pink-tinged materials were unfurled for our inspection until the counter looked like a galleon covered in collapsed sails. I chose a stiff, cream-coloured cotton.

'If I buy so expensive thing, I must wear at least five years and I will get too bored with always same.' Yadav chose the cheapest white cotton-synthetic fabric, and would not be induced to change his mind.

We left the material at a tailor's shop with instructions to finish the clothes by late afternoon. Back in the main market, Yadav stopped in front of a small cart. The owner was bent over the hand of a young girl, stencilling a pattern of henna on her palm.

'Now you will put henna on your hands. It will look too beautiful, and is custom for all newly wedded brides.'

'But Yadav, I am not a newly wedded bride.'

Taking no notice, he picked up my hand and held it out to the stenciller, who covered the palm first with a plastic hand-shaped stencil and then with a thick coating of dark-green henna paste. After a moment he peeled off the plastic, leaving a pattern of small green blobs. He repeated the process on the other palm, giving a final daub to my fingertips.

'Now you are even more my sweet wife,' said Yadav. 'When paste will be dry in two hours and you wash your hands, it will look even more beautiful.' He sighed with happiness.

We collected the kurta-pyjamas later in the afternoon. I thought they looked lovely, but Yadav was angry, telling the tailor he had made a bad job of them. He may or may not have meant it; he was always suspicious of being overcharged. The tailor seemed to enjoy the harangue. We parted amicably and bumped into the shopkeeper next door, who persuaded us to buy his khadi silk for another kurta-pyjama and some wool for a waistcoat. He took us on the back of his motor scooter to the 'best tailor in town.' When we went to collect the silk kurta-pyjamas and the Nehru-collared waiscoat, even Yadav was pleased.

'Now is time for your sightseeing. We will go first to Dilwara Jain temples.'

NO PHOTOGRAPHY OF RELIGIOUS STATUES
NO EMBRACING NEAR THE TEMPLES
LADIES IN MONTHLY COURSE ENTERING
TEMPLE ENTER AT OWN RISK

We passed the forbidding notices, entered the main temple and found ourselves in a wonderland of glittering, white-marble lace. Every crevice and corner was encrusted with carvings of animals, lotus flowers, gods and goddesses, all framed in a delicate latticework of stone. A tour guide rushed into the temple, brandished his stick to emphasise his shouted comments to the party of Indians trailing behind him, and ran the group out again.

'Now we would rather like to see temple of Hindu religion,' Yadav said. 'I think is very interesting and I never seen in my life before.'

The car park at the Achaleshwar Shiva temple was crowded with jeeps and minibuses. Honeymooners wandered, hands clasped, amongst stalls selling soapstone statues, religious pictures, fried pakoras and seashell hangings.

Inside the temple it was dark and dank. Yadav fell to his knees. The bell tolled to announce another pilgrim to Lord Shiva's shrine, represented not by the usual lingam but by a hole in the ground, decorated with dark-green leaves. The temple priest sat cross-legged beside it, muttering a mantra for each five-rupee note that fluttered into his brass bowl.

We rented a boat on Lake Nakki and pedalled from one end to the other. In the middle of the lake Yadav said, 'If you will be my wife, if we marry, we can live in Mount Abu. We can have milk and dairy shop and build our house like houses in these hills.' I didn't answer.

'Do not worry,' he went on. 'All things depends on time.'

I was beginning to accept Yadav's views on life. Time and Fate would decide our futures. There was nothing we could do; there was no point in worrying or battering our heads against brick walls. It was a comforting way to think. I looked at Yadav and hoped that time and Fate would keep us together.

After breakfast Yadav announced that we would go riding. 'I never did ride on a horse before in my whole life,' he said, swinging into the saddle of a sad, skinny nag. With my long knowledge of equitation (I had spent much of my childhood following the Chiddingfold Farmers' Hunt over Surrey's back gardens and barbed-wire fences), I mounted with confidence, feeling the horse's ribcage against my legs. With unexpected energy, the bells jingling on its moth-eaten plume, the horse bucked, almost unseating me. The pony-wallah swiped it with a stick. It bucked again. Thinking that a little coaxing would do more good than a beating, I led the way out of Mount Abu and up the road to the maharaja's palace, now a hotel. Friendly persuasion left my bad-tempered beast unmoved; it backed and bucked and snorted and bared its teeth. Behind me, Yadav and his mount ambled along.

'All right?' I called shakily. 'Very fine indeed,' he called back.

Yadav had never been to Gujarat and said he could not read a map. He refused to allow me to read one, either, saying they were useless things and he preferred to find roads in his own way. Between Mount Abu and Ahmedabad we lost our way several times. Much later, we discovered that with a pair of strong spectacles Yadav's map-reading was as good as anyone's.

Ahmedabad overflowed with traffic and unwary pedestrians. There were neither traffic lights nor policemen. We were looked at suspiciously and rejected by three hotels. 'All rooms are full,' they said, without even making a pretence of checking the register. Finally a salesmen's boarding house offered us a double room, by which time I felt so humiliated that I would gladly have slept in a hen coop in the backyard of a brothel. We sat on the edge of the twin beds, exhausted, deflated and feeling that one night in this unfriendly city would be enough.

The guidebook praised the Jami Masjid, the Gujarati bird baths and the old merchants' quarter. Yadav was worried about the foreignness of the Gujarati language and culture, but he reluctantly agreed to walk through the packed streets to the fifteenth-century mosque. We stood lost in the immense courtyard until a tall, thin man wearing a white lace skullcap on his silver hair came to our rescue. He took us into the hall of two hundred columns, and upstairs to a smaller area with its own entrance – the women's quarters for the Friday service.

'Now I must leave you,' said our self-appointed guide, holding out his hand. 'It has been my great pleasure to show you round.' It had been my pleasure as well. He was a kind and charming man.

Before we left town, Yadav went to the barber for his morning shave while I visited Gandhi's ashram. Walking round his humble house, I wondered whether his wife had minded being banished from his bedroom in favour of his young niece. I hoped I'd find a postcard to send to Amma at Vinobaniketan; she had met Gandhi as a girl, and the meeting had changed her life.

The next day, our tonga clip-clopped through the dark, empty streets of Palitana. 'Is all different here,' Yadav observed. 'Even our dinner. All food, it tastes sweet, is very strange for me. Language is different. Customs is different. Nothing is same as Haryana.'

Heat prickled the back of my neck. It was early, but not early enough to beat the sun, which rose faster than we could climb the steep path to the Jain temples. Our track soon turned into wide, uncomfortable steps, stretching upwards to infinity. Each step was an effort, despite the stout sticks Yadav had rented at the base of the hill. Many times on the way up we were tempted by dholi-wallahs to ride in their wooden stretchers, suspended by rope from two poles that rested on their shoulders. The price, they told us, was based on weight, but my conscience prevented me from inflicting myself on the thin, sweating men. For the sake of my 'conscience', they would probably go hungry that night.

The Jain pilgrims, swinging upwards in plump contentment, full of anticipation of darshan with their tirthankaras, had no such qualms. A procession of naked monks and shoeless, hairless nuns hurried past us on their way downhill.

Quite suddenly, as though they had been built that instant by the wave of a wand, the high, fortified walls of the temple city rose before us. Behind them the domes and spires peaked and poked as though they were eager for a view of the outside world. We picked our way through discarded dholi poles, lying like giant crutches beside their exhausted owners. Before entering the city, we stopped under the shade of a peepal tree to eat cool curd ladled from an enormous pottery bowl into little black clay dishes.

A couple from Bombay left to bathe and dress in unpolluted clothes. They explained that if they needed to urinate or perform some other bodily function, they would have to bathe and change again.

The temples are almost two kilometres from Palitana, six hundred metres up. Most of the original buildings were destroyed by Muslim invaders, but 863 temples have been built or restored in the ensuing nine hundred years by Jains 'in need of merit from our gods', as one self-appointed guide put it. We were soon lost in a forest of temples, large and small, each housing a tirthankara whose glinting glass eyes stared at us from a smooth marble face. The pilgrims sat cross-legged in two long lines in the forecourt of the seventeenth-century Shri Adishwara temple, men in front and women behind. A scent of attar of roses filled the air. The petal-sellers kept up a deafening caterwaul, but they had no shortage of customers – everyone wanted to arm himself with an offering. We entered the temple and stood at the back while pilgrims approached the inner sanctum for darshan with the jewelled statue of Shri Adishwara, chanting and scattering rose petals as they filed past.

We left the temple to climb to the highest point in the city. Below us, huddled within confining walls, the roofs and domes of the hundreds of temples mushroomed. Beyond the fortifications the wild hillside tumbled to the silver river, a diamond-studded serpent making its glittering way through the valley while the barely visible town of Palitana went about its Sunday-morning business.

I took Yadav's hand. He looked at me in surprise.

'What is wrong?'

'Nothing. It's too beautiful, that's all.'

'Different customs,' he said darkly. Still holding my hand, he led me to the city gates. I looked back, but already the temple city had vanished, a secret treasure in the folds of the hills.

Driving eastwards, we reached the tip of Gujarat in early afternoon and crossed a causeway to the island of Diu. Yadav stopped the car and got out. He stood staring at the vast expanse of ink-blue carpet, stretching away to the curved horizon where the hulk of a cargo ship followed the butterfly wings of tiny fishing vessels round the rim of the world.

'Is first time in my life I see the sea.' He choked on the words. 'And thanks so much you bring me here. Thanks to you, Mr Purdeep Kumar.' I had forgotten my alias. Yadav brushed away a tear and kissed my cheek. 'Chalo!'

We stayed at a ghastly guest house, ghastly because its surly proprietor permeated the place with his unpleasant aura. But it was the only hotel on Nagoa Beach. The door of our dirty little room opened on to a yard, and through clothes lines full of travellers' T-shirts, we could see the water.

Never having been swimming in the social sense of the word, Yadav had no bathing trunks. It did not matter. Apart from an English boy sitting beneath the shade of a faded umbrella, which stuck up like a wilting mushroom from the centre of a concrete table, there was no one on the beach. We had a long floating lesson until, feeling cold, I left Yadav, now a champion floater lying ramrod-straight on the water, to lie in the sun.

I must have fallen asleep. When I woke, Yadav was looking down at me and laughing. A group of giggling Indian boys stood staring at both of us. I sat up. Yadav had drawn a circle around me. Inside it he had written:

I LOVE YOU!

I jumped up, covering my face with embarrassment. The boys laughed aloud.

'Do you mind?' Yadav looked worried. 'But I can see you do not. Now I am going to tell you serious thing. The sea has taken my lunghi inside.'

'Inside?'

'Yes. When I stopped my floating it had left me and I couldn't find it on sea or under sea.' We went to have another look in the water, but it had gone forever.

'Perhaps a fish has eaten it.'

'You are right. This is India, and fish might have hunger.' Yadav was serious.

From the top of a sand dune at the far end of the beach, we could see down into the next bay. A Western girl knelt by a rock pool, scouring a tin plate with sand and rinsing it off in the salt water. Further along the beach her boyfriend squatted over a fire, stirring a pot. Yadav, unable to resist interfering, walked over to the boy and looked in amazement at the contents of his pan.

'And you can really cook?' he asked. 'Indian men, the most of us we cannot. For these things we have mothers and wives. Can you also make chapati?'

'Yes.' The boy did not elaborate. The girl came over with the cleaned plates and sat down by her boyfriend, barely glancing in our direction.

'Yadav, I think they want to be left alone,' I said, pulling at his arm.

'Why?' he asked. 'Western peoples is very strange. We in India, we do not like to be by ourselves.' But he came with me to our sand dune, where we sat watching as the deep-red sun set in majestic splendour, enthroned in its golden rays, behind a royal-purple sea. The African palms fringing the beach became silhouettes, and the dark rocks at our feet merged with the sea as the sun sank lower and the water turned from purple to black.

It was time to move on to Sasan Gir, a quiet village set in hilly, deciduous forest, and home to India's remaining 304 Asian lions. They keep company with cheetal, sambar, nilgai, wild boar, panthers, hyenas and monkeys in Sasan Gir National Park. We took the car and a guide through the forest and saw peacocks, spotted deer, squirrels and sambar, but no Asian lions.

'Doesn't matter, yaar. We will see tomorrow morning. Now come on, I want to eat my dinner. We will ask in village for restaurant.' Yadav strode off down the wide dirt track that served as the village high street, and stopped at the tea stall.

'They doesn't have restaurant, but he say if we like to eat in his house we are welcome.' We followed the wobbling backside of the overweight chai-wallah till eventually it stopped outside a blue door set in a white wall that dripped with dark-pink bougainvillea. Children, forgetting for a moment their game of cricket, pointed and stared at us. Inside was a courtyard where a woman squatted by an open fire, stirring a pan of sizzling vegetables. A grandmother rested on flabby haunches, mending a quilt. Two small children gave us a shy glance and scampered away to hide in the folds of their mother's sari. We were enthroned on the only two chairs in sight. Yadav leant across and whispered in my ear: 'Like prince and princess of Haryana.'

The children skipped over to a shadowy corner of the yard and clambered on to a monstrous form. It shifted on its sagging charpoy, its huge stomach rising and falling in time to its soft snores. The stomach's owner, a man twice the size of our already ample host, had been dozing. Awakened by his grandchildren, he engulfed them both with one giant arm, and they giggled and wriggled in delight.

'My father,' explained the chai-wallah, easing himself on to the floor beside us, 'and my nephew and niece.' A touch of sadness tinged his voice. 'I have been married for three years, but we have not yet been blessed with sons. My wife and I have planned to go on pilgrimage in the hope that the gods will grant us a child.'

The three men talked together in Hindi while we ate.

'Customs here is really very different,' Yadav said, not for the first time, in a shocked undertone. A young girl had come into the yard. 'See this girl. She is twenty-two years and will not get married for another two months. In my state, is too old.'

We were back inside the park by seven o'clock the next morning. 'Here we can see lion,' whispered our thin, khaki-clad guide. We drove through an open gate. Beyond, but for the rustle of peacocks in the undergrowth, frightened into sudden flight by the noise of the car's engine, there was silence. We were beginning to lose hope when the guide put his hand on Yadav's arm. Ten yards to our left, a lion padded slowly through the dry scrub, his colouring blended so perfectly with his surroundings that we would never have seen him without the sharp-eyed guide. Abandoning the car, we followed his retreat on foot. The guide bleated loudly, like a sheep in distress. The lion hesitated, listening – his great head swung round and he stood motionless, staring in our direction. Then, deciding there were no sheep in the offing, he turned away and plodded on, soon to be lost amongst the trees and undergrowth.

'He goes to his water hole,' the guide whispered.

'Now I don't care whether we see any more animals or not,' I said. 'Wasn't he wonderful?'

'Darling,' Yadav's voice was heavy with emotion. 'You and me, we see my first sea together, and now our first lion in jungle. Is too good for us.' Three or four Indians were wandering in the clearing, binoculars slung over their shoulders. Assuming they were tourists as well, I told them about our lion and asked if they had been so lucky.

'Not this morning,' said one of them, raising his old fishing hat to me. 'But I don't get so excited as you. I'm researching why the lions in this jungle have suddenly started raiding the villages. They're becoming man-eaters, you see. If you really want to see lions, you must stay quite still and quiet until you hear the sounds of deer breaking through the bushes. Follow the sounds. You are likely to find a lion in hot pursuit. If you do, and you happen to meet him face to face, don't be afraid. Stand your ground and look him in the eye. Ninety-nine times out of a hundred, he will turn and walk away.'

'And the hundredth?' I asked. 'Has it ever happened to you? It must be very frightening.'

'Oh yes, several times. Of course it is frightening. In fact, it makes my ticker beat nineteen to the dozen.' I smiled at the Billy Bunter language. He was a very nice man.

'I must go,' I said, realising that Yadav and the guide were waiting for me. The man again touched his old hat.

'So nice to meet you. Do enjoy Gujarat. And remember, when you meet one of my chaps face to face, just look him straight in the eye. Good day.'

'That,' said the guide, 'was the maharaja of Bhavnagar. He does much work in our jungle.'

We packed our bags and moved on to Junagadh.

Five times a day we heard the muezzin's call to prayer from the minaret of the mosque next door to our hotel. Hidden behind the spice shop across the street, piled high with coloured powders, were the ancient mausoleums of the nawabs.

'I will stay in my bed,' Yadav said. Allowing me out of his sight for the first time since the start of our journey, he urged me to go and see Uperkot Fort.

It was strange how quickly 'being together' had made me appreciate being on my own. Filled with a ridiculous sense of liberation, I went off to explore the ancient citadel. The air smelt of new-mown grass. The trees shaded me as I walked along the nawabs' pathways and climbed the ruins.

Curiosity led me to the palace where Mahabatkhan, the last and most eccentric of the nawabs of Junagadh, had held his durbars until Partition, when he was forced to retreat with his army of dogs to Pakistan. The dogs were his special eccentricity: he had them dressed in sumptuous clothes and wedded, bedded and buried with pomp and ceremony, holding them in far greater esteem than he did the people of his court.

The temperature soared. Our tempers rose with the heat. In Bhuj market, Yadav and I almost fell out for good over the colour of a pair of trainers for Yadav's six-year-old grandson, the real Purdeep Kumar. We settled for pale blue and headed for Delhi. Mr Kumar's car-rental period was almost up.

I should never have allowed Yadav to lie to his boss about the car. But the state of being in love is entirely selfish – it sees nothing but its own wishes. And I was in love with Yadav.

'Love is never blind,' Yadav said.

'Love *is* blind,' I corrected him. 'It sees the other person as it wants to see him, not as he really is.'

I had wanted to rent the car again so that going to Gujarat would simply be another job for Yadav. But he had insisted on telling his boss that it was his friend Purdeep who wanted the car, with Yadav as its driver – at a low price, of course. Not surprisingly, Ravi Chhabra had grown curious.

'When I ask him for car, he says this time he wants to meet with my friend. I tell him Mr Kumar, he doesn't want meeting.

Then Mr Chhabra say to me, "No Purdeep Kumar, no car." Next day I tell to him that my mother, she is dying at farm. I must have to go home minimum three weeks. Mr Chhabra he say, "More than three days and you're fired."'

True to his word, Mr Chhabra had given Yadav's job to another driver. Although Yadav promised me that his sacking had nothing to do with me, I flew back to London feeling guilty and miserable.

9

'Hotel? Taxi? Sightseeing? Money change? Carpets? Silk? Jewellery? Shawls?'

I ran like a hunted fox out of the airport building. 'No. No thanks! I don't want anything. I have a friend waiting with a car.' Did I really? Suppose he wasn't there?

'Do you know your friend?'

'Well, if I didn't he wouldn't be my friend.'

'Achha!' The heads wobbled from side to side. I was back in India.

There he was, swathed in a blanket, balancing on a railing with the help of a bamboo staff. A plastered foot protruded from the blanket.

'Yadav, you're here!' My relief at finding him robbed me of coherent speech.

'Of course I am. But as you can see yourself,' he said, pointing to his foot, 'nearly I was not. I come to airport in scooter. Is very difficult.' He had fallen while pruning the branches of a tree at the farm. We walked slowly towards the taxi rank.

'Crutches would help,' I suggested.

After six months away, my memories, like childhood recollections of the scent of sun on dew-damp grass, were only of good things. Disillusion threatened with the first bursts of dank December air.

'We will not worry, yaar. Now we are together and each we has our own personal blanket. But before our sweet night I have serious matter to tell you.' He paused to give weight to his words. 'Before the next time you will fly back to your country you must have to decide one of three things, and you must have to give me answer.'

I was tired from the flight, and we were staying in an unsalubrious hotel. I had to fight to keep my eyes open. 'Yadav, couldn't it wait till tomorrow?'

He shook his head, cleared his throat and spoke.

'You will agree to marry me, this is first thing. Or you will live with me and we will not have marriage, this is second thing. Or you will go back to your country for your whole life and we will not see to each other again and I will suicide myself. This is third and last.'

While I was away, I had thought of little but the first two alternatives. The third no longer seemed a possibility.

'All right, I'll think hard. But it's very difficult. There are so many problems. During the flight I was thinking about last year and about our trip and about buying a jeep so that you'll have a job again. I didn't sleep much. I'll try to tell you my answer soon.'

'"All right"! Is not "all right" and there is no problem. Only you must have to decide.'

'Okay, but now I want to sleep.' I felt warm and happy. Yadav was beside me, and tomorrow the sun would shine, and he would still be there and so would I.

Yadav finished his third glass of breakfast chai. 'So this is programme. To buy jeep is good idea. We will take my good friend Dinesh – he is barber – to meet my nephew Sunil. Sunil already tell to me he knows man who wants to sell old jeep. Sunil is in Delhi police. He will help to us in this work.'

Dinesh was lathering a man's stubbly chin. Wash basins and barber's chairs lined one side of his narrow slit of a shop. Above our heads, rats scuttled across the rafter. An electric fan danced on the ceiling. Dinesh was clean-shaven, with a neat head of hair and myopic eyes as large as saucers. His trim little figure was dressed in a shirt patterned with cornflowers. Tiny, polished shoes peeped from beneath the turn-ups of his well-pressed cornflower-blue trousers. When he smiled, he looked more like a prep-school boy than a father of five.

Forgetting his plastered foot, Yadav embraced his friend, lost his balance and collapsed into a chair. 'You are right,' he said, hauling himself up on to his good foot. 'I must have to buy scratches. Only, I do not feel to look like idiot beggar man.'

We found a mountain of wooden crutches at the back of a chemist's shop. The assistant picked two from the pile, one short and one long. With difficulty, using a coin that did not fit the grooves in the screws, he took the crutches to pieces and reassembled them. They were still unmatched. After half an hour of trial and error he succeeded in making a pair, and Yadav's mobility improved a hundred per cent. Dinesh hailed an auto-rickshaw and we squeezed in.

Sunil was doing shift work at the airport. He was a portly young man with a small moustache, liquid brown eyes, a stomach already falling over the top of his shiny policeman's belt, and an overtight trouser crotch.

The four of us rode back to our hotel in one auto. The men settled down on our unmade beds to count out my money, carefully licking their fingers between each note. I knew how much there was – exactly a thousand pounds – but for Yadav, counting, touching and feeling was believing. Satisfied, he stuffed the notes into a plastic bag. We walked out of the hotel into the sunshine and climbed into a new rickshaw, closely following Dinesh and Sunil in another.

'I tell to drivers, my nephew, he is in police, so he will not try to cheat us.'

We stopped suddenly, inches from Dinesh and Sunil. A boy jumped out of a parked auto and passed a paper and fifty rupees to our driver, who handed it to Sunil. Sunil scribbled something on the paper, pocketed the fifty rupees, and gave back the form.

'What happened?' I asked.

'He cancel fine for rickshaw driver under the table. This is how police, they makes their money.' I was shocked. 'I'm sorry, but this is India. I think you knows it very well,' said Yadav.

We turned into an alley and stopped. Dinesh and Sunil disappeared through a dark doorway. Ten minutes later they emerged with smug grins on their faces and a bag bulging with rupees.

'But we are not sure it will be enough to buy jeep,' Yadav said.

A nagging worry cramped my stomach: money, always more money, even in India. Suppose I ran out? What would we do? The fears left over from bankruptcy were deep-rooted. Spending large sums of money felt like an electric shock.

'Anyway, see what happen.' Yadav's voice was cheerful. It was all right for him; it was not his money, nor his worry.

I left the three men sitting on the beds in the damp hotel room, counting rupees and downing Indian whisky, while I went out to have dinner and Chivas Regal in Ranji and Rosemary's comfortable flat.

'Can I hope you enjoy your evening?' asked Yadav when I came back. 'Tomorrow night Dinesh, he has invited us to have our dinner at his own home.' Yadav's hair was rumpled. The room smelt of stale alcohol. An empty whisky bottle stood on the cupboard. The others had left.

Dinesh and his family lived in a village on the outskirts of Delhi. It was dark when we left the auto to walk the last half kilometre of muddy alleyway to his house. A star followed the crescent moon through an ink-black strip of sky between the high walls on either side of us. We turned into Dinesh's immaculately swept courtyard. He was squatting before a wood fire, frying onions and garlic.

'This is Sushila, wife of Dinesh,' Yadav said. 'She is as my real sister.' Sushila smiled, wiping her floury hands on the electric-blue polyester sari that enfolded her voluptuous body. Taking my hand, she led us into a room, seated us on a charpoy and ordered her five boys, still in their neat school uniforms, to wait on us with chai, snacks and sweets. They joined their hands in greeting, grinned and ran away to change and play a last game of cricket in the dark alley.

Dinesh had been lucky in life. His father had retired from barbering and given each of his sons a shop in which to ply the business of their caste. Dinesh had five sons, so there were no daughters to find dowries for. Anil, the eldest, was seventeen and Ravi, the youngest, was eleven.

Dinesh and his wife shared the cooking. Sushila squatted beside her husband, her smart sari tucked between her legs, chopping, frying and boiling on a two-ring gas cooker. Dinesh looked up from his stirring. 'We make kofta with kadhi and aloo gobhi and dal and mattar. You like mattar?' I looked at Yadav.

'Peas,' he explained. 'Dinesh, he is famous cooker in all village. Today, because it is Tuesday, day of Hanuman, is strictly veg.'

A vacant-eyed man shuffled into the room and hesitated, looking round as though lost. When he saw me, an angelic smile spread across his sad face. He took my hand and stared into my eyes.

'He is Dinesh's brother. Once he was very great mechanic,' Yadav explained in a whisper. 'Now he is always drunk man. He do nothing else. *Nothing*. Only he take drink.'

The man swayed and fell into a chair. The children brought rum and a pitcher of water. With a trembling hand their uncle reached for the bottle. Pouring himself a tumblerful, he drank deeply and, with great care, refilled his glass. Sushila set the food on the table. Her brother-in-law, paralytic from his second drink, was led away. We were joined by an outsized nephew, so gross that he had difficulty bending his body to sit down. When he had finished every last grain of rice, he sat back and, with a huge burp of contentment, bemoaned his great weight and his wife and daughters. The causes of his troubles stood uncomfortably in the doorway, listening and giggling. After a ritual finger-licking, mouth-swilling and spitting, we got up to leave. There was a gale of laughter from the women.

'Ravi, he ask if you are my real wife,' Yadav said. I did not see why it was so funny.

'Sushila, she want you come again tomorrow to stay in her house. She say she love you as her own sister,' Dinesh said.

A few nights later Fate granted her wish, if not under ideal circumstances.

The jeep was parked outside her owner's house in a downtrodden part of outer Delhi. Her duck-egg-blue paintwork was chipped and scarred. Stuffing oozed from her plastic seat-covers. Her canvas top and cellophane windows were torn, and her tyres were as bald as the pate of a tonsured monk.

'What do you think?' Yadav asked. I asked how old the jeep was and how many miles it had on it.

'Don't be silly, yaar – age and kilometres, no one can say about. I tell to you before, this is India. Clock and all things is easy to change. Engine, it should have to be all right. Once Sunil, he help owner a lot. Only for this we can hope he is honest man.'

After the owner had taken Yadav and me on a trial run and a further three hundred pounds had changed hands, Sunil came out of the owner's house with an empty bag and a bundle of moth-eaten documents. Mahindra (the jeep's trade name) was ours.

During our celebration dinner at a restaurant of Sunil's choice, Sunil got very drunk, crunched chicken joints until his uniform was smeared and splattered, and littered the table until it was a battlefield of bones.

'I thought you told me all your family were vegetarians,' I said to Yadav.

'They is. But Sunil, he change very much. Now he do all things, even he smoke. But please do not be angry – because he is policeman, he will get discount on dinner with identity card and we can save our money. You should have to be pleased.' We had just spent three hundred pounds more than our budget on Mahindra. How pleased could I be about a discount of two hundred rupees?

Before going to sleep that night, we made an ambitious plan to drive our jeep from Delhi to Kerala, a journey of several thousand kilometres. We would stop en route to see my friend Carlo in Bombay, move down the coast to Vinobaniketan, the ashram and children's home where I had spent three months last winter, and finish at Kanyakumari. The next morning Yadav went off to register the jeep, and I rang Carlo to tell him to expect me in Bombay at the end of the month.

From the moment Carlo and I had first met, he had behaved as though I was his personal property. When I had first written to him, I had introduced myself as having met his friend Sarah through the marriage bureau, so presumably he had assumed I was still looking for a husband. After my short stay with him he had written me an impassioned letter, leaving me in no doubt about his feelings towards me. I did not mention Yadav or the jeep. A telephone stand did not seem the best place to explain that I was living with my ex-driver and would quite possibly marry him.

'Va bene, Jillina mia, ti aspetto,' said Carlo.

The registration was done. Feeling very proud, we drove to dinner in Connaught Place. 'Now we is prince and princess of Haryana. No doubt,' said Yadav. 'And tomorrow I will take jeep to mechanic. We must have to fix gear box and steering before we leave Delhi.'

The next morning Mahindra had a flat battery. Yadav marshalled an army of rickshaw drivers to push her into the stream of Delhi's rush-hour traffic. She remained cold, silent and sparkless, unashamed of her inadequacy in the face of passing Marutis, Mercedes and even sister Mahindras. An elderly Sikh rickshaw-wallah offered his help and the wisdom of his years. His great hairy face vanished under the bonnet and reappeared in triumph with Mahindra's rusty air cooler. Like a conjurer with a box of tricks, he assembled old rags, newspapers and a drop of kerosene, lit a small fire on the pavement, plunged the air cooler into the flames, pulled it out and replaced it, red-hot. Mahindra, smoke pouring from her exhaust pipe, spluttered into life. Yadav embraced our turbaned friend, took his place behind the steering wheel and, with a farewell salute on the horn, drove us to our appointment with the real mechanic.

I passed the day perched on a chair outside the jeep seller's house while Yadav, encumbered by his plastered foot, helped the 'best mechanic in Delhi'. They dismembered Mahindra bit by bit, strewing her innards far and wide.

After lunch – a glass of Nescafé – I accepted the jeep seller's invitation to sit inside his house.

'How old are you?' asked a toothless hag with grey rats' tails hanging down her back. I told her.

'Then why isn't your hair grey? Why don't you have gold nose rings, and why no bangles? We thought Westerners were rich!' The questions, all in English, came thick and fast. The family pressed around me and fingered my shirt, my hair, my watch and my shoes.

'I am forty-four, ten years your junior,' cackled the hag. 'You are as good as my elder sister.' I went back to my chair in the street.

The evening grew colder. I'd had nothing but Nescafé since breakfast. By 9 p.m., when the mechanic pronounced the jeep roadworthy, I would have considered killing my best friend. Glancing at the bill, Yadav handed the mechanic two hundred rupees. He looked at the notes, spat on them, threw them down on the seat and, leaping out of Mahindra, evaporated into the night.

'He is cross on me,' Yadav said, stating the obvious. 'I must have to go after him.' Gathering his crutches, he hopped away into the darkness, leaving me in the middle of the heckling, flashing traffic of nighttime Delhi. He returned half an hour later. I was too angry to speak.

'You cannot understand, yaar. He is liar and cheat. I am sorry, but I will not pay to him.'

The jeep made it back to the hotel. We went to bed.

Mahindra's moods still took no account of people's feelings. Nothing, not even another pavement fire, would move her. Finally the rickshaw drivers pushed her into the middle of the road, where an obliging lorry reversed fast into her backside and, with us inside, pushed her down the busy road at high speed. She must have enjoyed it – her engine burst into life and she leapt forward.

'But I am too worried about gear box. Seal is leaking. Before we leave Delhi I must have to take to new mechanic. And now, if you will not mind, it will be better you stay with wife of Dinesh. With you I have too much of worries. I must think all the time, "Jill, is she all right? Jill, has she had her lunch?

Does she need coffee?" You understand, yaar. With Sushila you will be fine? Is only for one night.'

'Yes, of course I'll be fine,' I said. 'You shouldn't mind too much about me anyway. I'm okay.'

It was long after Dinesh had returned from his barber shop that we heard Yadav's crutches click, clicking across the concrete yard. He stood in the doorway, unsmiling, his face and clothes covered in oil and grease. Ignoring me, he sat down beside Dinesh and began to speak in Hindi.

'Please, tell me what happened – is the jeep all right now?' I interrupted, forgetting that when men were talking together, women were not necessarily welcome.

'Wait. First I will tell in my own language to my friend. After I will tell to you. Now, you will please not disturb us.'

I sat with the little boys, watching a Hindi film that I could not understand and trying not to mind Yadav's rebuff. I told myself that this was village India, and that if I wanted to live with a village Indian, this was what I had to accept.

Dinesh put a bottle of rum on the table and poured out three tumblerfuls. At least I qualified for a drink. Yadav took a mouthful, swallowing noisily.

'Mechanic, he say we must have to make new engine.' I caught my breath – more rupees.

'Please do not worry for money,' Yadav went on. 'At farm I will find money and I will pay you back.' I knew he wouldn't, because he couldn't. He had no money. I wished I had never thought of buying a jeep, but it was too late now.

Yadav looked so dejected that I leant towards him, meaning to kiss his cheek. A look of horror crossed his face. He drew back against the wall.

'You must not have to do that,' he said. 'Our sister, she must not see these things.' I looked at Sushila. Her head was bowed, her eyes cast down. The children stared at me.

'But I was only going to kiss your cheek.' My face was on fire.

'Well, you cannot. Now please do not talk about this matter again.' Dinesh handed me my glass of rum. I took a gulp. The heat in my throat matched my burning face. 'You looks me little bit tired. You can go to the bed if you want to.' Yadav took another swig of rum.

Anil, the eldest son, led me across the yard and into a small, cold room. I was scrubbing my face with cleansing cream when Sushila came in. She looked through my makeup bag, fingering and asking, with Anil as interpreter, about the contents of every pot and bottle. She came to a small white jar decorated with flowers and held it in her hand for a long time. I unscrewed the top and squirted scent on to her wrist.

'Would you like it?' She shook her head, but held on to it. 'Please have it.'

'Thank you!' she said in English. She and Anil left. Two minutes later they were back with Shashi, the fourth and naughtiest of the boys, always forgiven for his crimes because of his beguiling grin.

'Aunty,' he began. He was holding something in his hand. 'Mummy...' His English dried up. Anil came to his rescue.

'My mother says you accept her gift. It is key ring.' I looked down at the enamelled, silver-fringed locket in Shashi's hand.

'Please thank her. It's very pretty. But you're all being too kind to me.' From the doorway Sushila burst into Hindi.

'My mother,' translated Anil, 'she ask if you like it and she say, please do not give to any other person.' I said I did like it, and promised not to give it away.

'Okay. Yes. Goodnight,' said Sushila, airing her few words of English.

Many people passed by our gates during the day. Sometimes there was a snake charmer, his cobra's head darting inquisitively in and out of its sack; often a couple of cows looking for their daily chapati; every morning the newspaper boy; and once a toothless sadhu, draped in saffron, rattling his beads and his begging bowl. When I offered to give him money, Anil looked upset. He took a coin from his own pocket and dropped it into the bowl.

'You are our guest. We must give,' he said.

Dinesh's brothers and their families lived with his parents. I asked Dinesh why he had moved out.

'My father was always angry with me. He beat me often and hard. And I do like to live in my own way.' He gestured towards his sons, lying one behind the other on a charpoy watching a video, and through the doorway to Sushila, crouched over her chapatis. 'I only like love. I am not interested for the money. I am happy man.'

Several days later, Mahindra stood in the main road. When I saw Dinesh's and Yadav's heads hidden under her bonnet, my heart sank.

'Is perfectly all right,' Yadav said, looking happy for the first time in days. 'But is not self-start. We must first heat engine and start with wire, like this.'

Mahindra roared. Yadav, his head deep in the engine, revved it for several minutes.

'Now is okay. Get in.' We were off to Haryana.

Mahindra danced down the National Highway, rattling our bones until our bodies ached. She needed new shock absorbers.

'Please do not worry for money. I will borrow from my brother Ramesh. He has already borrow from his friend.' Yadav took a speed breaker too fast, and we hit our heads on the metal bars of the roof. 'Double sorry,' he said.

We found Ramesh doing guard duty at the factory gate. He told us his friend had already been at the bank for two hours arranging a loan for us. After waiting another hour, we left.

'Come, yaar, my sister, she is dying to see you. She will help us,' said Yadav. Outside Sarti's house the usual crowd of admirers gathered, giggling and pointing. Yadav shooed them away. One pop-eyed man, transfixed by my presence, stood his ground.

'He build new room for my sister. His job is carpenter.' Yadav pointed to a new wooden door, complete with nuts and bolts, in the middle of a brick wall on the upper floor of the house.

'How can anyone use the door?' I asked. 'There's no staircase.' Yadav pointed to a stairway on the far side of the building. 'But...' I gave up. Perhaps someone would build a staircase later. A phrase I had often heard came into my mind: *Koi bat nahin*. Thinking about it, I decided that it *didn't* matter. Very few things really do.

Sarti wanted us to stay the night. She had such a pleading smile and looked so kind in her long green Haryana petticoat, her scallop-collared green-and-white-checked shirt and her red chiffon chunni, decorated with golden stars and thrown back from her face, that we couldn't say no. She was senior to most of the men who came visiting, so she rarely had to veil herself.

Still penniless, we drove on the next day to see Yadav's daughter Sarita and her family. They were gathered round a fire by the well, cooking sweet potatoes in the hot ash. One of the women raked through the embers, pulled out a blackened potato, peeled it and handed it to me. Someone else gave me a white radish and a screw of salt.

'Now I ask my son-in-law to arrange with friend to lend money,' Yadav said. 'We might break down on road to Bombay and we must have to need extra rupees.' We drove with Sarita (whose husband was off teaching in his village school) and the children to the village and sat in a courtyard, waiting for the friend and his money. He did not come. Climbing into the jeep we found Purdeep, who, deeply impressed by his ride from the well, refused to move.

'All right, we will take him to our farm,' Yadav said. He put the child on my knee. His small body stiffened. He turned his head away from me and gazed at his grandfather, never taking his eyes from his face until an hour later, when we pulled up outside a doctor's open-fronted surgery.

'Plaster is very uncomfortable, yaar. And now I am sure my foot, it will be all right.'

He came out of the surgery having exchanged the plaster for a bandage. 'Now is more comfortable,' he said. 'Here, this is something for you.' I opened the parcel and found a pink rubber hot-water bottle. 'Now may I hope you can be warm at your farm. Chalo! Is barely half an hour before we will be at home.'

'Thank you,' I said, moved by his kind thought.

At 9.30, with Purdeep asleep on my knee, we drove through the village, where darkened doorways were lit by small kerosene flames. 'Electricity cut,' Yadav observed. The moonlight made silhouettes of stark trees, haystacks and chattris. A breeze whispered through the undergrowth.

'Come. We will see my new granddaughter.'

In Shanti's little room, a noisy Hindi film flickered across the television. Tin trunks holding everyone's best clothes and treasures were stacked against the wall. Shanti lay on a cot, squeezed between Bubli, her youngest son, and Purdeep, who had crept through the dark yard into the arms of his favourite great-aunt. A blanket with a small bulge in it covered the other charpoy. I was about to sit down when Shanti, raising herself on one elbow, shouted in alarm. The bulge was Chenamunia, Meenakshi's new baby – I had almost squashed her. She woke, gurgling and singing beneath the frilled brim of her crocheted hat. Meenakshi was sent off to rekindle the mustard stalks and prepare our dinner. I felt sorry for her.

'She is pleased,' said Yadav. 'She like to do things for us. Is her pleasure.'

At midnight we climbed on to our charpoy in the new room – a separate building, whose foundations I remembered from my first visit to the farm. Now it had *Om* written in Hindi over the entrance to its veranda. Inside, the walls were painted yellow, with green recessed shelves outlined in lilac. The crowning glory was the small mirror stuck in an alcove – a little dirty and misted, but the only one on the farm. Four charpoys filled the room from end to end. We were the room's only occupants. Meenakshi brought the pink rubber bottle, filled with boiling water. I wondered if she ever went to bed herself, and where.

'Of course she does. She sleep with her daughter – what else can she do? No baby knows it is night. They needs their food and loo same as day. It is Meenakshi's duty. She is mother.'

I slid off my charpoy, wrapped a shawl round my shoulders and went out into the night. Going into the fields to pee was one of my biggest problems in India. I could cope with hunger during the long hours between breakfast and the evening dinner (a few cashew nuts and some fruit dealt with that); with having dirty, unwashed hands because finding soap and going to the well took too long; with intense cold on winter nights and suffocating heat in late spring. I could get up at dawn, and had learnt that after 6.30 p.m., when the light faded and the inevitable power cut put an end to reading or writing, there was nothing to do but cook, eat and go to bed. But I could not come to terms with the lack of a loo. My bladder and bowels were often at the bursting point before I could bring myself to get down on my knees at the well to fill the obligatory bottle with water and make the trek across the fields, either through shoulder-high dew-soaked mustard or, after the harvest, across sunbaked land without a patch of cover for miles around – and all this in front of the family and whichever elderly farmers and neighbours might have come visiting.

Coming back, I climbed on to the charpoy and lay with relief, comfortable and warm, between my white cotton sheets printed all over with black elephants.

The faint light of breaking dawn touched the sky. Through the open door of our room, I could see and hear the sounds of the waking farm. Everyone was up and busy. Soon the morning work would be over and they would be squatting or lying on their cots, the women gossiping, the men ruminating round the hookah. Boss Brother's wife led the buffaloes out of their night quarters into the yard to the dubious freedom of a five-foot-long tethering rope. Birds flew, hopped, chirped and perched, sometimes on the buffaloes' backs. A pair of doves swung and twittered on the wire of our single light bulb; a third rested on a silver peg. Bapu, carefully carrying his hookah to the smoking fire, his turbaned head bent almost to his chest, flitted across my vision like a caricature. Beyond the fields and craggy hills, the sun (which I had missed in London almost as much as I had missed Yadav) rose, heating the world as it inched its way upwards. After chai and breakfast, I borrowed the only two buckets on the farm, one full of rag-stuffed holes, the other in better condition and always in demand. Sitting beside the well, I scrubbed and soaped our filthy clothes. We were learning that travelling by open jeep was a dirty pastime, especially on national highways.

Ma sat on a charpoy, playing with Chenamunia. Babies liked Ma and she liked them. When they were together, Ma stopped wailing and the babies stopped weeping.

Yadav went off to give Mahindra a polish for her puja party. I fetched my sketchbook and crayons and tried to draw a buffalo. Rama's little boy, Vini, was playing near me. He came to examine my crayons, and I gave him one to try for himself. His mother was turning the wheel of the chopping machine, making mincemeat of a baleful of greens for buffalo fodder. Suddenly she stopped, came over to us, grabbed her son and slapped him viciously, dragging him off into their hut. My blood ran cold as his cries of pain cut through the quiet afternoon.

'Why?' I demanded of Yadav later.

'She think he is touching your things.'

'But I don't mind if he does.'

'I know it, but she doesn't.'

Feeling sick, I picked up the paper and crayons and went inside. If my presence was going to cause small children to be beaten, I would stay away from them. I couldn't explain much to Rama's wife in Hindi, and Yadav would not have thought it necessary to explain anything at all to a niece-in-law.

Yadav looked in. 'Why you are cross? he asked.

'I'm not. I just don't want to get the children into trouble.'

'But now my nephew, he is very cross on his wife and she apologise. Do you want to come for walk? Weather is little bit cooler, is too nice.' He limped along beside me, between the barley and mustard, to the second well.

Corrupt Brother's wife sat outside the hut where we had slept last year, embroidering a circlet for her head. One end of a thick piece of wool was hooked round her big toe while she wove the other round and round the circlet with her right hand, mixing it with strands of red and blue embroidery silk. She had been sitting there all day, waiting for the power cut to end. As soon as the electricity came back on, she would turn on the pump and activate the sprays.

'And if it doesn't come in the day?'

'She must have to wait through the night. Is farmer's work,' said Yadav.

At dusk we drove into the village to invite people to Mahindra's puja party at the farm. Yadav stopped in front of each house, proclaiming the party like a town crier. We picked up Brahmin Aunt, a cousin's wife's father, and Yadav's best classmate, now the village sarpanch. Like Yadav and his family, he had film-star good looks, with a thin, lithe body, chiselled features and a nice smile.

'Now we will do puja. You must have to. Is your jeep.' Yadav placed on Mahindra's bonnet a small saucer of ghee with a lighted wick floating in it, scattered a few sweets around it, and bent his head till it touched the metal. Lifting it again, he joined and unjoined his hands.

'Now is your turn. Please you pray your own god.' I bent down and said a quick 'Our Father', hoping that at least one of our various gods was listening and would keep Mahindra in order on our journey.

A group of women arrived, huddling into the room where Ma was enthroned on her charpoy amongst the oxen and buffaloes. Undisturbed by the constant snorting, peeing and farting of the beasts, they began to chant mournful-sounding bhajans. Ma sang along lustily, her voice often rising above the others in an ear-piercing screech.

The chief village singer and his choir arrived and the men sat down in the circle of firelight, their shadows distorted by the leaping flames. As the singers sang, the others tapped out the rhythm on their instruments. Some of the men played cards, some smoked and others passed a surreptitious bottle of whisky from hand to hand, from mouth to mouth.

'Once I was part of group,' Yadav said, going over to join them. He sat down but did not open his mouth. The song ended and he limped over to the charpoy.

'Why didn't you sing?' I asked. He shrugged and said that he had suddenly forgotten the words.

10

Thunder rumbled. A drop of water splashed on to my nose and then the rain came down, not very hard, but hard enough to send everyone hurrying into the two fields closest to the farm buildings.

The crops had been cut. Sheaves of wheat lay in neat rows, waiting to be stacked. I went with Boss Brother and Ramesh to help, but they both started shouting at me.

'They say you must sit on charpoy and watch,' Yadav said. 'They are right. Is not suitable work for you.' I tried to explain that I did not want to sit on a charpoy, plagued by flies, listening to conversations I could not follow. Ramesh understood. The brothers stopped protesting and allowed me to help.

When the stacking was finished we went to the kitchen, where Shanti was lighting a fire of dried mustard stalks in the hearth. Ramesh chopped chillis, garlic, onion and ginger and began to fry his mixture in boiling mustard oil. We coughed and spluttered as the chilli fumes rose, engulfing us, infiltrating the pile of dried mustard stalks and driving the mice into their holes. Ramesh laughed, wiping his good eye.

'I am best cooker. You like spicy food, I think? I have put only six chillis, not too hot. Shanti, she will make roti.' The pile of chapatis grew steadily. Shanti rolled out one after another with a small rolling pin on a round wooden board barely larger than the chapatis themselves. She turned each one to cook on both sides in her tawa before toasting them beside the red ashes until they swelled and browned. Ramesh stirred the vegetables and whispered to Yadav in a confidential undertone. I felt excluded.

'What are you talking about?' I asked.

'My brothers, they are talking about new boy they have found for marriage with Puja. But I am not interested. Is their own business. They are older than me.'

'But she's your daughter. It should matter.'

'No, yaar, is job for my Boss Brother. Now leave it, please.' Realising that he did not want or need my Western opinion, I shut up.

The chilli fumes had abated. Ramesh spooned his vegetable dish into small katori and his sons sat and squatted, slurping and supping. Mice ran backwards and forwards from wood pile to chapati dough and played hopscotch up and down the flour barrel. I screamed as a small furry creature brushed my bare foot. Everyone raised their heads from the serious business of eating and looked at me.

Yadav reproved me. 'She only want her dinner. What can she do? She has no home, no mother.'

The start of our journey was inauspicious. The nephews loaded our luggage into the back of the jeep, and Yadav opened the bonnet and applied the starting wire. Mahindra looked smug. Her engine was silent, her body immobile

'Bearings is stuck,' said Yadav. Towed ignominiously away by a bright-blue Massey Ferguson tractor, we spent the first day of our journey at the mechanic's. That night, having only driven thirty kilometres, we stayed with Yadav's elder sister. The next morning Mahindra had a flat tyre.

'Doesn't matter! It could happen to anyone.' Yadav and his nephew fought to release the spare tyre from its rusted bracket. At midday we were finally ready. We sped down the National Highway playing a tape of Haryana folk music. Yadav, having found his voice, sang along with gusto.

'And shall I tell you, yaar,' he said, 'what bad people in my village, they say after you go to bed at puja party. They say, "So now you have jeep. We'll see how you do." I explain them that jeep is yours, I only looks after it. "You are lucky man," they say, "but your family, well..." I do not know what they means, but they do not want we have success, only go down the hill. I think they is not the real friends.' I said I supposed they were jealous, which made me wonder how many people in the village were waiting to see what the rich white woman, as they probably saw me, would do next for Yadav's family.

Four men took a lift with us from Jaipur to Ajmer. Each paid five rupees – Mahindra's first earnings.

'By five o'clock we will be in Jodhpur. Today we is getting on very well,' Yadav said with satisfaction. Avoiding the body of a freshly killed goat, he turned the wheel sharply to round a right-angle bend on a near-vertical stretch of hill, and the engine roared. We stopped climbing and began slipping backwards, finally coming to rest against a bank at the side of the road. Mahindra had a broken clutch plate.

'But I buy new one in Delhi only few days before. Was duplicate – I should have to buy real thing,' Yadav said.

He made two abortive trips into Ajmer. On the third he returned with a clutch plate of the right size and a mechanic to fit it. The delay cost us an unexpected night in Pushkar. Yadav looked unhappy.

I tried to cheer him up by reminding him that at least we were together. Time and place did not really matter. We had wanted to come back to Pushkar and we were lucky to have a jeep, even if it did break down sometimes. The last bit was a lie – the wish that we had never set eyes on Mahindra kept coming, unwanted, into my head. But it made Yadav smile.

'This is true. If I can hope you are feeling cheers, I also am all right,' he said.

The third day was uneventful. Mahindra developed nothing more serious than a leaking radiator, and by feeding her water at frequent intervals, we arrived at Merta. In the dhaba where we stopped for lunch, two lorry drivers gave us a curious look and said something to Yadav.

'They comes from Haryana, same state like me. They ask me, "Who she is?"' Yadav told them I was his wife. They were surprised, saying that I was too old – forty-six at least. Yadav told them he was forty-four, so what difference did it make? Since he didn't actually know how old he was, what difference *did* it make?

Before we left Jodhpur, I rang Carlo in Bombay. The date I had given him for our arrival had already passed. I tried to explain the difficulties we were having with Mahindra.

'Sell it,' said Carlo, as though this were obvious.

'I can't, really. I'll be there as soon as I can. And I... I... ' What about Yadav? Once again, my courage failed me when it came to mentioning him.

The sun dived downwards behind the fields of sugar cane and banana, turning our first view of Daman, a very Portuguese seaport, into a fiery haze of heat. Surrounded as they were by dry Gujarat, the streets were lined with shops selling Indian whisky, rum, beer and Goan port. The beaches were made of black sand, and in the evening light the sea, lapping the gravel-strewn shore, looked grey and forbidding.

Yadav was disappointed. He had thought Daman's beaches would be as lovely as Diu's. He cheered himself up by buying two bottles of port, one for us – which we drank that night, giving ourselves splitting headaches – and one for Dinesh. 'He will enjoy to try new sort of drink.'

Daman's hotels were not for tourists. Yadav inspected two and reported that both had 'very bad stinkings'. The third was an old-fashioned building with a rattling lift that took us up to a second-floor room, from whose windows we could keep an eye on Mahindra in the street below.

'Are these yours?' A smiling Gujarati waiter stood in the doorway the next morning, dangling a pair of Yadav's underpants from his forefinger and thumb. They had floated from our window to the ground outside the front door.

'Yes, bhai sahib,' said Yadav, covered in confusion at the sight of his sacred secret garments being aired in public. I couldn't help smiling. The waiter put them down and bowed his way out of the room. I rescued the rest of our dripping washing from the window ledge and resigned myself to a suitcase full of wet clothes.

A rickshaw took us across the bridge over the muddy brown river that split Daman in two, past Our Lady of the Rosary and the impregnable walls of Daman's huge fort.

'Before we leave this place, we would like to take special drink,' Yadav said. 'Once you did tell me you want to try it, and now we are in right place.' I thought for a minute and remembered that I had read about this drink in my guidebook. Yadav said something to the driver and we recrossed the bridge, drove through a maze of cluttered streets full of small houses and pulled up outside an open-fronted shop whose floor was lined with big ceramic jars. The shopkeeper poured two tumblers of cloudy, white liquid from an unlabelled bottle. It left a taste of bad eggs in my mouth.

'This is tari, drink from palm tree of date fruits.'

Yadav was like the genie from the magic lamp – my wish was his command. I had forgotten about wanting to try the date-palm drink. He had not.

In a maladjusted Mahindra, Bombay at dusk was a nightmare. Darkness overtook us, blotting out the shanty towns. The heavy traffic was almost at a standstill. Its deafening roar filled our ears, and its fumes our noses and eyes.

'I think we should find a hotel near Carlo's flat and ring him from there,' I said. 'He might get too much of a shock if we just turn up.' Yadav looked at me helplessly. Cars hooted at us from all sides.

'Where is Carlo flat? I must have to tell you, Mahindra is very overhot.'

A man crawling along in an adjacent car helped lead us in the right direction, but all the hotels we tried were either full or too expensive. We had no choice but to find Carlo's flat and ask his advice before Mahindra (or Yadav) blew up.

To my relief, Yadav said he would wait with the jeep, which gave me a bit longer to prepare Carlo for his presence. Hearing his voice on the telephone had brought back memories of the few days we had spent together last year, and I had an uncomfortable feeling that he might not be pleased to meet Yadav.

Ambrose, Carlo's south Indian servant, opened the door and led me into the pea-green parlour, where Carlo was dining amongst his collection of empty, dust-covered wine bottles. On hearing my voice, he leapt unsteadily to his feet and gave me a parmesan-flavoured kiss. I began explaining about Yadav and Mahindra and the difficulties of knowing when we would arrive.

'Jillina, you have deserted me. Who is this man? How do you know him?'

'Carlo, I haven't deserted you. We're good friends, as we were last year. I met Yadav ages ago. I didn't tell you about him last year because... well, there didn't seem any reason to.'

'Good friends! No reason to! But Jillina, when you told me about the marriage bureau, I thought... Va bene.' He sat down and put his large head into his frail hands. I asked him if he could suggest an inexpensive hotel for us. He drew an illegible map on the back of an old envelope, but could not remember the name of either the street or the hotel. I promised to come back in the morning.

We left Mahindra where she was and took a taxi. Our search ended in a dingy hotel on a street full of beggars and smack smokers. A fight was in progress: a group of women who had been encouraging their children to beg outside the restaurant next door were being beaten up by the police. Our first night in Bombay was not sweet.

The next morning, while Yadav moved down the road to a marginally better guest house, found mechanics and looked after Mahindra, I went to stay with Carlo. He had taken to his bed with fever, brought on, he said, by his discovery of the presence of another man in my life. When Yadav rang to say that Mahindra was ready to leave, Carlo rallied and, with a great effort of generosity, told me to ask him to lunch.

'Tell him that Ambrose will make good curry.'

It was already the third of February. Our hopes of arriving in Kerala, visiting the ashram, reaching Kanyakumari and being back in Delhi by the end of the month were fading with every day that went by. The journey was taking double the time we had expected. We had no time to spare, even for lunch.

Yadav came to Carlo's for coffee. We sat in the pea-green parlour, talked and took photographs of each other.

Later, Carlo inspected Mahindra. Peering into her engine, he shook his head.

'Is she very bad?' I asked.

'Very,' he said. 'Look at the tyres. They're almost bald, and the fan has a broken propeller. You shouldn't be driving it.' Suddenly he smiled. 'But I wish I was coming with you. Take this, and bring it back next time you come.' He handed me a canvas-backed map of south India, which would prove invaluable to me and to Yadav once he had acquired a pair of spectacles.

We never saw Carlo again. A year later Sarah from the marriage bureau rang to tell me that he had died, probably all alone, in his pea-green parlour. Someone who had become very much part of India for me was no longer there, and it wouldn't feel the same without him. We named our map of south India 'Carlo' and thought about him every time we used it.

I went to bed in Belgaum wondering if we were mad to attempt to reach the southern tip of India in our unreliable jeep. After hours of tossing and turning, I shook Yadav awake.

'Yadav.'

'Yes, yaar. I want to sleep. Is too early.'

'I've been thinking – perhaps we shouldn't go any further south than Goa. In three weeks I have to be in Delhi to catch my flight to London, and with Mahindra springing leaks and God knows what else...'

Yadav sat up, suddenly wide awake.

'Darling, you are right. I am hoping since long time you stop your wish to go Trivandrum. Thanks God. And now – goodnight!' And he turned over and went to sleep again.

The next day we started driving north, past fields of sultry sunflowers. Yellow reflections of the summer sun, their faces followed him, gyrating and genuflecting where he led.

Bijapur, the Agra of the south, is a city of mausoleums, mosques and palaces. We hired a tonga pulled by a bad-tempered piebald pony and clip-clopped through the streets to the Golgumbaz, a gigantic 1,700-square-metre mausoleum whose great echoing dome made every sound reverberate around us.

'I cannot stay high up in this place. I feel I must have to fall off,' said Yadav, backing away from the flimsy balustrade on the inner side of the dome.

The tonga took us to the Jami Masjid and on to a building with a low arched entrance, through which came the sounds of wailing and moaning. Inside, women sat, knelt and crouched in close proximity round the tomb-filled sanctuary. They rocked backwards and forwards, crying out and clutching themselves and one another in paroxysms of pain and despair.

'What they do?' Yadav asked another man who was wandering amongst the writhing bodies.

'They come to rouse the spirits. They are leaving their own bodies to enter those of saints buried in the tombs.'

'What do you think? Do you believe?' Yadav asked me. I did not know what to say; it was too strange. 'I can't say I do, but I can't say I don't.' He nodded. I was pleased; we did not often agree.

The afternoon was Mahindra's. A mechanic removed several steel hoops from her undercarriage.

'Now she will stop to jump too much,' Yadav said. 'Mechanic, he want to buy her. He even offer same we pay in Delhi. What do you think?' The man was walking around Mahindra, inspecting her in an intrusive way. Noticing Yadav's interest, he quickly lowered his offer.

'How dare he?' I thought. Despite Mahindra's misdeeds I had become inordinately fond of her. I couldn't bear the thought of this man, whose only interest was in making money, becoming the owner of *our* jeep.

'No, please don't leave her here,' I said.

Yadav decided not to sell. For the time being, Mahindra was safe.

It was St Valentine's Day. We drove 250 kilometres and parked in the forecourt of a guest house in a town called Bir.

It was rather desolate, but Mahindra's dripping radiator had decreed an evening amongst the Ashoka trees with dinner in the deserted garden. A pinprick of light from a single candle punctured our mini-world, a shadowed no-man's-land in a remote recess of the starry sky. A sentimental song from Bollywood's latest movie slithered over the garden wall from the local cinema.

'Happy Valentine's Day,' I said, raising my glass of water.

'Oh darling, you should have to tell me!' Yadav said. 'Before you came in India, I did not know this Valentine. And now I forget him. Doesn't matter, yaar – cheers!' And he raised his glass to mine.

Another hard-won 150 kilometres and Mahindra, after only one stop to be tinkered with by a red-haired mechanic with pale-blue eyes and fair, freckled skin, kept going until we reached a welder in Aurangabad.

'His grandfather must have been a British soldier,' I suggested, thinking of the fair mechanic. Yadav roared with laughter.

'Don't be silly, yaar; he is albino. You want I ask him his grandfather is British soldier? He will kill me.'

The caves of Ellora were filled with Indian tourists. Yadav was impressed by the gigantic statues of gods and animals carved out of the solid rock face, but his interest soon waned. I went on wandering and wondering for a long time. How had man sculpted those marvels all those years ago?

'Yaar, I cannot enjoy too much in these temples. The gods, they already left them. Temples are not the real thing.' Yadav liked his temples in working order. Artistic merits were superfluous adjuncts to worship.

An ill-assorted trio from Bombay – a fat midget with miniature feet, an elongated skeleton and their khaki-clad driver – insisted on following us round the ruins of Daulatabad's fort.

'I do not like these men. They are boring. Small one, he even ask you see his bungalow. Does he think you has not seen so many bungalow, even best in India? He want we eat his lunch. He want your address in London. I tell to him, "She have no address. She is beggar."'

Halfway down the steep, twisting hill to Ajanta caves, Yadav stopped to give a family of twelve a lift. 'Let us see how many Mahindra will take,' he said, enjoying the challenge.

Hoping to see something of the beautiful, faded murals in the poorly lit caves, we tagged along behind a group with a torch. By Cave 17, Yadav had had enough. He borrowed a two-year-old child from a family of tourists, sat on the wall and lit a bidi.

'Please carry on. I will wait you here and play with this baby. See how pretty she is!' He kissed the little girl.

On our last day together, Yadav woke up weeping. Determined to be cheerful, he pinched me when he thought I wasn't looking.

'Is not me; is mosquito. I want to give you smile. I think you have grown fat like buffalo. Now please you will laugh. And please also you remember, my love, what I have tell to you. If we cannot see to each other, and I doesn't know why it might be, I will keep you here.' He put his hand on his heart. 'I will never leave you. Goodnight.'

It was still dark when we revved Mahindra's engine for our last, short journey. Check-in at Delhi's airport took two hours. Yadav waited on the other side of the barrier, waving and smiling. I left my place in the queue and went over to him.

'Go now,' I told him. 'There's no point in waiting – we'll see each other soon. And please don't keep saying that we might not.'

'All right, I will not say, and now I will go. But yaar, please you must have to remember what I have taught to you. Sad

11

The Tube shot out of the tunnel and jitterbugged to a halt. The grubby envelope fell from my hand. A clear-skinned, blue-eyed girl, glued to me since Pimlico, fanned my face with soft garlic-scented breath. The robust black woman propping me up from behind moved, mobilising a whiff of Camay and underarm sweat. They shifted, shoved their way towards the open doors and disappeared into the crowds. I bent to pick up my envelope.

'Victoria. This is Victoria. Change here for District and Circle lines. Let the passengers off the train first, please. Mind the gap!' screamed the loudspeakers.

Before the new crowd surged forward to occupy the seats and suck all remnants of oxygen from the already airless carriage, I sat down beside a sleeping tramp. Stale tobacco, unwashed clothes and alcohol fumes filled my nostrils. Smells, so many smells.

A woman fell over my feet and tumbled into the seat opposite.

'Sorry!' She withdrew behind *The Times*.

'Sorry!' I tucked in my feet and opened my letter. It was written in capital letters on cheap lined paper.

7 September
Sweet and very sweetheart Jill,
It is too hard to tell about thing which happened and is happening in these days. I hope you will try to understand my poor spelling and English.

As you know, my father is getting old. He is not all right. I don't hope that he will get better. One day when I came to farm from bus stand, he tell to me he cannot pee all the day. I took village doctor at my farm, he make it so my father, he can pee with plastic pipe. Doctor, he want to go his home. This night I have to go to fetch doctor to my father at least three times. We all could not sleep. In morning my father, he begin to cry very badly. Ramesh, Boss Brother and me, we put him in our jeep and take him to our town. Stupid Mahindra, it break down, I can mend, but not too well. I left my father with other brothers at hospital and go to workshop. Mechanic, he is lazy. He take too long to leave his bed. When I come back to hospital, is too late, my Bapu he is expired. We take his dead body at home. About two hours later we have burning in our own village.

Many, many peoples they come to our farm, because my father he have much respect in our village and area. Now we must have big party for minimum 1800 villagers.

With eleven family members, we go in your jeep to take bone of Krishan Singh to Ganga River. On journey we have too nice time together, singing, joking and laughing very much. Even we did not pay Brahmin. Bloody fool, he say he want 1000 rupees to take my Bapu in boat and throw him in river, so we throw in ourselves.

On second day of return, by misfortune, I miss sleeping policeman sign. We goes too fast over bump and whole engine, it fell out on road.

So, my sweet darling, I hope you will not mind, I have decide to sell your jeep. Luckily I find buyer, he is very rich man. He will change all things. So please you try to find money from your work for new jeep. Will be much better for us. We can have our taxi business and make many rupees.

Sweet, now I am not feeling to write any more. Please go on with loving to me if you can. Darling, a stupid, poor and mad lover is sending his love to you. I promise by myself I will go on loving you till the end of my life. Even I will wait for you til the last breath in my life, because I do love you. I want to get marry with you. I could live without wife before you met me. But now is too difficult. Please, I request you, think what you want to do. You knows about me, I am poor man, so all the decision are depend on you.

Jill, did you find work for me in your country? I think you cannot.

Please write me back as soon as possible. I am sending my love to my new wife. 125 per cent sure. But in truth, love has no percentage.

From Yadav.

The train retched. The couplings groaned. The doors slid open. I crammed the letter back into its envelope and hurried out, up the moving stairs into the cool, grey light of Tottenham Court Road.

I remembered my last conversation with Yadav at Delhi airport. Mahindra was gone; I would never see her again. And Yadav...? The icicles of fear that I had felt when we said goodbye stabbed at my heart. I shivered and hurried down the road to meet my clients for another day of Bath, Salisbury and Stonehenge.

Exhausted after eight hours with a bus full of tourists, I wrote to Yadav. I couldn't keep his question dangling in the air any longer.

'Darling, I do want to – yes, please, I will marry you.' For better, for worse, I had made up my mind.

1 October
My dearest love Jill,
I was waiting for your letter many days, feeling very sad because I saw you in my dream, but not clearly, so I was worried you

189

was not all right. At last I get letter on 20 September. Thank you very much. Now I am very happy you are all right.

'If you're not waiting for this bus, I am. Either get on or let me pass,' breathed an indignant voice behind me. 'Some of us have to get to work.'

'Sorry.' I climbed on to the green-and-grey 24 bus to Victoria.

... I am not well. After my father expired I catch pneumonia. Nobody at farm they cares about me. Even my youngest daughter, Puja, she does not bring me water when I call. At last Ramesh, he take me to Delhi. I saw lady doctor. She make X-rays and give me tablets and the pneumonia, it is better. But now I have other problem. Is 'depression'. Jill, I am too frightened, I think I must become mad. All time, thoughts, they comes in my head and I cannot send away. Please you come back quickly. Or I think I die before you are at your farm. Lady doctor, she send me to nice Dr Prakash at her same hospital, but his tablets, they doesn't help. Ramesh and me, we tell him, please send to new doctor. He agree and he send me to very great doctor of depression. He is famous in whole world, this he told me himself. He say he will make cure in one month only and he will.

Sweet love, you say in letter you will get marry with me. I am putting my hand on your head and telling you, when you will come back, we will arrange all things and you will be my real wife...

Yes, it is good idea you have, we will open travel agency with new jeep. I will be driver. You will be guide. We will have too many clients. Believe me.

We crawled round Trafalgar Square. Lord Nelson stood on his column. The pigeons massed, awaiting the day's crop of tourists. Nothing had changed.

Gulf Air. London, Bahrain, Muscat. One hour's wait. Muscat, Delhi.

Where was Yadav? The heat of the day did nothing to melt my ice-cold fear. A strange young man stepped from the crowd.

'Uncle is here.' I looked over his shoulder and saw Yadav. His eyes were glazed. His hand trembled as he took mine. His lips were thick and hot.

'Is my nephew. I could not wait in front line. I was frightened to come alone. Is my depression.' His voice was slurred and indistinct.

'Yadav, what's wrong? What's happened to you?'

The bloated lips smiled. 'I did tell you in my letters, yaar, is only my 'depression'. But now I have new doctor. We must have to stay for some nights at hotel to buy our new jeep, and tomorrow you will meet with doctor. He is badly waiting to see you.'

We said goodbye to the nephew and took a taxi into Delhi.

'I have very great surprise for you,' Yadav said. 'I have built loo for you at farm. We dig deep hole, forty foot, and then builder, he made small concrete house with water tank on outside wall. Government, they give free seat, but is not good. We make Indian-style – no seat. Government one we will use for chimney in kitchen. Now we will save our rupees. We will not have to drive for twenty-five kilometres to tourist complex.' I had made a habit of visiting town to make telephone calls, have breakfast and use the loo.

The morning after my arrival Yadav took me to meet his new doctor, a young man from south India. He rotated from side to side on a shabby swivel chair in a poky consulting room above a chemist's shop. His once-white shirt hung loose outside his trousers, the cuffs tightly buttoned over dainty wrists. He did not get up. While Yadav talked about his depression, the doctor stared out the dirty little window, an abstracted expression on his face.

When Yadav paused for breath, the doctor leaned across his desk, breathing enthusiasm and half-digested onion over me. 'Now,' he said, 'I think, Madam, you will be interested to ask me many questions?'

I asked him if he was a qualified psychiatrist. 'Actually,' he said, evading my question, 'I am specialist in gentlemen's troubles.'

'Gentlemen's troubles?'

'Yes,' he warmed to his subject. 'I am specialist in all matters of impotency and related problems. I have invented unique, infallible cure. The lid is on the teapot for all who come to me.'

What could I say in answer to this astounding announcement? 'I have heard that cocoa and oysters are excellent aphrodisiacs,' I parried.

'Cocoa, that I do not know. Oysters, I can say, are most useful, as are all foods resembling the male sex organs.'

After some persuasion, Yadav decided to go back to Dr Prakash, a man whose head was full of common sense and whose face was wreathed in smiles. He was sitting in a clean consulting room that smelled of disinfectant and ether.

'I am not here to tell Mr Yadav what to do,' he said. 'He decided not to take the medication I prescribed, and naturally his condition did not improve. Unfortunately the young specialist I sent him to has left for America.' He looked at the prescription that the specialist in gentlemen's troubles had given us, and spread his hands in an eloquent gesture. 'Of course, I don't know this man. But I am delighted to have Mr Yadav back as my patient.'

He kept us for a long time, curious about how we had met.

'So I would like to ask Mr Yadav,' he turned in his chair. 'You have told me that you may marry this lady. Isn't that perhaps the cause of the tensions you are suffering in your mind? Are you not worried about your family's feelings in this matter?'

'No,' Yadav said. 'You are absolutely wrong. My daughters, they are married. Last one, we find husband for her and she is married in summer to Raja Ram, my son-in-law. If my family do not like I marry with British lady, I do not care. I am free. But they will not mind. Already they respect and honour her too much. Is true thing.' He looked at me and took my hand.

We dined at the Kwality Inn in Connaught Place. Our usual place, a dive behind Janpath, did not seem grand enough for two people about to buy a brand-new jeep. I felt hot and prickly at the thought of exchanging the thousands of pounds I had brought from England, and at the thought of calling more friends of friends in Delhi. After our disastrous time with Mahindra, I wanted some proper advice on buying a jeep.

'Only one thing is important. We must have to buy new jeep on a Friday, Saturday or Tuesday.' Yadav had visited the Brahmin near his elder sister's village and had been told that those were the auspicious days.

Skyline Automobiles was in a bazaar full of cars and spare parts. We climbed a flight of broken steps into half an office. The other half was being demolished. A man looked up from his papers without interest. When we told him we wanted to buy a jeep, he looked even less interested and waved us towards two seats in the ruins.

'Repairs,' he explained, pointing to crumbling walls and a jumble of naked wires where three men sat behind a long table, talking on three telephones.

At last, one of the men put his receiver down. He re-rolled the sleeves of his striped shirt, smoothed his baggy trousers and lit a cigarette. 'Yes,' he said, looking at me rather than Yadav.

Yadav explained our mission. After a long interview, interrupted by phone calls and other conversations, it was established that if we arrived the next morning with the money, a new jeep would be delivered to our hotel that evening. No, we could not choose the colour. No, we could not see the jeep. The salesman yawned. The interview was over.

The next day, having changed my travellers' cheques into a thick bundle of rupees, I spent the morning looking up contacts. The director of Delhi Tourism was retiring that very day. She was busy, but spared me a few minutes.

'You want to open a travel agency? I'm afraid I cannot help. You would need to be registered by the government of India. Do you have an office and a telephone?' I shook my head. 'Jeeps are uncomfortable, but perhaps you will take young people? I suggest you go to the AA. They will make you itineraries with appropriate lunch stops.'

Back at Skyline Automobiles, we handed over our bag of rupees.

The jeep was parked outside the hotel. Yadav stroked its shiny, army-green paintwork lovingly. As usual, I felt apprehensive about the money we had spent. How many Oxfords and Stratfords, Waleses and Scotlands had it cost?

On our way to the garage to have the rods for the canvas roof shortened, we stopped at a Hanuman temple. Yadav bought prasad, rang the bell of the sanctum, abased himself before the image of the monkey god and handed a few of the sweets to the priest, who stuffed the sticky yellow balls into the mouth of the grinning effigy and passed me a garland of yellow flowers in exchange. Outside, a group of beggar children pounced on the remaining prasad. We hung the garland on the rear-view mirror. Our new Mahindra was blessed. We drove on to the garage.

The mechanic studied the rods and, with a great show of force, bent them one by one until they fitted into the holes.

'But Yadav, it's a new car. They ought to fit properly.'

He shrugged. 'This is India, and now they does work very well.'

We spent the night with Dinesh and Sushila. 'Is because I promise to Brahmin I will never drink and drive, and tonight I want to drink.' Despite Yadav's insistence to the contrary, he and Sushila did not get on. During dinner they ignored each other.

'Why you do not stay any more with us?' Sushila asked me through her eldest son.

'I can't just now. Yadav and I are soon going to the hills.' It was an excuse that might come true.

'Yadav. Yadav. All Yadav. He is bagra.'

'Backward tribesman from Rajasthan,' the young man translated. Yadav was at the water tank, making a lot of noise cleaning his teeth.

At the border between Delhi and Haryana we found a roadside garland maker.

'We will decorate only bonnet,' Yadav decided. The man assembled a geometrical pattern of strings of yellow flowers, sticking them into place with cellophane tape. 'This is decoration for newly married couple.'

'Rubbish. It's for the new jeep. We're not married at all, and certainly not newly,' I said.

'No, but we will be. We will.'

An hour later we turned in at the gates of Ramesh's factory. A guard stepped forward, smiled and said something to Yadav.

'He ask, "Who she is?" I say him you are my good friend. I cannot say my wife.'

I felt unreasonably hurt. 'Then why can you say it to people you don't know and don't care about, like that flower seller?

As we are going to get married, it would be nicer for me if you could tell the people you take seriously.'

Ramesh arrived to admire the new jeep. 'Very best.' He beamed, chatted for a few minutes and, putting on his black beret at a jaunty angle, went off to do guard duty.

We stopped for coffee in Gurgaon. 'Anyway,' I said, going back to our earlier conversation, still feeling cross and unhappy, 'if you're too ashamed to say we're getting married, perhaps we had better stay just good friends.'

Yadav took the two spoons from the cups and put them on the table. 'Look at spoons,' he said. He put the sugar bowl beside them. 'I can use these spoons, you too can use them, but they is not ours. We cannot keep them.' He put one of the spoons into the bowl of sugar and stirred it round. 'We must first buy spoons; after that nobody he can tell us what we must do with them. The same when we will get married. We will belong to each other. No one he can tell us any things. Isn't it?' I was not sure about the spoon metaphor, but I nodded, feeling happier.

We stopped again beside a tinsel seller just beyond Gurgaon. The jeep was going to look like a Christmas tree. The man sat in the front seat with two balls of plastic twine and bound the steering wheel in green and white string.

'Much better,' Yadav said, turning the wheel to the left and right. 'And now I think you will like to meet father-in-law of Puja. I have told him we will get married. He thinks it is good idea. He is waiting to see you.'

Puja's father-in-law's brother led us across the ploughed fields by torchlight. The family welcomed us and fed us aloo gobhi and chapati. While we ate, a succession of neighbours dropped in to have a quick word with the family and a long stare at me. They had already made up theiir minds that I came from a place where everyone was rich and powerful, that at the drop of a word I could transform their lives, find jobs for their children and give them heaven on earth, as I myself must surely possess. They wanted to know how old I was, whether I was married, where my husband was, how many children I had and how much money I earned. Nothing beyond that was of any interest to them.

Chaudri Sahib, Puja's father-in-law, smiled and chuckled from every fold and crease of his ample kurta and spotless white dhoti. His eyes laughed and sparkled from beneath the shadow of his outsized turban. His wife was his foil, going quietly about her duties but capable of a sly quip when gently teased by Yadav.

It was not many months since Puja had been the rejected bride and Yadav's brothers had renegotiated her hand. Now she was the happy wife of Raja Ram. She appeared to be pregnant, though how she found the time and the privacy for lovemaking was hard to imagine. When her father-in-law was present, Puja veiled her face and talked in a whisper.

'Is she having a baby?' I asked Yadav. He looked shocked.

'How can I know? I cannot talk with my daughter about such things. With her mother-in-law I can have joke, but for this conversation there is border I must not cross.' He didn't seem to notice the distinct bulge under Puja's petticoat.

Raja Ram was learning to be a village doctor. 'Not a proper doctor, you understand,' Yadav explained. 'Only he can give injections and tablets to villagers.' He had a smattering of English and was anxious to practise it on me. 'I love my Puji,' Raja Ram confided. 'She is beautiful. And you are my respected aunt.'

Chaudri Sahib's sister sat on the only chair in the yard, knitting. 'For my son,' she said. 'He has followed his father into navy.' She delivered her explanation in a superior tone. 'My husband was important gentleman. Officer, I believe. He has recently expired. Now I am alone in this world.'

We slept in our clothes, on two charpoys in an open-fronted shed. The strings creaked and strained at their oblong wooden frame, rolling me into a dip in the middle. Yadav snored. On the other side of the wall the family slept peacefully, sharing their room with three buffaloes. From where I lay I could smell the acrid scent of urine mingled with the sweet, cloying odour of warm dung. Hot and grimy from my travels, I lay awake, tossing and turning and watching the white shadow of the moon disappear slowly as the sun rose, painting the morning a pale primrose-yellow.

A bird chirped its first noisy note of the day.

'Tomorrow I will go to doctor. I am not all right.' Yadav's plaintive voice came from the other charpoy. I looked across at his unshaven face and crumpled, dirty clothes and erupted into criticism.

'You should take more care of yourself. If you smoke and drink whisky all the time, and don't change your clothes or wash, how can you hope to be well? You don't take responsibility for yourself, or have any discipline in your life.' With every word I grew more furious. Was this nagging woman really me? The same who, a few days earlier, had longed for nothing more than to be with the man I was now berating?

'I will change. I promise you I will. But now I am not well.'

I felt ashamed. Why should he change? He was a farmer and a driver. If I could not accept this, I should not be there, lying beside him in Chaudri Sahib's barn.

'I'm sorry. I shouldn't talk to you like that. Please forgive me.'

'But you should, and I am very thankful to you for what you tell me. Only say in polite voice and I will not mind. And soon you will be my sweet wife.' Yadav slept again.

Should I really marry him? Could I ever fit in with the simple ways of his family and friends? Would I be upsetting him and his way of life? Why was I choosing to live in circumstances which would be uncomfortable and frightening to most people with anything like my background? Why was I contemplating marriage with a man who was, at times, uncouth and unkind?

Because I loved Yadav and I wanted to belong to him, not just for a day or a month or even a year but forever, as long as forever might last. I wanted security and propriety, a life in which no one smiled wryly about my living with an Indian taxi driver, or suggested that he was one of 'Mum's afternoon delights'.

'Love is not blind.' Yadav had got the saying inside-out; love is very blind. But right or wrong, I wanted, at whatever cost – and at the moment I was not counting the cost – to be married to Yadav.

'Darling, what you are thinking?' Yadav's voice was muffled beneath his mound of discoloured bedding.

'Nothing. Nothing at all.'

'Is seven o'clock.' Raja Ram stood between our charpoys with a cup of hot, sweet chai for Yadav and a bottle of water for me.

'I am sorry, Aunty, we haven't coffee and I think you cannot drink chai?' He held up the bottle. 'For latrine,' he explained. I stuffed some loo paper discreetly down my bra and stumbled out into the wet mustard field. Through a forest of thick green stalks, bright chunnis and turbans broke up the sea of yellow flowers. I marvelled at the clockwork timing of the village bowels. Before the cock crowed, their 'work' would be finished and the day would begin.

'We must take Chaudri Sahib and Puja to farm with us. And before we go back, if you will not mind, we will see to Sarita and family for jeep puja party.'

'Another puja party?' However smart the new jeep was, I did not feel any affection for it. Old Mahindra had become a personality, a friend; this one was just a jeep.

A coat of paint and a few repairs would have transformed the dilapidated home of Sarita and her family into a grand village house. We passed beneath a Moghul archway into the pillared courtyard. Sarita and her sisters-in-law squatted on the ground, preparing dinner. Children played and chattered. Minute four-year-olds struggled under the weight of baby brothers and sisters. Older girls ran errands for their mothers and aunts. Squeals and shouts joined the yaps of a tormented black puppy whose efforts to escape the yard were blocked by four little boys, egged on by their youngers. Whichever way it turned, the puppy was cornered, kicked and teased. Nobody noticed its distress. Under the shade of a mulberry tree, a baby lay on a charpoy, its face blackened with buzzing flies. It cooed and sang, reaching out its hands to a flock of tiny birds as they rose and fell through the branches above its head.

I was a better game than any puppy. Followed by the other children, the boys left the little dog and made a circle round me. 'Ringa, ringa,' shouted Purdeep, who grew taller and thinner each year. 'Ringa, ringa,' chorused the others. I joined hands with them. They galloped me round and round in a circle until the song came to 'All fall down.' We fell with a bump.

'More, more!' they cried. We danced down the village street singing 'Ring-a-ring-a-roses,' collecting children as we went.

'Chalo!' shouted Yadav. Purdeep rushed back to the jeep and was first on the front seat. I sat beside him. Sarita had changed into a sari for the journey. Cradling her screaming daughter, she climbed into the back and undid her blouse, pulling the pallu of her sari over her head and the child's. As

Sunita nuzzled her mother's breast, the screaming was replaced by sighs of contented sucking.

We bumped down the track between tall, feathery grasses, soon to be cut and used for thatching. The sprinklers shed crystal drops across the fields. A gentle *thump*, *thump* from the well proclaimed electricity. The family, hearing the jeep, were waiting to welcome us. The evening echoed with *Ram Rams* as Yadav tore the wilted yellow flowers from the bonnet and threw them to the ground. Our luggage was shouldered into the room where we would sleep.

Hanuman took Sunita from Sarita's arms and bore her away on his shoulders. Purdeep clutched his Aunt Shanti's hand and Puja went off with Ramesh, who had taken leave in order to cook dinner for the new jeep's puja party. Meenakshi put Chenamunia into my arms and went to the kitchen to help Ramesh and her sisters. Ma shambled round the jeep, touching and talking to it. She bumped into me and rubbed my head in blessing.

'You did not yet meet with my Boss Brother. You should have to touch his feet,' said Yadav, taking Chenamunia and throwing her up in the air. She laughed and wriggled from his grasp.

'But Yadav, I don't think he likes it, and anyway I'm probably the same age as him.'

'Doesn't matter, yaar. In family you are youngest sister-in-law.' At the farm Yadav stuck strictly to protocol.

To please him, I bent down and touched Boss Brother's feet. Boss Brother protested, looking as embarrassed as I felt.

Darkness and a power cut came suddenly. They usually fell at the same time. Bubli, Ramesh's youngest son, could see in the dark. He stood in our room and stared as I unpacked, picking up and fingering everything, demanding explanations for the things he did not recognise. The older children had a fascination for anything that came from the West, thinking that anything you wanted there was superior to its equivalent in India and, more remarkably, was to be had for the asking.

'Roti khale, roti khale,' Chenamunia called, taking my hand and leading me across the yard to the kitchen.

'I am cooker for tonight,' said Ramesh, tearing up aubergines and potatoes with a blunt knife. 'Shanti, she is no good.' Shanti smiled and pulled her chunni further over her face.

Ramesh stood up. 'And now, let us take drink.' We shut ourselves into Shanti's small room and drank duty-free Johnnie Walker out of smeared glasses. 'Very best,' said Ramesh, tossing a tumblerful down his throat. 'Mrs Jill, I am interested to know about your farmers. Which are crops that they grow? And for milk, they have buffalo same like us? I think your farmers, they are more rich peoples than us?'

I told him about the the acreage of our farms, the absence of buffalo, the use of machinery and lack of need for human labour. He registered his amazement.

'Please, next time you go in your country you bring back wheat and barley seed, and we will grow here on our farm. Will be very interesting for me.' (I did bring back two bags of grain. But the next season, when the crops came up, I asked Yadav where the English seed had been sown, and he said that Boss Brother had mistakenly mixed it with the Indian seed and didn't know.)

I suggested offering a glass of whisky to Rama and Raja Singh, Yadav's nephews. Both were married men with children of their own, but Ramesh was shocked. 'They are our children! They are strictly not allowed to drink or smoke in our presence.'

'Barfi?' asked Deepak, a farmer from across the fields.

'Deepak says there is drama in his village. He want we give him one kilo barfi for new jeep, bloody fool,' said Yadav.

'What is drama? Is it theatre?'

'Yes. Is really quite boring. Men make play about the gods. We will not go.'

'Please, Yadav, I would love to.'

Deepak added his pleas. 'Yes, yes, you must have to bring her.' Yadav relented. We finished our drinks and got into the jeep – Deepak, two nephews, three great-nephews, Yadav and I.

We bumped along the dark track. A hare paused for a second, caught in our headlights, before bounding into the undergrowth. Squirrels scurried from our path. A huge nilgai, half horse and half deer, stood stock-still for a second, caught in the glare, listening, and then galloped away into the darkness. A single candle here, a kerosene flame in a window there, the beam of a stroller's torch lit corners of the sleeping village. Late-night walkers flattened themselves against walls or stepped into archways as we passed.

Deepak's village, also suffering from a power cut, was black as a coal hole and empty as the desert. Nothing stirred but the pye-dogs in the dust. Disturbed by the jeep, they clambered to their feet and, one taking its cue from another, set up a fearful wail, splitting the silence in a long, drawn-out howl.

The jeep skidded in the soft sand, out of the dark little streets into a dazzle of light. The stage was a glittering planet in a universe of gloom. Caught in the sparkle of the generated light bulbs, three hundred pairs of eyes were riveted to a shimmering world where gods and goddesses, spangled in gold and silver, trod the boards, reciting the drama of the *Ramayana*.

At the sound of the jeep, the heads swivelled for a moment, then returned to the lighted stage to join Lord Rama and the brave, scarlet-clad Hanuman as they planned their flight to Lanka. Neither the man in a Western suit – a woollen hat pulled over his ears, incongruous as he jumped from stage to audience, soliciting cash – nor the prompt who shouted forgotten lines from a corner, nor the whir of the generator spoiled the audience's enthusiasm. Deepak pulled us to the front.

'Cover yourself and they will not stare,' Yadav said, throwing a white shawl over me. But nobody gave us a glance. The musicians on the stage rolled their drums. The voices of the actors echoed across the village, competing with the howling dogs.

'Is story of Lord Rama and Sita and Hanuman monkey god,' Yadav yelled above the booming drums and the shouting actors. Now the audience turned to stare.

'Come,' Yadav said, leading the way to a canvas enclosure beside the stage. He lifted the flap. Inside a pretty, dark-haired girl in an electric-blue sari was practising a dance routine. Deepak beckoned to her.

'He is man dressed up like woman. He will dance in sari,' Yadav said with relish. It was true. The arms were thick and muscular, and the coarse-grained chin needed a shave. 'And now he is going to do dance especially for you.' We left him practising his delicate steps and went back to our places.

The actors stopped acting and grouped themselves silently at the back of the stage. An unearthly hush of anticipation awaited the dancer. He stepped from the wings. The musicians struck up. Disappointingly clumsy, he pirouetted and wriggled his hips beneath the blue sari. The man in the suit wandered round the audience collecting donations. With each fistful of rupees he returned to the stage, and the drums rolled as he announced the name of the donor and the amount given. When he came over to us, he and Deepak had a long, deep discussion ending in a peal of laughter.

'They say that because of you, we are rich. We must give fifty rupees. Bloody fools.' Yadav felt for a five-rupee note. Deepak looked pained. 'If Deepak wants we buy him barfi, we cannot afford more. Is enough.' Deepak smiled at the mention of his favourite sweets.

'Only fifty rupees,' the man wheedled.

'I will give maximum ten.' Grudgingly, Yadav held out another five. The man took the money and pranced back onstage.

'Mrs Jill from London and Lal Singh Yadav – ten rupees.' The drums rolled. The blue sari began a seductive sashay across the stage.

'Chalo,' said Yadav. 'Now you have seen drama long enough.'

'And I enjoyed it so much. Thank you for bringing me.'

The next day, Yadav led me to the edge of the fields beyond Rama's hut. He pointed across the plough to a small oblong of concrete. 'There,' he said with pride. 'There is your loo.'

'But it's miles away,' I couldn't help saying. 'Why didn't you build it near the farm?' I may have sounded ungrateful, but I had been the one to pay 150 pounds for this unsolicited structure.

'My Boss Brother, he would not like it. It would not be all right.'

We walked across the field. The small building lacked a door, but that was not the main problem. The pink plastic tap did not fit the water pipe from the outside tank, and the tank would have to be filled with water from the well. 'This is not difficult,' said Yadav. 'Childrens, they will carry water pots on heads.'

Yadav asked the carpenter to make a door out of some old planks of wood. He did his best, but it still would not close. Hari Ram was sent to the village to look for another tap. He came back with something in delicate baby blue, but it still did not fit the pipe. The loo has never worked. It stands in the middle of the mustard, a white elephant covered in green creepers, a monument to Yadav's idea of Western ways.

The yard was filling with people. 'You want to drink?' Yadav asked. We sat behind closed doors in Shanti's room. Ramesh came in with a bottle of rum.

'Very best item. Impossible you buy in shop. Army issue only.' He handed me a generous glassful and downed his own. Deepak, from across the field, looked in. 'Barfi?' he inquired. Yadav opened a box of sweets and gave him half the contents.

This was a grander party than old Mahindra's had been. There were three big bonfires. Shanti cooked puri and subzi, and chai flowed. The musicians played louder and longer. Ramesh was quite carried away – he knelt, he stood, his one eye gleamed in the firelight. He reached out, flinging first one arm and then the other in impassioned, supplicating movements while twisting his body backwards and forwards.

'You are very happy?' he asked, breaking off from his dance. 'But now I think you are tired. I will show you to your bed.' Yadav had long since gone to bed in the room we usually slept in. That night it was full of guests, so Ramesh took me to the room where Shanti was already asleep on the charpoy she shared with Ashok, Purdeep and Sunita. 'You will sleep very well here,' Ramesh said, offering me the empty cot.

Feeling guilty, but not guilty enough to offer to share the cot, I climbed on to it. Another night without changing or washing. Through the open door I could see Ma's strange silhouette, kneeling up on her cot and raising and lowering her arms as she swayed drunkenly in time to the music.

On Monday Yadav drove most of his daughters, grandchildren and nieces back to their own farms. We kept Meenakshi and Chenamunia. 'Shanti, she must have help with buffalo and cooking and we do need baby at farm. Is too difficult to live without childrens to play with.'

Left to myself, I reluctantly began writing an itinerary for 'Safaris in India à la Carte', the name we had decided to give our travel agency. I was not at all sure that I wanted to import to India the work I had escaped from in England, but I was still worried about my part in Yadav's job loss and wanted, if I could, to help him to find something to do. He was excited by the prospect, and had already begun to calculate how we would spend our first million. My idea was to offer a forty-day jeep trip from Delhi to Kanyakumari. As I wrote, I forgot my misgivings, and my mind filled with thoughts and ideas for the journey. I wrote for myself, not really believing we would find anyone to come on our tour.

It took less than a day without Yadav for me to realise how lonely I was when he was not at the farm. Everyone was kind, of course; they boiled water that smelt of woodsmoke for me to wash in, while Chenamunia sat on my wooden charpoy-table and played with my paper clips and cellophane tape. Meenakshi cooked me pakoras and Ma hobbled over with a kettle of chai, a cushion for the seat of my chair and a spate of Hindi, of which, to my shame, I could not understand a word. At 6.30, when the sun was setting and the white disc of the crescent moon appeared, I heard the jeep's engine and thanked God that Yadav had decided against staying the night with one of his other relations.

'Here.' Yadav handed me a wad of dirty notes. 'This is first earnings of new jeep. Tradition say I must give to my wife.'

The next morning Hanuman gave me a letter he had written in English. '*Dear Aunt. Now you have new jeep, my college friends, they want party. Please help. My god will keep you. Hanuman.*' I thought we should give him a hundred rupees.

'Fifty is too much. Please give money from jeep,' Yadav said.

'But you said it was a tradition for you to give it to me.'

'We have made tradition yesterday. Now it doesn't matter we give to Hanuman. I did give to you first. Important thing is done.'

After three days' work and a lot of help from Yadav, I finished Day 40 of our itinerary. Since I had no typewriter, I sent off my longhand scrawl to a friend in England with a list of possible clients, and a postscript to say that I would ring him once a week for the results. 'Safaris in India' was launched.

At about seven o'clock every morning, when the older nephews who shared our room went to the fields to do a few hours' work before school, Chenamunia and her cousins Anu and Vini, the latter a serious schoolboy with thin little legs and knobbly knees, came to wake us up. 'Khadi ho, khadi ho, Naana, Naana!' Chenamunia shook Yadav and he swept her off her feet and under his bedcover, hugging, kissing and stifling her. She squealed to be released, and he threw her on to my charpoy. After climbing all over me as though I were Mount Everest, she, Anu and Vini helped me to dress.

'Le, le,' they urged as they passed me my earrings, bangles and necklace and then stood back, waiting for me to get up, chase them from the room and finish dressing. As soon as I was dressed they trooped in again, giggling, a threesome of wicked garden gnomes. Under toadstools of coloured crocheted hats, they sat round my makeup box, digging and delving, picking and poking into mascara, eyeshadow, lipsticks and rouge. They chattered and chortled, applying this and that. They begged for toothpaste and scrubbed their teeth with their forefingers. They held out small palms for hand cream and sat still while I gave them each a squirt of French scent. Our morning pantomime became a daily ritual.

'Jill.' Yadav interrupted Chenamunia's lipstick application. 'Is time we think of our marriage. We will go Pushkar and ask Beni Gopal to marry us. Today we will go to buy corn and ask Brahmin man, who live in same village, auspicious day for marriage. Brahmin is very great man. Many peoples they go to ask his advice. We must have to hurry. If we get late we will lose our turn.'

He need not have worried. As soon as we entered the Brahmin's house, overflowing as it was with people, we were taken to the corner of the room where he sat, cross-legged, waving a handful of peacock feathers over a deaf-mute child. His beige face was unlined, and his silver-grey hair was neatly cut and combed. Over his ample stomach he wore a white kurta, turned pale-blue in the wash. Seeing us, he dismissed the child, smiled broadly and gestured to us to sit down. Three cups of chai were passed over the heads of the waiting crowd. I sipped mine. Yadav stared at me.

'Many times you tell me you do not like chai,' he said, trying to take the cup from me.

'I don't, but it would be bad-mannered to refuse. I didn't want to hurt their feelings. It was so kind of them to make it for us.'

He shrugged his shoulders, non-plussed. 'Rubbish. Stupid British way. In India, we doesn't like, we doesn't drink. Chai, it has no feelings!'

'But I didn't mean the chai, I...' Yadav was deep in conversation with the Brahmin, who nodded, listened, spoke and nodded again. The people closest to us leant forward to hear. They smiled and occasionally laughed out loud. The Brahmin handed Yadav a set of metal dice, opened a tattered book and began to read, muttering the words under his breath. Yadav passed the dice to me.

'You please throw first,' he said. I tossed the dice. Yadav scooped them up, studying each one intently. 'Very good. You have best luck.'

'Why?' I asked. Without answering, he threw the dice himself. He and the Brahmin studied the uppermost numbers. 'Second luck,' he said.

The Brahmin spoke. The people were silent, hanging on his words. He finished, measured yellow powder into a tiny screw of paper, gave it to me and hung a metal talisman on a string round Yadav's neck.

'He say if we get married we will have good and happy life. Marriage must be after December ninth and before end of month. About depression, he say if I stop to drink I will be all right by fifteenth November.' Yadav pronounced the words as though God himself had spoken. 'For our travel agency, we must not have to travel on Friday or Saturday, or even before that date. That is all.' He felt in his pocket and gave the Brahmin one rupee. The Brahmin accepted it and asked Yadav if I could bring him a present from England.

'I say certainly not. What he think? He say he even give you yellow powder to throw on fire for puja. Nonsense. Stupid.' We picked our way through the seated people.

In spite of the Brahmin's prediction that Yadav's health would improve, he collapsed on the back seat of the jeep in black depression, leaving me to drive back through the town. At the bus stand we met his sister's nephew's son-in-law.

'Please let him drive. He knows very well,' Yadav urged. The young man crashed the gears and slammed on the brakes, and he was only going as far as the next bus stand. We stopped to let him out and were immediately besieged by hundreds of would-be passengers.

'Get off, all of you! This isn't a bloody taxi; it's a private car!' I yelled, forgetting that we had bought the jeep with the idea of giving Yadav work as a taxi driver. The tone of my voice was enough to make them fall away. Sometimes, in the heat and dust, under the pressure of crowds of strangers, things got too much for me. This was one of those times.

'You shouldn't have to say like that. Deepak farmer, who you knows very well, is here, and four peoples from your own village. We will lift them.' I recognised Deepak and tried to smile through my bad temper. 'Now my sister's nephew's son-in-law is not here, you will drive again. Please be careful with jeep. Your way of driving will break it too quickly.'

'I think your sister's nephew's son-in-law is a terrible driver.' I was furious.

'My sister's nephew's son-in-law is not bad driver. Is you who is worst driver I meet in whole life,' said Yadav. I turned to answer the criticism. 'Look out!' he shouted. An old man on a bicycle was weaving down the centre of the road. I could not find the horn; I swerved violently. 'You see? You almost kill him. Now please do not take risk.' I drove on. He and his friends gossiped in the back.

Yadav let out a great guffaw. 'Deepak, he tell my friends you are seventy years old, and now they are having joke about you and me. Is really very funny.' To me, alone in the front seat, it was not funny at all. I felt like bursting into tears. 'Jill. Why you do not laugh? You looks me very sad.'

'I am. And now I don't think we should get married. Everything about us is too different.'

We dropped the men at the village bus stand and bumped on between the mustard fields towards the farm. It started to rain. Lightning lit the sky. It grew colder.

'It will be so good for crops if it can rain, really. Come, we will make share with my shawl.' Yadav put half his shawl round my shoulders. I was glad of it. The wind battered at the grasses beside the track. I felt hot tears running down my cold cheeks and tasted the salt on my lips. Yadav wiped his own eyes. 'And now you will tell me why you cry? You and me, we must not have secret. And if you say again we will not get marry, I will lose my life.'

I told him that I could not bear the men sitting in the back laughing at me. Or his criticism of my driving. Or the mob who had tried to get into the jeep in town. Or his dirty clothes and unshaven face. 'We're too different,' I repeated.

'Yaar, please do not say again. I do not shave this morning because, you knows, I am not so well. Men, they are joking, passing time. I tell them stop, but they doesn't want. One man, he even ask, "Does she want to come in my wedding?" For driving, I have often tell to you – you are very British driver. In India is not good. In villages, jeep is taxi. How villagers, they can know you do not want to lift them?'

'Shall we go to his wedding?' I asked. Yadav looked surprised.

'He didn't mean it, yaar. He say to me, "All people they will stare at her. You do not bring her."'

'But why doesn't he say what he means?' I asked pointlessly.

The night before we left for Pushkar, I was not well. My stomach turned upside-down and my legs felt like jelly. I slept fitfully and woke early to find a mouse sitting on my pillow, staring at me. Forgetting my weak legs, I leapt from my cot to Yadav's, yelling at the top of my voice and bringing the entire family rushing into the room. 'Is only chuha,' Yadav told them.

'Chuha, chuha, chuha!' The boys shuffled out, chuckling. That was not the end of the story, however. Every night thereafter, the mouse made a dash across my bed, and once, when I was sweeping behind our tin trunk, it hopped out in broad daylight. Hari Ram and Rama mixed a dinner that should have delighted the most discerning of vermin, and sprinkled it with rat poison. The food was left untouched.

One day Bubli came back from the village with a very small, very skinny kitten. On a sparse diet of half a cup of buffalo milk and half a chapati a day, the kitten became a puny little cat. We never again saw my mouse, nor any one of the army of mice that had once lived behind the kitchen walls.

I staggered from tin trunk to suitcase, neither knowing nor caring what I packed. Yadav looked in. 'Chalo,' he said. 'Before we leave village, we will like to see Boss Brother's best friend's new grandson.'

I liked Boss Brother's friend. He always wore an immaculate white kurta-pyjama and turban, and his colourless, plastic-rimmed spectacles gave him a comforting air of middle-class respectability. His mouth turned up in a friendly smile. But that day I did not feel like seeing anyone.

'Do we have to? I really feel very ill.'

'Yaar, is our duty. Is his first grandchild and he is friend of my Boss Brother. Chalo.' Hari Ram and Bubli loaded our luggage into the jeep. It was a beautiful day, neither too hot nor too cold, and the sun shone on the green shoots sprouting in the fields. Tiny striped chipmunks dashed across our path. When we slowed down at the level crossing, a pair of doves flew through the jeep and out the other side.

In Boss Brother's friend's village, I was stared at mercilessly.

'Must be different climate,' said one boy, seizing the chance to practise his English and give my skin closer scrutiny.

'Chalo,' Yadav called to me from outside the dark little room where the mother and baby lay, protected by a group of women squatting in the courtyard outside. It was unthinkable that any man should enter, least of all the father of the child. Lunch in honour of the birth was puri, subzi and laddu on a tin thali. Someone brought me a teaspoon.

12

Yadav's prudent principles made him disapprove of my buying new clothes for our marriage.

'Of course is important day. But why you do need new clothes? I do not understand. Okay, I see from your face that you must have. We will buy sari in Delhi, and for our night I would like to take you in hotel on bank of very beautiful lake. Is on right road to Rajasthan.'

Buying the first sari of my life, I spent hours walking up and down rows of exotic lengths of neatly folded fabrics, not sure what I was looking for. Yadav followed with great patience. 'Please remember, you cannot choose white; is for widows. Blue and blacks is also not suitable.'

From the government emporium we went to the khadi shop. The assistant sat on a platform unfolding sari after sari. I could not decide. 'Doesn't matter, yaar. The womens in all the world, they are famous to take long time for shopping.' At last I found one that I liked, a dark-pink silk with small yellow flowers. Yadav was ecstatic.

'But we haven't bought the necklace,' I said. 'I thought you said it was important.'

'Of course mangal sutra is important – without it we cannot have ceremony. Is like you have finger ring. We will buy in Jaipur. Now, chalo.'

The pink city of Jaipur was under a curfew, with police lurking at every corner. The shops were shuttered and barred. All of India was afraid. We had just learnt that the Babri Masjid, built, according to Hindu mythology, on the site of Lord

Rama's birthplace, had been destroyed by Hindu extremists. Two hundred people had already died in riots in Delhi. Unrest and fighting were expected everywhere.

The broad streets felt hollow and empty. A group of policemen, fidgeting with their revolvers, blocked the narrow entrance to the jewellery market. 'Curfew will be lifted at one o'clock,' one of them said.

'Bad luck. Is too late. We must arrive in Pushkar in time for auspicious marriage date. I wanted you choose mangal sutra from between many shops.'

We found one shop open, a bakery-cum-jeweller. The shopkeeper lifted a tray of necklaces from amongst packets of biscuits and dried fruits. He picked three and held them out to me.

'They are not valuable,' sighed Yadav. 'Please, you take one. At least they are right sort of beads.' I chose a double string of tiny black beads joined at every twelfth bead by a silver link. An oddly shaped medallion hung from it – a half-open lotus flower.

Pushkar teemed with Western tourists. Yadav grumbled as we walked the length of the main street to the only authentic Indian restaurant. 'They have foods only for the foreigners. Pancake, apple crumble, what is this rubbish?'

The following day, according to the village Brahmin, was the auspicious date for our marriage. I spent the morning at a beauty parlour learning how to wear a sari. When I told the beautician that Yadav and I were getting married, she gave me a disbelieving look.

'But you are very old.'

When she had finished tucking and pinning the silk into the tightly drawn waist string of my cotton petticoat, she stood back to admire her work. Yadav looked pleased.

'Indira Gandhi, she looks like,' said the girl. Was she emphasising my age, or paying me a compliment? Both, perhaps.

With Yadav carrying the sari, carefully folded into a plastic bag, we trudged skywards to Beni Gopal's hilltop temple. The climb would have been doubly difficult with the encumbrance of long clothes I was not used to wearing and gold chappals most unsuitable for mountaineering. We had no appointment and no idea whether the priest could or would marry us, or even whether he would be there. If he was and he could, I would dress in my sari on the spot.

'I feel too excited to see Mr Beni Gopal. I have been waiting for his help. Tonight, yaar, we will have our sweet honeymoon. And you, you do trust to him?' I nodded, too out of breath to speak.

We arrived at Beni Gopal's temple home hot, tired and full of expectations. There was nobody there. Yadav went in search of the priest and came back with his small daughter, who told us that her father was sleeping off a bad fever. Yadav, who had come to Pushkar and climbed the steep hill with marriage in mind, was not prepared to be fobbed off with a fever. 'Beti, you please go to wake your papa and tell him we are here.'

Beni Gopal's eyes were glazed and red-rimmed, his beard was straggly and his shrunken body was wrapped in crumpled saffron cloth and a brown shawl. Apologising for his condition, he sat down carefully on a piece of goatskin and told Yadav to unroll a small rug. In a deferential voice, Yadav explained why we were there. Beni Gopal sat in silence. When he spoke, his voice was grave.

'This is a serious matter. Have you thought through the difficulties? You have different nationalities, different religions, different everything. Do you want to change?' He looked at me. I explained that for many reasons, work, children and others, it was better that I stayed British and Christian.

'And your children, they are happy about this marriage?' We admitted that we had not told our children. 'You should. They will not mind if you give them love. Love is the important thing.

'For yourselves, if you love enough and you think you can make each other happy, you should marry. The chances of your meeting and deciding to live together must be millions to one against. Perhaps it is meant.'

Yadav was impatient to get on. 'We will like to come to your temple tomorrow to get married.' Beni Gopal reached for a book and flicked through its pages.

'This is not the right time. I can see two dates, one for each of you. I think for your religion,' he said, looking at me, 'twenty-fifth December is the birthday of your god. For you, according to Hindu thinking,' he said, looking at Yadav, 'the date should be twenty-eighth January. What is the date of your birth?'

'I do not know. Only what I have written myself in passport, and this is not proper day.' Yadav had had a passport for many years, just in case he was ever offered a job in the Middle East.

'It is not important,' said the Brahmin. 'Often we people in India do not know. For many years I thought that I was born on a date in nineteen thirty-six. Not long ago, I discovered it was nineteen thirty-eight and on quite a different date. Immediately I gained two years.'

'It would be so nice if you will marry us. But we cannot know where we will be on those days. We can hope.' Yadav knelt down before the priest and touched his foot. I moved to do the same.

'No, no. Not you,' he drew his feet beneath his robe.

'Are you disappointed?' I asked Yadav as we left. I could not help being thankful that I would not have to climb the hill in a sari.

'No. He has given blessing and he tell me in Hindi, "Get marry in any temple." In front of figure of my god, in presence of five peoples, I must have to put garland on you and you on me. That is all. So we will marry on your day, twenty-fifth December.'

'It's very kind of you to suggest it, and of course it's a special day. But not for weddings. Everyone's too busy celebrating the birth of Christ.'

'I see. You mean your prophet have his birthday? Very good, we will choose twenty-eighth January. According to Hindu religion, twenty-fifth December is not auspicious day. And thank you very much you choose my day.'

Our mission semi-accomplished, there was no reason to stay in Pushkar.

'We will have one night at Sariska before we reach to farm. Is big park with tigers. You will enjoy to it too much.'

I dreamt my way through the hot Rajasthan afternoon – dreams of flower garlands and Yadav and marriage and dairy farms full of buffaloes...

'SARISKA! Where were you? Did you fly to the London?' asked Yadav.

The *Times of India* lay on the reception desk. The news was better now; few disturbances had been reported in the last twenty-four hours. But the official death roll had reached 1,500. In London, John Major announced the official separation of Prince Charles and Princess Diana.

The receptionist's jungle report was encouraging in one way, dire in another. 'Twenty-two tigers living in jungle, perhaps today you see one. Last week, blind deaf boy, he has habit to walk alone in jungle. Warden, he find pug marks and boy's jaw bones. Now we are afraid of man-eater.'

Yadav raced the jeep through the forest, upsetting a group of serious tiger-spotting Westerners. They glared at us from behind expensive binoculars. 'Unluckily, no tigers. To see one would be so nice!' Yadav shouted above the noise of our roaring engine. But his mind was on other things. From the thickly wooded jungle, we came to a temple in a clearing.

'Now I would like we see real Hanuman temple,' Yadav said. 'When Hanuman was alive, many thousands of years before, he lay down here and changed himself into monkey. He wanted to prove to Bhim, who is very strong hero of *Mahabharat*, that he, Hanuman, is even stronger. Bhim was very proud man, he did many things to show his strength. He made lake in ground so his mother could drink. Here, in this place, you will see where he cut whole mountain in half only with one hand. But Hanuman show him there are some things he cannot do. "Please, you move only my tail," he said. Bhim, he try and try to shift tail, but he cannot, not a single inch. Temple is called Pandupol, temple of Bhim and his four brothers, sons of Pandav.'

We offered sweets, and the Brahmin gave us a garland for the jeep. Outside, the temple monkeys pounced on the remaining laddu. Behind the building, stone steps led up a steep ravine.

'And now, my very sweet darling, we will climb to see how Bhim split mountain.' Yadav started up the steps. My legs were still aching and stiff from my illness and from the climb up Pushkar's mountain. I followed him, pulling myself up with the help of an iron handrail. At the top we had to walk across a narrow ledge of rock, a natural bridge crossing Bhim's great cleft in the hill, hundreds of feet deep. I kept my eyes on Yadav's back; to look down would be fatal.

An old blanket, fixed across a cave formation in the rocks, blocked our way. We pushed past it. A naked sadhu sat on the bare ledge beside a pile of smouldering logs. Seeing me, he half covered himself with a ragged cloth and looked at us incuriously with eyes as deep and fathomless as wells, in a face as empty as an unpatterned plate. An economic covering of satin-smooth skin barely stretched across his bones. He patted the rock, inviting us to sit, and listened to Yadav's eager questions, answering each one briefly in Hindi. Yadav translated for me. He had lived on the rock for six or seven years, he estimated. He kept the fire going to discourage tigers and other beasts. For recreation, he sang songs. Sometimes he descended to visit the market, but more often, people brought him his scant provisions.

'I am sure he see his god, so I ask him how farmers like me, they can see to the god. He answer that God is everywhere for everyone, only we must look. This is true. Chalo!' We left him perched, like his companions the roosting pigeons, singing along to their gentle cooing. It was actually from a song I knew – 'Daisy, Daisy, give me your answer, do.'

The great bonfire hissed and spat. Heat and shadows shimmered and danced across the courtyard of Sariska Palace, once a maharaja's hunting lodge.

We dined with the tiger-spotting group Yadav had upset with our noisy jeep in the park. Luckily they did not recognise us. The London stock market was collapsing, the price of Chelsea property was rising, and wasn't Waitrose loo paper much better value than Safeway's?

'Have you enjoyed India?' I asked a woman from Esher, in Surrey.

'Oh yes, but I'll be glad to get home to Ember Lane. You know where you are there, don't you?'

'Yes,' I said, thinking of the sadhu on the ledge and wondering if his fire was as warm as ours. 'Yes, you do.'

'Anyone for a morning bird watch? Six o'clock start?' asked the enthusiastic guide.

Unanimously they declined. India was safely behind them; Esher beckoned.

13

I finished rinsing our clothes, hung them in the inner courtyard and emptied the last bucket of water. Hanuman came over to the well, waving a pair of Yadav's dirty kurta-pyjamas.

'Tomorrow,' I said.

'Today. Uncle wants them today. Is your duty.' He pushed the clothes into my lap.

'Fuck Uncle,' I said under my breath. Snatching the kurta from him, I refilled the bucket and sat down again on the wet stone. He stood smirking down at me while I scrubbed.

Later, as I lay reading on my charpoy, Yadav came in with the underclothes I had just hung on the line.

'Shanti, she say they is dry,' he said.

'They're not. They're still wringing wet.' But I knew he had brought them in because I had hung them in a public place. 'Why does anyone mind? We all have to wear underclothes.'

'This is village. We cannot,' he said.

'What, wear underclothes?' I snapped. Yadav took me seriously.

'Yaar, how can I know about the womens? I don't think so they do. Hang outside, this they absolutely doesn't.'

Darkness came and the electricity failed. The boys lit the new gas lamp I had bought and put it on the window sill to light the veranda where Chaudhri Sahib, Puja's father-in-law, and Boss Brother reclined on charpoys, smoking the hookah and waiting for their dinner. Cooking only by the light of the mustard-stalk fire, we burned the onions and had to pick out each little charred bit to make the dish edible.

I went to our room to write a letter, moving the light so I could see the page. Rama rushed in.

'Please leave chimney in window. My father and my uncle will not see to eat their food.' He picked up the lamp and put it back on the window sill.

After dinner, I climbed disconsolately on to my charpoy. Ashok, Yadav's son, was sharing our room. A plague of wasps kept us awake. The more Yadav swatted them with a dusty exercise book, the more they buzzed. Some committed voluntary suicide, battering themselves to death against the wooden shutters in frantic fury, while others whirred round and round in an endless, futile dance. I pulled the covers over my head, but then it was too hot... Across the yard, Ma wailed loudly. I reached across to Yadav's cot and shook him awake.

'I think your mother's ill,' I said. We found her rocking backwards and forwards on her cot, holding her stomach as she retched and vomited. Yadav banged on the door of the inner courtyard, yelling for Shanti. She came out, rubbing the sleep from her eyes, and handed him a bright-green pill. Yadav tried to feed it to Ma, but she knocked it from his hand. It fell to the ground and was lost in the sand. I stroked her hair. She pushed me away.

'She does not take medicine. She will not help herself or us. All family members, they prays she will die quickly. She is too old and too bad-tempered. If you understand what she say, you could not stay at farm with her. She tell all village we give her no food. Now she even has pain. Is too much.'

We left Shanti to minister to Ma and walked back to our room. The wasps were quiet. We slept.

Later in the night, going out to pee, I hit my foot against a tethering stake. The next morning it was too painful to stand on. Rama made a poultice of hot cane sugar and wheat and strapped it on with an old rag. 'Complete cure,' he said. It was not. The swelling and the pain got worse.

Yadav had an appointment with Dr Prakash in Delhi. At the little hospital where he had his consulting room, they X-rayed my foot, wrapped it in plaster up to the knee and told me to come back in a month. I left the hospital in a wheelchair, immobile. It took some time to convince Yadav that I could not manage the rigours of farm plumbing with only one leg. When at last he saw that I was serious, he agreed that we should stay at the tourist bungalow in the district capital until the plaster was taken off.

Our room was not beautiful, but it did have a bathroom, somewhere to put clothes and electricity most nights. It was luxury to be able to read, write and see after sundown. I cleaned the room, put a spray of bougainvillea in a mug and arranged some books on the dressing table.

For Diwali, however, our presence at the farm was imperative.

It was late afternoon when we arrived. The small figures of Anu, Vini, Chenamunia and Raja Singh's son came running towards the jeep. Bubli, now twelve years old but wishing he was still a child, brought up the rear. They rummaged through the parcels of sweets, fireworks and bananas we had brought, twittering like excited little birds.

My plastered leg was a novelty. I was seated on a chair in the middle of the inner yard and given a cup of coffee. Ma gesticulated wildly, moaning and berating the elements. 'She say you must cut off plaster. You do not need it,' said Yadav.

Hari Ram was busy up a ladder, fixing swags of fairy lights on buildings and branches. As soon as it was dark the children began to light sparklers, dazzling us with a million falling stars. Bubli went from room to room lighting tapers in tiny saucers of ghee, as Lakshmi would not enter in the dark. The light of the main altar, on a corner of the kitchen floor, was kept alive all night.

'Come. We will pray the god for peace,' Yadav said. He knelt down before the flickering flame. 'Shanti, shanti, shanti.' I hopped back to my seat, leaning heavily on my crutches.

'You must stay at farm tonight. It is custom. I beg you,' Ramesh said.

'Please, Yadav, tell him I can't. I do need to stay at the tourist bungalow for the moment.'

'It is up to you. I cannot decide for you,' Yadav said. He walked away.

I spent the night in furious misery, sitting on a charpoy while Yadav snored beside me. At two o'clock I woke him to help me into the fields. Why hadn't he built the loo closer to the buildings, and why hadn't he made it work? I felt defeated by the farm, by Yadav's family, by India itself. I decided to go back to London on the next plane. Having been born one of its seven million citizens, I supposed I must belong there. Hell, I must belong somewhere.

The farm came to life when the sun was already high in the sky. Stiff and unwashed, I levered myself off the charpoy. My foot had stopped throbbing. Thoughts of flights to London faded back into the unreality of night. Today was a new day, bringing with it what it would. Since I had come to India I had learnt to open the book of life at a blank page, to be filled in as the day progressed. Anything could happen at any time.

If I had known what this day would bring, I might never have got up. I might have delayed our departure; I might have hastened it. But we had no crystal ball. How could I have foreseen that by evening, I would have learnt an entirely new kind of fear and mistrust?

In the afternoon we left the farm to drive the twenty-five kilometres back to town. Rama and Hari Ram came with us. Ma stood by the jeep, weeping. She didn't want me to go back to the tourist bungalow. We laughed and joked as we drove through the tall grasses and fast-growing crops.

On the far side of the level crossing, the boys got out. A couple of men flagged us down. 'They are my friends, yaar. We will give them lift,' Yadav said. They climbed into the back. Five minutes later, they demanded a stop to pee. Yadav pulled over to the side of the narrow road and told them to hurry.

We turned in our seats, watching the men disappear over the edge of the grass verge and down the bank beside us. A busload of people, topped by three or four sitting on the roof, was some distance behind us, coming up fast. As it approached, rather than slow down, it gathered speed, swerved on to the verge, accelerated and began to pass our stationary jeep on the wrong side. The driver lost control. The bus lurched, turned on its side, rolled over and came to a standstill at the bottom of the bank, wheels up. Yadav's friends, wary of trouble, did not reappear. Yadav started the engine.

'Yadav, we ought to stay and help. We might be needed as witnesses.' He turned off the engine and sat waiting.

The bus had been carrying a private wedding party. People were screaming and shouting and clambering up the bank. I reached for my crutches and started to get out.

'Stay in the jeep,' Yadav barked. A curious crowd was pressing round us.

A boy of about twenty-five had been riding on the roof. His friends jumped clear, but as the bus rolled over it had caught him by the hips and pinned him to the ground. Four young men dragged him up the bank by his arms, his legs dangling from his body like a rag doll's. They manhandled him on to the back seat of the jeep. His face was streaked with blood and vomit, and he groaned and cried terribly. The others crowded in with him. We revved the engine to part the crowd and drove back the way we had come, stopping at the first village doctor's shop we came to. The boy was dragged out, only to be bundled back into the jeep a minute later as the village doctor could not handle such a case. We drove once more towards the town, which had a hospital.

At the scene of the accident, the road was now blocked by an ugly crowd of threatening men. I asked Yadav what they wanted.

'They want to kill me,' he said simply. 'They are going to put all blame on us.'

A human barricade barred our way. The boy, once again screaming and crying, was dragged from the jeep and hauled into a waiting van. The crowd parted for the van to drive away and then quickly re-formed around us, the men shouting, pointing and raising their fists. I was pushed back in my seat. Someone leant across me, took the key from the ignition and threw it far into the scrub. Hands tugged at Yadav, pulling him from the drivers' seat. Faces leered at us, hungry for violence. I tried to hold on to Yadav, scratching, pinching and biting the nearest arms and hands that tore at his clothes and face. A sharp slap stung my face, and a brutal wrench sent a stabbing pain down my arm. My hold loosened.

'Let me go,' Yadav gasped to me. 'You can do nothing. They will kill me. Let them. If you try to interfere, they will hurt you more.' With a vicious jerk they ripped his kurta from my grasp; I was left with a scrap of cloth in my hand. Yadav was manhandled out of the jeep and thrown to the ground, where the men began beating and kicking him.

I moved into the driver's seat. My head did not know what my body was doing or vice versa. My knuckles turned white from gripping the steering wheel. Perhaps my instinct was to stay in control, but I was helpless against so many thugs. I sat slouched over the wheel with the bleak certainty that I would never again see Yadav alive.

He was back. I don't know whether it was minutes or hours later; time had taken on a different dimension. He was sitting beside me, battered and bleeding but alive. His voice came in a breathless croak. Two of the men had tried to strangle him.

'I pretend I am dead, yaar. Others, they gets frightened. "Leave it," they say. So I am here.' He fingered his bruised throat.

The hostile crowd still pressed round the jeep, hemming us in and blotting out the daylight. Operations were directed by a fox-faced man wearing a dhoti and white turban, with pale-pink plastic-framed spectacles balanced on his bony nose. He leant across me, pressing so close that I could feel his bones and smell his hookah-scented sweat. He pushed the gear lever into neutral. I tried to turn the steering wheel, but he grabbed it from me and, far from parking neatly out of the way of oncoming traffic, he and his friends pushed us broadside across the road, our bonnet facing the overturned bus. With a threatening gesture, and a backup of fifty men, he ordered us to get out.

A photographer arrived. Suddenly I realised what was happening: they were creating false evidence against us. I hopped round until I was in front of the jeep. If they were going to take photographs of it, they would have to take me, too. 'It's not true! It's not true!' I shouted. They pushed me to one side, and my crutches fell to the ground. I was powerless. They took their photographs.

The police arrived. Flourishing lathis, they dispersed the crowd. 'Now everything will be all right,' I thought with relief. The policeman with the shiniest belt and the most stripes on his shoulders began questioning the crowd. An officer of lower rank stood beside Yadav. I was ignored.

'They're arresting me,' Yadav said. I hopped over to the officer carrying out the inquiry, convinced that he would put things right and release Yadav as soon as he understood what had really happened.

'What are these people saying?' I asked him.

'They are telling me how and why this man caused the accident,' he said, uninterested in my version.

On the way to the police station, Yadav told me some of the stories the police had written down as evidence against him. 'Some said we were parked across middle of road and a camel cart was coming in the opposite direction. Some said we were drunk and were trying to pass the bus. And some said we were sitting in middle of the road kissing and hugging to each other.'

'And why did the police believe such rubbish?'

He shrugged.

It was dark when we reached the police station. Yadav was kept inside for a long time. A policeman placed a wooden chair in the yard outside the door and gestured to me to sit. Voices and the glare from a naked light bulb were my only clues to the goings-on inside. Some time later, Yadav was pushed out.

'They will lock me here for this night,' he said. 'Boy, he has died in the hospital. Is very bad.'

The chief officer swaggered out after him. He had changed into mufti, a pair of fawn-coloured trousers and a checked shirt. Buttons strained over the beginnings of a paunch. The sight of him filled me with impotent fury. I asked him why he believed the stupid stories of the thugs who had beaten Yadav, and why he had not asked me a single question.

'Madam, I am carrying out my duty.' A supercilious smirk parted his fleshy lips. 'All people say he is guilty. What can I do?'

'But they're all lying. Anyway they're all telling different stories. How can what they say be true?' My voice rose in despair at the hopelessness of our situation. Was there no one to help? No one to tell the truth? No one to believe us?

'I cannot help you.' He shrugged his heavy shoulders.

Yadav was locked in a cage, and I was driven thirty kilometres back to the farm by a man who did not know the way. Somehow, on anonymous farm tracks, crossing identical fields in pitch-darkness, we arrived.

I was trembling. My teeth chattered. Shanti brought food and I swallowed it automatically. Many hands helped me on to my charpoy, piled heavy quilts on top of me and left me to sleep. I lay, half suffocated but ice-cold, sobbing great, shuddering sobs. Ma came and stood beside me, leaning on her stick. She stared down at me, patting my head, weeping and muttering.

I sat up. Had I gone to sleep at last? Was I dreaming? No – Yadav had walked into the room with an old man, the father of a niece-in-law. He had spoken. He had touched me. He was real.

The old man had bicycled ten kilometres to the prison to bribe the police with seven hundred rupees. Yadav was told to return to the police station in the morning. 'I did have to come back to you. I know if I do not, you will cry all the night.'

Yadav had to be at the police station at six a.m. I went later with Hanuman and Rama. Boss Brother, the sarpanch (one of Yadav's best friends) and a few other villagers were already there. We waited around for a long time. The unpleasant chief of the station had become very solicitous, and instructed Hanuman to take me into a small private yard. Left alone, I opened my book – I always carry one, as reading keeps me calm in difficult situations – but was almost immediately disturbed by the chief police officer, who exhorted me to admire the view of the hills behind the temple. He was on his way there for his daily puja.

He was back in a few minutes. 'I like you,' he began condescendingly. 'I would be most happy to have dinner and drink. I am sure you like drink. You are Western and Western women, they drink. Please name your day, the time and the place.' I hated his arrogance, but Yadav had told me to be polite to him. I said Yadav and I would be delighted, especially if it meant going to his home to meet his wife and family.

Hanuman looked into the courtyard. 'Uncle said you might need me. We will leave soon.' At my suggestion of a foursome, the policeman's ardour cooled. He had no more to say.

We stopped to offer our condolences at the hospital where the boy had died. A group of villagers hung about outside, and I recognised the man with the spectacles. Yesterday afternoon's horrors had become part of our lives.

Outside the magistrate's court, we waited for another long time with the sarpanch, Yadav's two elder brothers and Jagdish, a young lawyer whom Yadav addressed as his grandson. Jagdish assured us that the penalties would not be too heavy. 'Only six months in prison or a fine. Of course, the case will take five or six years.' His voice was matter-of-fact.

'Only? Five or six years?' I tried to tell him that the evidence was all false.

He smiled. 'This is India.'

At last it was Yadav's turn. Handcuffed to a policeman, he was led into the court like a dog on a chain. The magistrate charged him with dangerous driving leading to death, and released him on bail. The bus driver, who had run away, had been found and was being charged for the same crimes. It was small consolation.

Through the village network, we heard that the police station would drop the charges against Yadav in return for five thousand rupees. Jagdish said it would be a good idea, but Yadav did not agree. 'They can quite easily take money and leave me with challan. We cannot have guarantee. No.'

Two days later we returned to the police station to collect the jeep. Since we now had no key, Yadav started it with a piece of wire. The police had drained the diesel tank dry, so we were forced to buy a can from them just to reach the nearest garage.

On Sunday we drove round the village with the sarpanch, trying to collect witnesses. Yadav's two friends (but for whose need to pee we would not have been in trouble) refused to help us, afraid of losing their teaching jobs. We drove to the neighbouring village at the base of the hills, which I had often looked at and wondered about from my 'washing seat' at the well. Some of these villagers had been in the ill-fated wedding party. They stared at me and offered us chai, but they were too frightened of the consequences to be witnesses.

'Now we will go to see man who arranged for men of his village to fight with me,' said Yadav. There were the pink spectacles again, perched on that predatory nose. The memory was fresh enough to give me feelings of revulsion, causing a white-hot fire to burn within me. The man advanced on the jeep, inviting me to sit with him and the others on the ground outside his house. I stared into his eyes, hoping to burn him alive with my eyeballs. My body was as stiff as a rod, but inside I trembled like jelly. I turned my back on him.

When I asked Yadav why he sat with such a loathsome creature, he said that the man was now willing to help us. I did not believe it, and would not have wanted his help even if it were true.

At Boss Brother's request, Spectacles took us to the farm of the dead boy. A group of women sat on the ground, their veiled heads bowed, keening quietly. We sat with the men in silent sympathy.

There were so many plots and counter-plots. Sometimes it seemed that the police would drop the case; sometimes we found witnesses willing to swear that they had seen what had happened. We visited endless farms and drank countless cups of chai. I sent letters explaining events as they had really happened to the *Times of India*, the superintendent of police, the head of the Haryana police force, our local member of Parliament and the British High Commission. The only answer came from the High Commission, who sympathised but could not help. We simply had to live with the situation; Yadav would have to appear twice yearly at the local magistrate's court for the foreseeable future. We would live in the hope that he would not eventually go to prison.

My leg felt heavier and more uncomfortable every day, as if all the sand in Haryana had collected under the plaster. One evening I could bear it no longer. I went to a doctor across the road from the tourist bungalow and he and his assistant, equipped with two rusty saws, freed my leg of the impeding plaster. There was no longer any reason to stay in a hotel; Yadav and I packed up and moved back to the farm.

14

It was already the week before Christmas, too late to plan anything. We decided to stay at the farm and drive to Delhi on Christmas Eve for midnight Mass at the cathedral.

'But I must buy you Christmas present of gold earrings. Every bride in India, she must have earrings.' I said I would rather have a ring. 'I know, is custom in your country. We will buy both.'

Yadav's family jeweller lived in the next village. The old man greeted Yadav affectionately and led us into a room where his son sat cross-legged on the floor with a blow lamp in one hand and an anklet in the other. A child brought a piece of sacking for us to sit on. The jeweller blew out the lamp, put the anklet away and, at Yadav's request, showed us samples of the earrings he could make. There were studs, hoops and sheets of paper covered with designs for customised rings and necklaces. I chose medium-sized silver hoops, thinking this would keep the price down. Yadav said nothing.

The old man's wife brought glasses of chai. To her incredulity, I refused. Yadav elaborated on my dislikes. 'She doesn't drink milk or even take ghee.' Between appreciative sips of chai, they looked at me in amazement. I studied the dog-eared pages of samples and asked Yadav how much we would need to spend.

'Earrings will not be too expensive. Now, please choose a ring.' The jeweller tipped a box of rings on to the floor. They were all silver, painted with peacocks in bright enamel colours. They were not wedding rings. I drew a diagram of a wide band with plain borders and a middle band of flowers and explained that it should be made of gold. The jeweller understood. He took a metal strip and softened it with the blow lamp. 'Please show him width,' Yadav said. After more firing, hammering and banging we decided on the width, with the help of a special measuring stick.

Eventually, when we had been with the jeweller for over an hour, Yadav had had enough. Halfway down the street he turned and shouted something back to the jeweller. 'I tell him if he has not made jewellery by Monday, we will not buy. I have cancel silver earrings and order plain gold ones in small size. As I have said, I do not like silver. It will not be pretty for you.'

I did not bother to explain that gold meant little to me. I would not care if the earrings were made of tin, as long as they looked original. But all village wives wore gold, even if buying it beggared the family. Customs were customs.

The next day we agreed to give Hanuman a lift to his 'engineering college', where the teaching equipment consisted of a few broken bits of old cars and tractors. Hanuman showed us around with great pride, insisting that we take photographs of every boy and every stick and stone. He was taking me back to the jeep when a small man in a tweed suit stopped us.

'What are you doing here, Madam?' he demanded. 'I am director of this college. I have watched you taking the liberty of walking around our institution and taking photographs. Who has given you permission for this intrusion, may I ask? You should know better.' I explained that I was Hanuman's aunt, and apologised profusely. He was not placated.

In the evening Yadav, Shanti, Chenamunia and I went to hear the village women sing in the temple. Having settled us into our places, Yadav disappeared, probably in search of a friend with a bottle of whisky. Dressed in the sari he had insisted I wear, I sat with Chenamunia asleep on my knee while Shanti gossiped with her friends. The singing rose and fell.

The women smiled at me and felt the fabric of my sari. 'Bahut mahenga,' they said, shaking their heads and inviting me to feel their synthetic materials. They touched the bangles Yadav liked me to wear on my wrists. 'Sona?' they asked. I shook my head. They looked shocked, and fingered my fish-shaped mother-of-pearl earrings. 'Fashion,' I said. They sighed despairingly.

Back at the farm at last, we found Hanuman and a college friend asleep in our cots. Yadav shook them roughly and ordered them out. In December, the cold set in after sundown. I was afraid they would freeze to death on the veranda, but the next morning they came to wake us up.

'Madam Jill, I heard from Hanuman about the headmaster. He is very stupid, very rude man. If I had been there, I would have told him to shut up. He only wanted to show how great he was.'

Hanuman's friend's English was good. Although he had slept in his clothes like everyone else on the farm, his blue-and-white striped shirt looked clean and fresh, his hair was brushed and his small moustache was neatly clipped. He bounced into the room in new white trainers.

'I am in the Indian Navy,' he told me. 'I was sent on this course by my ship. But it is no good. It is government school, therefore we learn nothing. The teachers know that they can never lose their jobs, so they do not bother to teach.'

'This is for you,' he continued, holding out a white envelope. 'I know about your special twenty-fifth December. We also celebrate it in the Navy.' It was a Christmas card, inscribed: *'To wish you joy and happiness, dear Aunty. With love, Hanuman.'* I thanked Hanuman and his friend for their kindness. They beamed and asked me to take their photograph.

Then the impossible happened. The grandchildren of Brahmin Aunt, whose son was the village postmaster, ran across the fields with a telegram for us: 'YOU HAVE THREE CLIENTS FOR YOUR 40 DAY SAFARI. PLEASE PHONE.'

We really were in business. I could not quite believe it. We packed our things once again and left for Delhi, calling at the jeweller's village on the way. My ring was, and is, beautiful. The earrings were never a great success, as the posts were thick and painful. The jeweller suggested I enlarge the holes in my ears by sticking peacock quills through them at night. Eventually I lost one earring in the sea, and Yadav took the other back to the jeweller and sold it for its weight in gold.

'Yaar, in town is best chai stall. You will not mind if I stop?' He knew I would mind. As soon as he left me in the jeep, gawping youths surrounded me with intrusive staring eyes. He ordered his clay cup of chai, and while he stood drinking it, chatting with the chai-wallah, all the town's youth began to muster. My temper rose. I got out, took one of the boys by the shoulders and turned him round slowly, scrutinising every part of his anatomy and finally looking straight into his eyes.

'Now you can see what it's like!' I shouted. There was no response. They only stared. Yadav threw away his cup and pushed through the crowd.

'Chalo!' he shouted in an authoratitive voice. They melted away. 'You shouldn't have to do that. I don't mind them, why should you?' he remonstrated.

'You don't mind them because they don't stare at you. How can you know what it's like?'

'Now, yaar, I have found five customers to go Delhi. Is very good. Jeep will not bump, and they will pay our diesel. I hope you will not mind to drive. I have bad headache and I am not well.'

On the verge of tears, I climbed into the driving seat and drove, poker-backed, through the thick traffic of the National Highway while Yadav chatted with his five passengers, packed tightly behind me.

When we arrived in Delhi, I telephoned my friend who had found us our clients. They were a British couple with a grown-up daughter, and they wanted to start their safari on 27 January. 'Now,' said my friend, 'send the names of the hotels and prices as soon as possible, and do stop gasping and get on with it.'

I hung up and hugged Yadav. 'Now we must buy a typewriter. Typed letters will look more professional, and we do need a travel agent to help us with hotel bookings.'

Yadav looked as pleased as I felt. 'Yaar, first we will go to travel agent. I knows them all very well. I have worked many years for many travel agents.'

Mr R.K. Das sat dwarfed behind a giant double desk in the office of 'Happy Travelling Days'. In spite of being small, squat and middle-aged, with receding grey hair, a pudgy nose and a pot belly, Mr Das was king of the company. Nobody argued with him.

Recognising Yadav as a driver he had once or twice employed, he wasted neither time nor manners on him, focusing his charm and his gold-toothed smile on me. He assured me that he would be delighted to help with our forthcoming tour, and with any others we might conduct in the future. He then stroked his stomach and winked at me. 'We Bengalis enjoy our food. It will be my great pleasure if you, and – er – Mr Yadav will dine at my house tomorrow.' He beamed, unzipping his homespun grey woollen cardigan to reveal a clean shirt and a knitted Argyle tartan waistcoat.

Mr and Mrs Das and their sons lived on the outskirts of one of south Delhi's smarter colonies. Mr Das welcomed us in a none-too-clean kurta that fell comfortably over his paunch. With reverence, he produced a bottle of Johnnie Walker Black Label and offered me a glass, filling another tumbler for himself.

'Only for those who appreciate it,' he said, giving me a golden grin and pouring Yadav a glass of Indian rum. 'You see, Jill,' he downed his drink and refilled the glass, 'I can understand real quality when I taste it. Perhaps you could ask your clients to bring a bottle? I'll reimburse them, of course.'

His wife came in from a political meeting. She changed into a pair of bedroom slippers, bowed to me and started to hum to herself.

'She doesn't speak English, and she's not so interested in cooking. That is why I have myself prepared tonight's feast,' her husband said. 'I also concern myself with dusting and all household chores. Each morning I rise at five a.m. in order to complete my tasks and do my puja before going to the office. Idleness, you know, is bad for the spirit.' He disappeared into the kitchen.

Mrs Das forced the gladioli I had brought into a small vase behind a large statue of Ganesh. The Dases' son came in from a day at university, went straight to the stereo and put on a loud American pop song. His father hurried back in from the kitchen and turned it off.

From then on, Mr Das helped us with our tours, and his suggestions for good hotels in places that I did not know were almost infallible. But his services were not free. Not only did his son ask me for a baseball cap, but Mr Das himself wrote to me in London. It was a short letter with a long list attached.

Dear Jill
Please bring –
One hundred Dunhill cigarettes.
One dozen refillable lighters.

One dozen packets Willkinsons sword edged razor blades.
Two and a half litres Johnnie Walker Black Label whisky.
One bottle ladies French scent, best quality.
One ladies gold coloured watch.
One tune playing wall clock.
Jovan Sex Appeal after shave lotion.
I will of course reimburse for all items.
Your most cordially
R.K. Das

'You shouldn't have to do it,' Yadav said when he saw the list. 'He already ask me for black partridges and mustard oil and wheats while you was away.' But Mr Das was always at the end of the telephone, ready to help in an emergency. Without him and his agency, we would never have managed. And when we returned to Delhi on 26 January to meet our tourists, we were greeted with a large envelope containing hotel vouchers for forty nights.

We went in search of a typewriter and found a small second-hand Olivetti in a typewriter market in Old Delhi. We found a good map of India in a map shop tucked away on the second floor in an alley off Janpath.

We dined in a restaurant decorated with Christmas trees, tinsel and baubles, surrounded by well-to-do Delhiites who, after eating, would bop the night away at discos in five-star hotels. The smart set turned every festival of whatever religion or creed into a fine excuse for a party.

'Will you come and see the crib at my cathedral?'

Yadav nodded. 'All gods is one god,' he said.

Outside the cathedral, the traffic police waved their batons as if conducting the Philharmonic. Crowds milled backwards and forwards. Huge bunches of balloons floated on high. Beggar children ran between legs, tugged at skirts and pulled on trousers while their maimed and disfigured elders crouched in every corner and cranny.

'Happy Christmas,' I said to a man standing at the church door.

'Yaar, you are very stupid. How can he know what you say? He is Muslim.'

The crib had a brand-new straw roof and brightly painted figures. I explained the Virgin birth and St Joseph and how they had had to use a simple stable because there was no room for them at the inn. Yadav looked bored until the cow caught his eye.

'See, you have our mother cow. And all peoples they pray her.' He fell to his knees beside a south Indian mother and child, dressed in their frilly best. 'Why you must pray her and then you eat her? Is too bad.'

The church was full. The congregation settled down for the long midnight service. 'I will wait for you in jeep. Please you enjoy till worship is finished. It will be my great happiness and please you have your happy Christmas.'

Later I found him hunched up in the jeep, half asleep. 'Happy Christmas, darling,' he said, smiling. Yadav had a wonderful capacity to share other people's happiness, even when it had nothing to do with his own.

'Thanks. Happy Christmas to you, too,' I said, and I kissed him.

The next day, while Yadav went to the doctor, I telephoned my children to wish them a happy Christmas. My youngest daughter was staying with friends in Normandy. I had spent Christmas with them two years ago, and hearing their voices I suddenly missed them all terribly. I remembered champagne after midnight Mass in a tiny village church, the cold walk in country lanes after too much Christmas lunch, games of *Trivial Pursuit*, crumpets and Christmas cake in front of a roaring log fire. I sighed down the telephone.

'What did you say?'

'Nothing.'

'Right, then! Mary Jane's in the bath; I'll tell her you rang. Happy Christmas!'

'Same to all of you. Give her my love,' I said, wondering why she was in the bath at lunchtime. Then I remembered the time difference.

I rang my ninety-five-year-old aunt in Chelsea. 'Happy Christmas, Aunt Honor!' I yelled. Aunt Honor was deaf.

'Who's that? I can't speak, you know. I've lost my voice. My ridiculous doctor won't do anything about it. I shall change him. Who did you say you were?'

'Jill,' I shouted. The telephone bleeped twice and cut me off.

Before leaving Delhi, we stopped to buy a bright-red tricycle for Chenamunia, socks for the older nephews and plastic bats and balls for Vini, Anu and Raja Singh's small sons. At a sweet shop we bought boxes of barfi, laddu, gazar halwa and balloons for everyone at the farm. 'Bas,' said Yadav.

'Don't forget we're going to buy potato crisps and namkin. Do you think they'd like Coca-Cola?'

'Certainly not. We will buy namkin. That is all.' Afraid of doing the wrong thing, I said no more.

'Very costly,' said Ramesh disapprovingly when we dropped into the factory to show him our purchases. 'What is this Christmas?' I tried to explain.

'Mrs Jill, then can you tell me why you buy these presents? Is not our Hindu festival. Childrens, they do not understand. Better we spend money on seeds for buffalo. And Chenamunia, she needs new pants.' I felt deflated. 'Now, please, you and Mr Yadav come with me. My friends, they are waiting to meet you.'

Hari Ram and Bubli unloaded our parcels and waited expectantly. We gave the bats and balls to the children, and pleased expressions appeared on their faces. Without a word they hurried away to their huts to hide their toys, like squirrels with their winter nuts.

The boys took their socks in silence. Perhaps they were disappointed. 'No, yaar. They doesn't know to say thank you. That is all.'

Chenamunia's tricycle was the greatest success. Bubli and Vini pushed her round the yard, faster and faster with every turn, until she fell off. Without a tear, she picked herself up and sat hastily back on the saddle, determined to allow no one the chance to usurp her throne.

'Shall we have the food now?' I asked.

'Yes, and then all will be finished.'

Meenakshi laid a sack on the ground. We spread out the snacks. The others stood round, waiting for their rations and disappearing to eat them in private, afraid of thieving hands.

Christmas was over, and a few days later the year came to an end. In our restaurant in Connaught Place, the lights went out. Yadav kissed me. It was New Year's Day.

Ma had disappeared. Hari Ram cycled off to look for her and found her walking along the path, already halfway to the village. Her entire wardrobe was balanced on her head, and her savings were screwed up in a cotton handkerchief. She was chatting with a farmer friend, telling him how her family was trying to steal her things and, worse, doing their best to poison her. She refused Hari Ram's offer to escort her home.

'Chalo, yaar,' said Yadav. 'We must have to take jeep to fetch her. I think she will go to house of my Brahmin aunt.' We took Bubli with us. Though just twelve, he was the only one who could deal with his grandmother. We found Ma resting on a cot in Brahmin Aunt's courtyard, singing a bhajan.

Without demur, she allowed herself to be pushed into the jeep.

Brahmin Aunt's son gave me a typed envelope postmarked from France. It was from my brother: he wanted to join our tour in Goa and travel through south India with us. I was delighted, but apprehensive. For a variety of reasons, it was now more than twenty years since we had spent any time together. I wrote to R.K. Das asking him to book an extra room from Goa onwards in the cheaper hotels, along with Yadav and myself.

Yadav was overjoyed. 'Now I have first chance to meet with my dear family member,' he said happily.

15

We had decided to be married on Yadav's auspicious day, the day after our tourists arrived in Delhi. Dinesh had agreed to be a witness, together with our clients if they were willing.

'That makes four. We will ask waiter to be fifth,' said Yadav. 'It will be special surprise for tourists. Extra thing they did not expect. They can enjoy with us.' I had no idea what they were like, of course, but thought they might be amused to help.

I was suffering from the worst cold sores I had ever had. My lips looked like bloated bubble gum. I felt hideous, seedy and sorry for myself and suddenly had no enthusiasm either for our wedding or for the tour.

'When this tour's over, it will be almost time for me to go to England,' I said. 'Tonight's our last night as proper private people rather than public tour guides. And this morning we ate our last bazra roti at the farm.'

'Don't be silly, yaar. We will have our nice time with tourists. And tomorrow we will have our marriage.'

We waited outside the arrivals hall at Delhi airport. On the stroke of midnight the plane landed. An hour and a half later, thousands of air miles weary, our tourists straggled out, two middle-aged misses in linen safari hats and a girl in cut-off jeans and a tight T-shirt. Yadav eyed her with appreciation. It had never crossed our minds that the 'couple' might be two women. Jostled by the crowd, they waved frantically at our placard.

'Terrible flight,' said one. 'Nothing but spicy food. My sister can't eat it. My name's Ruby Richie.'

'And I'm Rachelle, and this is my daughter Suzanne.'

I made polite inquiries. 'We come from North Yorkshire. Both retired, and Suzanne's doing her degree in applied mathematics. I was a staff nurse in a big hospital; Ruby finished up as a senior police officer in the North Yorkshire Constabulary. She never got married. I did, but it only lasted two years, enough time for Suzanne to be born. Who needs men? Right lot of nerds, if you ask me. We both earned decent salaries. Now we've good enough income between us from pensions and the bits and pieces we've saved.'

This quick resume was all we ever knew of Ruby, Rachelle and Suzanne's lives. The porter threw their luggage into the back of the jeep. 'Eh lad, go easy then,' said Ruby.

We dropped them at their hotel. 'We'll come to pick you up at eleven o'clock in the morning,' Yadav told them. 'Please you take good rest.'

'What did he say?' asked Rachelle, addressing no one in particular. 'Doesn't speak very clearly, does he?'

I translated Yadav's good wishes.

They were waiting for us on the hotel steps the next day. 'We asked for a hot-water bottle last night,' said Ruby. 'When it eventually came, it was a bottle of hot mineral water.' We all laughed except Yadav, who had not understood.

The day went well, apart from the Qutab Minar being shut. 'You would have thought the guide would have known,' Rachelle said. Having been in this situation a number of ghastly times over the years, I stayed calm.

That evening I rang their hotel. 'Rachelle has fallen off one of your ridiculously high curbs, and hurt her knee and ankle,' Ruby said. 'Your Mr Das phoned. He's coming round to help.' This did not seem the moment to mention marriage. We drove round to see Dinesh and cancelled the wedding arrangements.

I felt so apprehensive about our already obviously difficult clients that I was glad to cut one possibly fraught event off the list.

The next morning Rachelle's knee was well enough to travel. Via the seven-storied palace of Datia we came to beautiful, dreaming Orchha. Yadav and I were given the once-magnificent state bedroom in the Sheesh Mahal Palace, the very hotel where we had spent our first night together three years ago.

I looked around at our suite's bygone glory. 'Yadav, I think they've given us the wrong room. This should be for them.'

There was an impatient knock on our door.

'Please do not say anything. We would like to sleep in this room,' Yadav said.

It was Ruby. 'We are in an indecently small room. I insist on changing.'

Yadav stood squarely in the doorway, blocking her way. 'Jill will try to make change,' he offered. The manager found them a better room, but I spent a guilt-ridden night in our decadent boudoir.

After a morning wander through the temples of Khajuraho, the afternoon was free. We left our tourists to shop and swim and returned to the waterfall, with its deep, round pool.

'From another life,' I sighed.

'Other life? Don't be silly, yaar. Other life will come later. Before we died from this one, we cannot have. In new life I will meet you again and we will have our own sons and I will be rich and we will be truly prince and princess of Haryana.'

Yadav's depression, manifesting itself in black moods, was becoming a problem. At times he sat ramrod-straight at the steering wheel, unsmiling and grim. At others he gave up, insisting that I drive while he lay inert in the back, casting a stifling cloud over everything. 'I cannot help it, yaar. I am not well,' he said.

I woke one night to find him sitting up beside me. 'When do you think we will have our marriage ceremony?' I asked.

'I will marry you tonight.'

Getting out of bed, he began rummaging in my bag. 'I can't find it,' he muttered. 'Doesn't matter.' He went to the dressing table and took something out of the plastic bag in which he kept his anti-depressant pills. He came back to bed.

'And now we will marry.' His voice was serious. He opened a small packet and shook a little sindoor into his palm. With his other hand, he parted my hair in the centre and rubbed the red powder in.

'Should be my own blood, but I cannot find pen-knife in your bag.'

'Thank God for that.'

'Now, yaar, you must touch my feet and then join your hands. After, you will be my truly wife.' He looked lovingly at the red streak in my hair. I did as he asked. 'Now you can say we are married. Later we will have other ceremony, but important thing is done,' he said, never taking his eyes off the bright-red line.

'Do you really think it counts?'

'Count? Of course it does count. I promise you, by my god now you is my real wife.'

I was very touched by what he had done, but couldn't help feeling that we needed a more substantial ceremony.

'Ruby's hungry,' said Rachelle. We were in the middle of nowhere, halfway through a four-hundred-kilometre drive from Mandu to the painted caves of Ajanta. Yadav pulled up at a chai stall.

'Will this do?' he asked.

'Well, it'll have to, won't it?' snapped Ruby. She stood well back from the stall while Yadav ordered and paid for a newspaper packet of pakoras.

'And I'll have a bottle of mineral water,' she said. We had bought a crate a few days earlier, suggesting that we share the cost between us. The bottles had disappeared, and so far there had been no contribution.

From the caves of Ajanta and Ellora we had another long day's drive to Matheran, Bombay's prettiest hill station. This was the first place on our journey that was new to Yadav and me. The road wound up and up, through double twists and hairpin bends. Yadav seemed near collapse. He seldom spoke, not even to Suzanne, who usually commandeered his willing attentions.

'Hubby's not too happy today, then?' Ruby remarked conversationally. I pulled the jeep round another blind corner and found a lorry bearing down on me.

'No.' I tried not to look down as I edged past the lorry, with centimetres to spare between us and the valley below. 'No, I don't think he's feeling well.'

The outsized orange sun finally sank behind the hills. 'You can take the toy train down the hill tomorrow,' I said.

Early the next morning, I watched the sun climb back into its infinite sky-blue ceiling and prayed for a peaceful day.

My prayer went unanswered. 'Very dull, really. And you told us the wrong time. We've been waiting for you for half an hour,' Ruby snapped when we picked them up at the little train station at the bottom of the hill. 'Well, I hope you've got us a decent hotel in the centre of Bombay.'

'It's on Juhu Beach, much nicer than central Bombay.' I desperately hoped this was true.

The lobby was filled from wall to wall with salesmen attending a rag-trade fair. My heart sank. Rachelle's face lengthened. She had a bad cold, and all through Bombay's crowded traffic she had been talking about the lovely rest and hot shower she was going to have when we reached the hotel. Alas, it was definitely not 'decent'. Even without the salesmen, it would have been unkempt and down-at-heel.

'Is brothel,' Yadav whispered to me. 'I have already seen prostitute.'

'Shut up,' I whispered back.

'We can show you one of the rooms now; the other will be ready later. As you may have observed, we are labouring under extreme difficulties,' said a harassed young receptionist.

'You may have difficulties, but I have clients. Please take us to the room.' My nerves were twanging. The Richies, Yadav, I and the porter, with the Richies' luggage, followed the receptionist into the lift.

'See?' Yadav said. Now on the fifth floor, we were walking behind a young woman wearing a Western skirt and high-heeled shoes a size too big for her. 'She's one.'

'Oh, please shut up!' My whisper was too loud. The Richies turned round. Looking very uncertain, the young man was putting a key into one of the locks. He opened it a crack, peered in and quickly withdrew his head.

'I'm afraid it is already taken,' he said apologetically.

Wedged between sweating salesmen, we descended to the ground floor. My clients were beyond speech.

'I want one triple room NOW!' I shouted.

The young man found another key, and we retraced our steps to the threshold of another room. The bedcover was crumpled, the carpet stained and the washbasin cracked and grimy. There was a pervasive stuffy smell of dirt and mildewed plaster.

'Is too bad,' Yadav said. 'Next door is Holiday Inn. Better we should take them there.' Once again, the Richies and their luggage came down in the lift. Yadav was right: they were happier in the Holiday Inn, and we were poorer.

The Richies decided to fly from Bombay to Goa. They had had enough driving, they said, and would not be missing much in the way of sightseeing. We would meet my brother at Goa's airport before we saw them again.

'I like you sit in front,' Yadav said. 'That lady, she always take your seat. She never offer to anyone else, not even her sister.'

'Well, they are paying,' I reminded him. 'And I thought you liked sitting next to Suzanne. You seem to get on very well with her.'

'Please do not speak rubbish.' Yadav's reply was too brief.

'Do you know tomorrow is St Valentine's Day?'

'I did forget it. But thanks to my sweet wife, thanks God, now I remember,' he said thoughtfully.

'Do not mind if I leave you by yourself with cup of coffee, yaar,' said Yadav. 'I have urgent and very secret work.'

The next morning, in Pune's best hotel, we breakfasted in blissful solitude in the comfortable room the Richies would have occupied. Yadav handed me a white envelope and a packet done up in pink-striped paper. 'This is for my girlfriend. Please you read card.'

To Jill with love from Yadav.

'Now please open parcel.' Yadav was so excited he could hardly keep from tearing off the paper himself. Inside was a bottle of two-in-one shampoo-conditioner and a very small, very thin, golden ball-point pen with one refill. 'I do not know what is in bottle. But it was much and much more expensive than pen. Do you like it?'

'I love it and I love you. Thank you very much. I have never had such a nice Valentine present.'

Yadav looked as though he might burst with happiness.

'Is my pleasure,' he said.

I looked forward to seeing my brother John. Our paths had rarely crossed. Ten years older than I, he had been away during my childhood – at school, in the army and later at Oxford. I had worshipped him from afar, and he had treated me as a very small, not very sensible sister. He and my first husband had not got on with each other. This was the first time in many years that we would be spending several weeks together.

Yadav and I waited outside Goa's airport, ready to present the huge garland Yadav had insisted on buying.

'John, he is my own relative. I must have to give garland,' he said, trying to guess which of the unlikely men coming out of the building was my brother.

'He's very tall, six feet four,' I said.

'Then that is him. It must be him!' Yadav shouted in excitement. It was. John had to stoop for Yadav to hang the flowers round his neck. 'No,' he said firmly, as his brother-in-law tried to hug him. 'The flowers are quite enough, thanks.' Yadav soon came to learn that my brother did not expect physical contact from his brother-in-law.

We crossed the border from green Goa into the arid browns and reds of Karnataka. Yadav had never been further south than Goa, so everyone except me was on new territory. Ruby, having changed places with Rachelle and Suzanne, sat beside Yadav, studying the map.

'Well! He certainly can't read it,' she said, looking at Yadav. We had just taken a wrong turn and added twenty kilometres to our journey.

Rachelle and my brother sat together on the middle seat, discussing literature. Suzanne was silent, a faraway expression on her face.

I sat in the back, repeating to myself in time to the jerks, 'We're halfway through... bump... halfway through... jump. Charade must end... hup... Charade must end... phew... We'll say goodbye... Yadav, mind that lorry... say goodbye... eek... in

251

twenty days, thump... bump... jump... twenty days... That was my head... ouch.'

'Sorry, yaar, is very horrible road. You should have to sit in front.'

Didn't he see that I couldn't? Why was tourism so depressing? Why had India lost its golden glow? It was becoming just like another 'Wednesday Oxford and Stratford' or 'Sunday Bath, Salisbury and Stonehenge'. Travelling alone was so much more amusing. Tourists were only interested in getting their money's worth, in being pandered to and not having to think for themselves. I wanted to jump off this homogenising merry-go-round, to stop riding back and forth on its destructive path.

Blinded by the setting sun, we entered the town of Hospet, knocked an ice-cream vendor off his bicycle and arrived at the Maligi Tourist Home, where we were welcomed with garlands.

'Don't let them put one of those things round my sister's neck. She suffers from chronic hay fever.' Rachelle clawed frantically at the yellow and white flowers that already adorned Ruby's gnarled, unwilling neck.

Peace came with nightfall. The Richies were on the other side of the door that divided the deluxe rooms from our less salubrious quarters.

'Yaar, I think we are very tired. So goodnight. Tomorrow we will take Ruby and Rachelle and my brother-in-law to Hampi. Porter, he tell me it have very great temple with live-in elephant. Will be good for them.'

'Perhaps. Goodnight.'

Yadav and I sat breakfasting in the garden. When the Richies arrived Yadav sprang to his feet. It was Suzanne's twenty-first birthday. 'Happy Birthday, Suzanne.' He fished in his pocket and brought out a small packet. 'Please sit.' Going down on one knee, he opened his packet, brought out a pair of silver anklets and fastened them round her ankles.

'Thanks, Yadav. That's kind of you.' She looked down at her legs. 'I think one at a time's enough. I'll use the other for a bracelet.' Yadav was about to tell her that that was not the custom, but thought better of it.

The Richies' energy was flagging. They wandered disconsolately around Hampi's emotive ruins. 'Enough's enough for one day,' snapped Ruby when I suggested walking on to the farthest and most beautiful temple ruin. 'We'll go to our hotel if you don't mind.'

In Bangalore, the Richies went shopping while Yadav, my brother and I walked in the botanical gardens. Yadav was talkative and cheerful. I teased him about his crush on Suzanne and he responded in kind, neither admitting nor denying it. Then, for no apparent reason, he was struck down by one of his black moods. It lasted until the following morning.

In Ooty, our tour almost ended on the sharp bend of a slippery road. It had been raining, and I was slow to change gear. With no handbrake to stop us, the jeep slid backwards, its wheels almost off the side of a steep, muddy bank. Yadav leapt out and planted two stones behind the back wheels. For the rest of the day, he drove while I sat in the back nursing my nervous tension. We flashed like a runaway spinning top down the tortuous road, passing tea gardens, terraced vegetable plots and eucalyptus forests,

'Could you tell your other half to drive more slowly? It makes me nervous,' Ruby said. She never spoke directly to Yadav.

'I like it, Ruby, and he's quite in control.' Rachelle was leaning forward in the front seat, enjoying the roller-coaster ride and making sure she did not miss a single tea bush.

'As you please, but I'm hungry. It's a long time since I had my breakfast, if you could call it that. A bit of black pudding, that's what I fancy.'

We stopped at a café in the first small town we came to. 'What, I'd like to know, would they do if I said I didn't like rice?' No one bothered to answer. Ruby always had the last word.

In Cochin, a short walk from our hotel on Willingdon Island took us to a jetty where we hired a fishing boat and cruised the lagoon. Yadav and Suzanne lay sunbathing on the for'ard deck, talking in low voices. I pretended not to notice.

In Matancherry, Yadav was late back to the boat. I seethed with fury at his lack of professionalism. Only weeks later did I discover that he had been buying me a little silver box of sindoor.

On our last evening in Cochin, we all dined together. 'I think I'll have some more of that beef. Quite tasty for India,' Suzanne said, getting up to head back to the buffet.

'Beef? Do you mean they have dish of cow? Did I eat cow?' Yadav looked down at his half-empty plate in dismay. Neither he nor I had thought to wonder what all the buffet meats were.

'Aye, you did, that. And what's wrong with a bit of beef, I'd like to know?'

I wished she would shut up, but Yadav was not listening. He sat with his head in his hands, rocking backwards and forwards and muttering.

'Meri ma, meri ma, I have eaten my mother. Oh my God, I have eaten my mother.'

Poor Yadav.

Kanyakumari! Yadav and I hugged each other, danced for joy and hugged each other again. 'Yaar, we've done it... DONE IT... DONE IT!' yelled Yadav in time to the breaking waves and chanting pilgrims. We were standing on the slippery rocks of the southernmost tip of India, watching the sun set and the moon rise over the meeting point of the three seas.

'Done what?' Ruby enquired, almost losing her foothold. 'Look out, for God's sake, Rachelle,' she shouted at her sister, who was wet and dripping from the waves. But Rachelle only laughed and shouted back that she had lost one of her sandals. Yadav slithered gallantly over the rocks to rescue it. Rachelle embraced him, and they roared with laughter as another huge wave drenched them both.

My brother, not fond of noisy celebrations, found a Japanese journalist to chat with. Suzanne stood staring at the rising moon. Ruby scowled. The Richies forgot to complain about the hotel's inadequacies. We were all, in our own ways, held by the spell of the sacred sangam.

It was almost over. The Richies were booked into the best hotel on Kovalam Beach. Nothing could go wrong now, nothing.

'Mrs, Mrs and Mrs Richie?' asked the receptionist.

'More or less,' said Ruby impatiently.

'You are in the cottages. Non-A/C.' Rachelle's face was like a black sky before a thunderstorm. My stomach muscles tightened.

'The cottages are lovely – round the swimming pool, down by the sea.' My voice came from somewhere else, a place outside me.

'We'll see the room before we decide, thank you. I insist on air-conditioning. We can't be expected to sleep without it in this hothouse of a climate.'

'I'm sorry, Madams, all other rooms are taken.'

'I've heard all that before,' came Ruby's icy voice. 'They needn't think they can pull the wool over our eyes. You use your authority, Jill. DO SOMETHING.' The porters re-loaded the luggage and we drove downhill to the cottages.

Pretty as they were, the Richies were not going to admit that they liked them. 'We'll stay here if we must,' said Rachelle.

'We'll see you tomorrow, then. We're staying at a small hotel at the other end of the beach.'

Ruby was standing by the jeep, grumbling to my brother. 'Bloody wogs, the lot of them,' she said.

John leant out the window. 'Ruby, my dear.' His voice was silken. 'I've only met one "wog" since landing in India... AND THAT'S YOU!'

When the Richies were gone, I could no longer contain my fury and despair. It was Yadav, however, who started crying.

'Why are you crying?' I asked him. 'Because you fell in love with Suzanne, and now she's gone? What do you think it was like for me? It was so obvious!'

Yadav looked utterly miserable. 'Yaar, I know what you say. I didn't do anything, only talk. I cannot help to myself. She is too pretty. But now is completely finish. I'm sorry, darling, because you is my true and real wife. You must have to forgive me.'

'I'm not your wife just because of some red powder you put on my hair. You can do what you like – look for more pretty girls if you want to. I don't care.'

Before we left Kerala, Yadav stopped to buy a large sack of green coconuts.

'Is good present for childrens at our farm – they have never seen coconuts. Also, weight will stop jeep from bumping.'

By early afternoon we were in the temple town of Madurai. Yadav went off to buy a bigger and better horn. When I complained about the price, he pointed out that in India a good horn is far more important than a handbrake.

My brother and I threaded our way over scorched dust through religious processions, ornately caparisoned elephants, half-naked pilgrims and motor scooters, whose speakers spewed political slogans and Indian pop music.

After the noise of touting traders, blind beggars and pestering pye-dogs, the sudden silence of Sri Meenakshi temple was almost deafening. Past the towering entrance, we confronted our own images in the green waters of the great tank, mirrored, as in a frame, by the surrounding columns. Behind, against a bright-blue sky, rose four of the twelve massive gopurams. A Western woman sat sketching on the stepped ghat. The temple slumbered, gathering its strength for the evening onslaught.

Picking our way round sadhus on siesta, supine hunks of saffron folded in sleep, we entered a lightless forest of sculpted beasts four times our height. Their stone heads stared down at us with toothy, slavering grins. We trod the endless halls, lost in a labyrinth of hoary giants. Suddenly the beasts were behind us – with a final leer they had rocketed us into another world, a bustling temple bazaar full of bright lights, picnicking pilgrims and stalls piled with sweets, garlands and gewgaws. My brother, tired by the heat and chaos of the city, went back to the hotel for a rest.

The temple came alive at four o'clock. People flocked in, splashed in the tank, rang brass bells and wended their way to puja at a hundred altars, gaudy with golden gods and goddesses. My ears rang with drumbeats, clanging bells and the eerie rhythm of flat, chanting voices.

Yadav was sad. He had found his horn, but he had also learnt that tomorrow was Holi – a festival not celebrated in south India. By chance, we found a group of Rajasthani boys who were all too anxious to play. We returned to our hotel transformed into red devils. My brother stared at us.

'Most uncomfortable,' he said. My brother is very sparing with his words. After a year or two of celebrating Holi at the farm, I could have done without it; but I was glad it had made Yadav happy.

Our hotel in Trichy, described in the guidebook as having 'a faded touch of the Raj', was in an advanced state of dilapidation. The staff looked and behaved as though they were in a silent movie, inefficient to the point of uselessness. The redeeming feature was a flower-filled courtyard, where we ate breakfast and drank afternoon tea served with multi-coloured cakes. They smelled and tasted like those in the suburban bakery in the town where I had grown up. Such memories, from the time before my life had been turned inside-out, were pinpricks of sad nostalgia.

The 437 steps through the Rock Fort temple sent us to our rooms to rest until the next day, when we decided to visit the ashram of Dom Bede Griffith.

I had first heard about Father Bede from the elderly father-in-law of one of my best friends. 'If you do go to India,' Nigel had said, 'look him up for me. You won't be sorry.' I did, and I wasn't.

Father Bede had come to India as a young Benedictine monk. Caught in the thrall of India after working in the jungle for some years, he had founded the Santhiravan ashram at Saccinananda. It all seemed very remote, but Father Bede's name had stuck in my brain. Two years ago, during my stay at Vinobaniketan, I had visited Trichy and taken the bus out of town to meet Father Bede in his small pink cottage. I had found him half sitting, half reclining on a bed, reading, his eighty-five-year-old face quiet and smooth. He was a wonderfully peaceful presence.

Now, two years later, when I returned with Yadav and my brother, we learnt that Father Bede was in hospital in Trivandrum.

'Father is not with us. He had a bad stroke. We do not expect him back.' The Belgian woman's guttural voice did not falter, and the tear that glittered in her eye did not fall. A man sat alone at the end of the dining room, reading aloud from a book on the life of Mother Teresa.

After lunch there was a silent hour. We rested on the veranda and then walked around, looking at the books in the library, the well-fed cows and the brightly painted statues that sweltered on the prayer-hall roof, mercilessly exposed to the afternoon sun.

'How can a Catholic ashram have statues of Hindu gods?' I wondered.

My brother looked up. 'But they're not. They are Matthew, Mark, Luke and John.' He was right. I wasn't used to such colourful portrayals of Christian saints.

Spring, and the London guiding season. I was half listening to the news on Radio 4, half thinking about the day's work. Windsor and Oxford... what year did William of Wykham found New College? Was the guard change at Windsor in the Quadrangle or down by the guard room today?

'Father Bede Griffith, the Benedictine monk who spent most of his life in the jungles of south India, died early yesterday morning in hospital in Trivandrum. And that conclude's this morning's news. Good day.'

I turned off the radio and let myself out the front door. The sky had been washed in the night. The sun warmed the London pavements. The sparrows in the plane trees chorused a greeting.

16

My brother caught a train from Hyderabad to Bombay. Yadav and I were alone at last, and very tired. By evening we arrived in Nagpur, in the heart of India's orange groves, and collapsed in a comfortable hotel room far beyond our means. After two days of watching mindless Bollywood movies on TV and eating delicious subzi and ice cream in the pretty blue-and-white restaurant, we were ready to move on.

The weather was uncomfortably hot. Twenty kilometres outside the chaotic city of Jabalpur we found Bhedaghat, a peaceful village on the banks of a lazy jade-coloured river that flowed through a deep gorge of solid white marble, then gathered speed and crashed in a gushing cascade of silver on to the flatlands below. The Motel Marble Rocks was tucked away in a garden that sloped steeply down to the gorge, filled with sweet-smelling tobacco and many-coloured bougainvillea. The manager and his family were from Haryana.

'Tomorrow is Wednesday, an auspicious day,' Yadav said. 'Still we have not found time or place for marriage. Shall we ask manager to come with us in temple?'

The manager agreed to help. His wife, his two daughters and the hotel's waiter would be our five witnesses. Yadav gave them a present of six coconuts and took the hotel's TV to the menders in Jabalpur. But when I asked him if we should buy sweets for our marriage party, he was hesitant, doubting the validity of the manager's promise.

'First I want to be sure he does not joke with us, yaar. He took me to meet his wife, but only in front of house. He did not ask me in. This I mind too much.'

'It'll be all right. You'll see.' I was sure that this time our wedding would take place.

A short walk through the village took us to the jetty. A rowing boat, overflowing with people, stood waiting. 'Room for more. Room for more,' shouted the boatman in English.

'Let's take a boat for ourselves,' I said. We rowed past the other vessel, weighed down by its human cargo. Our boatman, said his assistant, was deaf, dumb and married with two children. We slid into the gorge, dazzled by the orange, pink and yellow rays of the sun as it struck the tall marble cliffs. For an hour we glided through an unreal landscape, a natural gallery chiselled and chipped by centuries of water and weather. At times, the gorge was so narrow that I could reach out and touch the smooth stone on either side.

The next day I woke early, inhaling the strong scent of tobacco flowers mixed with the smell of muddy river water. My mind was full of marriage: I remembered my first wedding to a penniless barrister at the Catholic church in Chelsea on a cold December morning. Now, thirty-five years later, far from Chelsea, I was about to marry a second penniless husband, this time without even an A-level education to his name. And we were still not even sure whether the Haryana hotel manager was taking us seriously.

Shall we? Shan't we? Shall we be married today? See what happens, I told myself, trying to be Indian about it. But I wished I knew. I had a cold bucket-and-jug bath, washed my hair and painted my fingernails.

Yadav woke up. 'What do you think?' I asked him.

'About what?'

'Our marriage, of course.'

'All depends if manager is serious or not. See what happens.'

The manager came to sit with us at breakfast. Yadav asked if he had meant what he had said. 'Certainly I did. I do not say what I do not mean. I am from Haryana, remember.' He turned to me. 'And my wife is waiting to help you to put on sari.'

I felt a twinge of doubt and fear. I could still say no. I could still go back to England, to my house and my financial worries and the Oxfords and Stratfords and half-day Londons as if nothing had ever happened. I had still not told my children about my marriage plans.

We fixed the time for three o'clock at the Chausath Yogini temple, dedicated to the goddess Durga and sixty-four yogini, and drove to Jabalpur to buy garlands and sweets. The garland seller made two large newspaper parcels. We laid them on the front seat and went into a dark little shop to buy two kilos of barfi, one plain and one chocolate-flavoured. Yadav groaned at the price.

'They are too costly, yaar.' It wasn't worth arguing. Yadav complained about the price of any item that cost more than one rupee.

'And we need a kilo of namkin.'

He sighed. 'Yaar, is too expensive to get marry with you.' We had spent 140 rupees.

Yadav's clean kurta-pyjama was with the dhobi-wallah, whose shop was shuttered and padlocked. A child showed us the way to his house and we retrieved the pressed clothes.

'Now is your turn to get ready,' said Yadav. Once again I was tucked and pinned into my pink wedding sari, this time by the manager's wife and giggling daughters. I could hardly believe that, after so long, our marriage was actually about to take place.

Yadav was waiting outside the hotel, immaculate in his white kurta-pyjama.

'Please collect all items and we will be complete,' he said in an important voice.

I put the 'items' into a bag: two garlands, twelve bangles for each arm, the mangal sutra from Jaipur, my gold ring, a bottle of hand cream in case the ring got stuck halfway down my finger, and the small silver box of sindoor that Yadav had bought me in Cochin.

Together we climbed two hundred steps to the tenth-century temple, which stood like a miniature fortress on the hill. The inner side of its surrounding wall was a gallery of statues of the sixty-four yogini, each in her own niche.

'Waiter is Brahmin,' said Yadav with satisfaction after the waiter had volunteered this information. 'Is good we have Brahmin at marriage.' He gave the temple bell a push, and its jangling note echoed round the dark little interior.

'Come,' he said. There was just enough room for the seven of us. 'You and me, we will stand in front of goddess.' He felt around in our bag and brought out the garlands. 'First I will put on you.' He slipped a garland over my head. 'And now you do same.' He handed me the other necklace of flowers and I arranged it carefully round his neck.

'Very good,' he said. 'Now I will put red powder.' He opened the silver box, dipped his finger into the scarlet powder and rubbed it into my parting. Then he took my hands, one at a time, and slipped twelve bangles over each.

'Now you must touch my feet as Hindu wife.' I bent to do as he said.

'And will you touch mine?'

The vertical lines between his eyebrows deepened. 'No, I do not.' I felt his shock. A hot flush spread through me. Why had I tried to turn something that was so sacred to Yadav into a shallow Western joke?

'I was only teasing you,' I said.

Yadav saw that the manager and his family were laughing, and his grim expression turned to a smile.

'Now the ring. This is for your religion.' He slid the ring over the third finger of my left hand.

Kneeling before the statue of the goddess, he prayed for a moment before patting the ground beside him. 'You should also pray. Remember there is only one god for all peoples.' I knelt beside him and looked up at the face of Durga, the inaccessible, one of the many manifestations of the wife of Lord Shiva.

We got up. It was over. I wished we could kiss each other as a Western couple would, unashamedly, in front of everyone present. But I knew that for Yadav, a husband and his new wife would never kiss in public. Ideally, they wouldn't even look at each other.

I wondered if it was true. Could such a simple ceremony really bind us together for life? I knew that in the eyes of the world, we would have to have a civil marriage as well – but perhaps what we had just done had forged a stronger bond than any piece of paper could do.

Climbing down the worn, uneven steps in a sari was difficult.

'Only hold it up with one hand. In a sari you must be very ladylike,' laughed the manager. We sat in the garden. The waiter brought a tray of tea, coffee and water.

'Where's the champagne?' The manager's twelve-year-old son handed round a plate of barfi.

'Please you take namkin. We do not need. And thank you very much to help us,' said Yadav when the manager and his family got up to go.

'And now, my very sweet wife, I would like to take you in jeep to see waterfall. Please do not take off sari. I like it too much and you looks me very pretty. Tomorrow we will go to hill station for one-day honeymoon. We still must drive many kilometres before we reach our farm. My family, they will get worried. Harvest will be going on. We must have to help. After farm we will go straight to Delhi magistrate's court to get marriage certificate; will be easy thing. Later we will have new honeymoon in Uttar Pradesh Himalayas. I thinks you will like too much.

'All things is very good for us, yaar. We are lucky. The god is too kind to us. So, goodnight.'

Pachmarhi, our honeymoon hill station in Madhya Pradesh, was invisible. Sheets of heavy rain blotted out the vicarage, a cottage called Evelyn's House and the church hall. Garden gnomes, left over from an earlier age, dripped sadly in would-be cottage gardens.

'... OLF CLUB. MEMBERS ONL...' Both ends of the notice board were splintered and broken. Thunder rumbled around the brown mountains. The Mrs Simkins, Major Johnstones, Misses Broadstairs and their polite little dogs had long gone, and with them the jolly, hygienic life of the Raj, leaving only a mocking tradition of chhota pegs, gin, hunting trophies and 'jolly good shows'.

'I will not stay here. I feel my depression coming very badly,' said Yadav. From our pink-and-green bedroom we had a bird's-eye view of the village below, where lighted windows winked at the wet street and bedraggled villagers hurried home.

By morning the rain had stopped. The sun climbed into the sky. The waking village steamed in its warmth.

A cock crowed. Shawled figures emerged from cottage doors. Opposite the hotel the dry cleaner's shutters rattled open, revealing a neat row of suits and saris. Schoolgirls with brightly ribboned braids chattered and dawdled along the road. Two little boys nursed their broken tricycle across the street.

A dog lapped puddle water. The determined ring of a bicycle bell sent pedestrians scattering. According to a peeling poster on the wall of the next-door 'Backet Hotel', Pachmarhi offered three days of non-stop sightseeing. With half a day to spare, we hired a guide and set out.

It must have been on just such a sunny day in 1857 that Captain Forsyth, a Bengal Lancer at the head of a column of troops, first glimpsed the beauty of a saucer-shaped plateau girdled by the Saptura hills. Humans had lived here for ten thousand years. According to legend Pachmarhi got its name from the five Pandava brothers, who had taken refuge in the rock-cut caves from which we could now see the town's very English church spire. Captain Forsyth's discovery had turned Pachmarhi into a sanatorium and summer retreat for the British.

The tortuous track played havoc with our springless jeep. We stopped at a small temple in the shade of a monkey-infested tree. Painted tridents leaned against the wall. A fire burned on the altar before a huge painting.

'He is saint,' explained our guide. 'The saint's disciple must sit always outside temple of the highest hill. See,' he pointed to a temple on the summit of a nearby hill. 'Until temple is finished with roof, he will never go inside. Now we must walk.' He took us to several more rock-cut temples, at each of which Yadav sank to his knees and worshipped.

We had been away for two-and-a-half months and driven more than eleven thousand kilometres.

The children's pleasure at seeing us was outshone by their delight at having the jeep back. Yadav fetched an old axe and lopped off the tops of the coconuts. They had grown old on the journey; half the milk had turned to flesh. The family sipped cautiously.

We did not tell anyone about our marriage. I did not know then, and I still have no idea, what they think of our relationship. It must seem a strange union, but they have always accepted me without question. I am part of the wheel of their fortune, decreed by Fate. It would not occur to them to ask how or why.

We went to Delhi to have our marriage officially licensed. A voice behind a locked gate at the British High Commission told us to apply for a marriage certificate at the magistrate's court near Kashmiri Gate in Old Delhi.

Arriving at the magistrate's court, we scanned the rows of lawyers seated beneath hand-painted signs outside corrugated iron lean-to offices, and settled on a man in late middle age. His back was hunched into a dusty black jacket. His cracked shoes, barely concealing the holes in his nylon socks, stuck out from beneath his trestle table.

'You go yourselves to Marriage Room,' he said, picking his nose with his little finger. 'Collect form and list of documents required. With these items, it will take barely three days to get certificate. Now is closed. Return tomorrow.' Convulsed by a fit of smoker's wheezing, he spat with gusto.

The Marriage Room was a Dickensian dream. Its cream-coloured walls were spotted with damp and filled to bulging with people. Accompanied by numerous family members, couples dressed in their best jostled for position with eager touts and advocates in black jackets and sneakers. We elbowed our way to the reception desk, where a bored girl sat passing out forms. 'Wait is thirty days after depositing papers,' she said.

The list of required documents was endless. We returned to the British High Commission for a letter stating that, as far as they knew (how could they?), I had not remarried since my divorce.

Back in our own district, Yadav went to the hospital for a copy of his wife's death certificate. 'I do not know it will be all right or not,' he said, waving a flimsy sheet of paper covered in smudged Hindi. He had waited ten hours to get it, and it wasn't even the one he needed. 'Clerk made bad mistake. He gave wrong woman's papers. Tomorrow I must return for proper document, but no one can stamp it. Clerk, he has locked stamp in desk and taken key to his home for weekend.'

We drove back to Delhi and had our photographs taken. 'Dinesh says he has friend, a very great transporter, who knows good lawyer. He arrange marriage for Dinesh's own brother in only one day. No waiting. Dinesh, he will take us. Chalo.'

Dinesh's friend's lawyer had a grander office than our previous advocate's, one of a line of open-fronted concrete boxes outside the Supreme Court. The lawyer was small, with grizzled locks that poked from beneath a moth-eaten pillbox hat. Last night's dinner had left yellow stains on his Nehru jacket and baggy trousers. Dinesh's friend sat beside him, a leather briefcase balanced on the knees of his dark, well-pressed suit. Sickly-smelling oil ensured that not a hair on his well-groomed, silver-grey head went astray.

'He is truly great man,' Yadav said in an awed whisper.

Every five minutes a boy passed with a wire basket full of glasses of steaming chai. It seemed to keep the men's throats lubricated throughout a discussion in Hindi that I thought would never end.

'Dinesh, he is right. This lawyer is proper person for us. He will get certificate tomorrow – no doubt. Documents is all right. Only we must have to explain we already married in temple. Is expensive, but it is good we will finish this matter. He wants five thousand rupees.' Yadav looked pleased. 'We will give three thousand only today. He does need your passport. He say letter from British Embassy is not all right, he want you get new one.' I handed over the money and the passport and asked for a receipt.

'Don't be silly, yaar. This is India.'

I signed an affidavit stating that we had married in Bhedaghat temple on 25 March 1993. We arranged to meet the lawyer the next day at Kashmiri Gate. The nice Indian man at the British High Commission assured us that the letter verifying my divorce was standard form; they had written thousands just like it.

'Just be careful of these casual lawyers,' he warned.

The court at Kashmiri Gate was awash with people. We panted down the dingy corridors after the lawyer, afraid of losing sight of him as he wove in and out of the crowd. At last he stopped in front of a door, knocked and beckoned to us to follow him in. A fat, overdressed man sat behind a desk at the far end of the room. He thumbed through our papers. He had grown the nail on the little finger of his right hand and he picked his teeth with the forefinger of his left, chewing the pickings and spitting them onto the floor before he spoke.

'You need proof of your temple marriage – invitation cards, photographs,' he said, handing back our documents with an air of finality. 'Not my day on duty. Go to Room twenty-nine.'

Outside Room 29 we shared three broken chairs with seven Rajasthani farmers. Yadav played tinny Haryana songs on his Walkman, turning it up to full volume for the farmers' benefit. Their moccasins, loosely attached to feet beneath their white dhotis, tapped in time to the raucous rhythm. Their darting eyes looked out from wizened faces, half hidden under huge turbans. An hour passed, then two.

'Let's go,' Yadav said abruptly.

'Why? I thought we were going to get married!'

'I don't think so we can without marriage invitations. Chalo.'

Another morning wasted, more money lost. The next day we returned to Kashmiri Gate to deposit our papers and start our thirty-day wait. 'Apply one day in advance to appear before magistrate,' said the clerk, when at last we reached her desk through throngs of brides and grooms.

After a quiet month at the farm, during which I caught up with my diary-writing, we again inched our way through the congested corridors. 'You will need three witnesses and the names and addresses of their fathers. Better you use my services,' a henna-haired tout-cum-lawyer whispered in Yadav's ear. We engaged him for the following day and, in the absence of Dinesh, who was away on a pilgrimage, asked Mr R.K. Das if he and his family would be our witnesses.

'I shall be pleased to assist,' he said. 'My wife and I and our son will accompany you tomorrow. I know the name and address of my wife's father, and naturally of my own and my son's.' He laughed at his own joke.

But Mr Das's son could not come. 'This is not a problem,' he said, beaming. 'I shall suggest to the magistrate the absurdity and extravagance of demanding three witnesses. Two is more than adequate.' Sadly, he was wrong.

'But where is your third witness?' asked our red-haired lawyer. 'I told you to bring three.'

'Of course he doesn't know what he's talking about... Anyone can see he's not a proper lawyer,' said Mr Das in a loud voice. He and his wife shifted from foot to foot like a pair of crows. The lawyer offered an unknown youth a bribe to masquerade as Mr Das's son, but after some deliberation the young man turned the offer down. The following day was Shivaratri, a festival of fasting and vigil and, of course, a public holiday.

When the court reopened, we again fetched Mr and Mrs Das from their quiet little garden square in south Delhi. Our problems seemed endless. Mrs Das had no ration card. 'How can she prove she is Mr Das's wife?' queried the lawyer. In a paroxysm of fury, Mr Das led his wife and the lawyer off to find a magistrate and returned triumphant.

'Of course, when I explained the situation he immediately agreed to accept my wife without the card. Now, I hope we can proceed with no further delays.'

After a long wait, the lawyer came back. 'You did not come to get papers sanctioned by magistrate on the day after depositing,' he said accusingly.

'But nobody told us to.' I was close to tears.

At Mr Das's suggestion and my expense, we went to a dreary three-star hotel near Kashmiri Gate to drink beer and eat platefuls of pakoras. Mrs Das rounded off her snacks with cassata ice cream.

'Italian,' said Mr Das with a knowing grin.

Squashed between Mr and Mrs Das, I jerked up and down in time to Yadav's stop-start driving. The jeep squirmed and skirmished with the traffic.

'Does he usually drive like this?' asked Mr Das of no one in particular. 'I always think it is so much better to drive slowly. Drive with care. Arrive alive. Eh, Jill?' No one was listening. 'I wonder, Jill, if you could bring me a gold coin of your Queen Elizabeth when you return in the autumn. Not your present queen, you understand; the previous one.' I told him I would probably have to sell my house to raise money for such a thing. This did not register.

'Perhaps you mean Queen Victoria?' I asked.

'Yes, yes,' he said. Mrs Das squinted at me through thick lenses and gave my arm a quick squeeze.

My flight to London was only two weeks away, and we were no closer to being officially married than we ever had been.

'Doesn't matter, yaar. Next year will be good.' Yadav believed in a fortunate future. I hoped he was right.

The following autumn, through our greatest English friends in Delhi, we met Sangita Kumar, a lady of statuesque build and determined manner. She agreed to help us.

'The marriage certificate will be no problem. I will telephone a friend at Kashmiri Gate.'

We went to Kashmiri Gate to meet Sangita's lawyer. Sangita said he had asked an exorbitant fee. 'But don't worry – I have settled with him. Do not pay any extra money without consulting me. Now, if you want to get the certificate quickly we must arrange photographs of your actual temple marriage.'

She took us to a bazaar where we bought a red, tinsel-bordered veil and two garlands. Sangita rubbed red powder into the central parting she had instructed me to make in my hair and pressed a large red *tilak* on to my forehead. In ten minutes the passport photographer had taken and developed head-and-shoulders photographs of us, garlanded, veiled and with our arms round each other. It was Friday afternoon. The court was closed till Monday.

On Monday morning we were back at Kashmiri Gate. The lawyer arrived in what Yadav called 'Indian time' (an hour late). He told us that before we went in front of the magistrate, we would need a written certificate from a temple priest stating that he had married us, and a government servant as our witness – someone we had known for at least five years. My heart sank. We had neither.

'Do not worry; I can arrange everything. Only you must wait till tomorrow,' the lawyer said.

On Tuesday, 6 December, we returned to the court. Everything was organised: a certificate from a temple we had never been to, an elderly civil servant we had never met and a visit to the inner sanctum of the Marriage Room, where the magistrate sat combing a sparse crop of carrot-coloured hair. Without looking up, he signed the certificate. We were legally married.

'And now we will arrange our sweet honeymoon,' said Yadav. 'We will like to go to Andaman and Nicobar Islands. I have seen sea; two things are left to do. One is to travel on sleeping ship. The other, and I do not know I will have chance in this lifetime, is to fly once in aeroplane. That is all. After that – enough – I will like to stay at my farm.'

We sailed on a 'sleeping ship' to South Andaman Island and spent Christmas and the New Year on deserted beaches, fanned by gentle breezes. Hermit crabs in borrowed shells raced each other across silver sands fringed by tropical jungles, and the crystal seas were alive with rainbows of aquatic life. I thought we had discovered yet another Paradise.

But Yadav, always surrounded by people, found the islands – surrounded only by water and devoid of crowds – depressing and lonely. He could not wait to leave. The highlight for him was the New Year's Eve dinner-dance, at which we won first prize – a pressure cooker and a digital watch – for being the oldest couple on the dance floor.

17

Another year had gone by, but Yadav's romantic spirit had not flagged. 'Please you pack all things for hill stations,' Yadav said. 'We must have to finish honeymoon from last year. In mountains we will buy Alsatian, or special mountain puppy. Will be good for farm and friend for me when you are in your country.'

I protested that a mountain dog would feel too hot in Haryana. 'And why did you give the old kuta away?' I asked. The kuta's village lineage was as long as anyone's. He had grown up with little food and had learnt to avoid the worst of the kicks and blows that were a farm dog's lot. I did not want to bring another dog into such a life.

'Chaudri Sahib, Puja's father-in-law, he wanted him. So we have to give him. Now we do need new dog.'

After Dehra Dun, the road began to climb. Yadav stopped the car and got out. 'Please you drive. To look down hill does make me very frightened. Is my depression.' Reluctantly I changed places, sure that we would have one of our driving arguments, and we did. Yadav leant across me to change the gear. I asked him to tell me when I should change again. He thought I was being cross, and refused. The road got steeper. I could think of nothing but the absent handbrake.

'Yadav, I can't drive on these roads.' I stopped, stalling the engine. Before he had time to tell me that I was going to break the jeep, I burst into tears. 'Yaar, why you are crying? I do and say nothing and you cry. Is not sensible.'

'Because I think you will be pleased when I go back to England.'

'Yaar, you think you are alone in London. I too, I am alone on your farm. My Boss Brother, he does not like me. No one at farm they cares about me. Please do not say I will be happy when my wife she will fly to London. Now I will drive, but is very difficult for me in high places.'

He drove very slowly and safely, in the middle of the road, until we reached Mussoorie.

'I'm feeling to take whisky because of cold. Will you allow me?' The early-evening sun lit the bottles in Mussoorie's wine shop, turning them into sparkling fantasies. Yadav had only just promised me and his god that he would not drink again.

'Have one and the next will be easier,' I said. I walked on, leaving him to go into the wine shop alone. Back in our hotel he disappeared into the bathroom, coming out with an empty quarter bottle of Royal Challenge.

'I drank only one drop – the rest I pour down loo. Please will you excuse me?'

'Yadav, I can't. It's up to you and your promises.'

The next morning, walking down the Mall in search of breakfast, we met a furry black-and-tan puppy with disproportionately large paws. Yadav negotiated with its owner but decided not to buy it. 'I do not want to lose our honeymoon. Perhaps Rishikesh hotel will not allow puppy. You are more important for me.'

'Thanks,' I said, glad that I rated higher than a dog.

The jeep wound slowly down the valley road, lined with bright-blue flowers, to the holy city of Rishikesh, full of fervent commercialism and religious fever. After parking the jeep in our hotel's underground car park, we took an auto to Lakshman Jhula. The suspension bridge swayed gently as the crowds crossed and recrossed it; far below, the Ganges foamed and frolicked. The river was in its last dash, falling like strands of milky shredded-wheat cereal from the heights of its Himalayan birthplace to its long, slow journey across the Gangetic plain towards the sea.

On Easter Sunday there was a strike. 'Roads will be dangerous. Strikers they stop all traffic and take air from tyres, sometimes worse. Better you drive, yaar. They will not touch foreigner.' We retrieved our car from underground.

A small, multi-coloured cockerel strutted across our path, followed by his demure brown hen. 'Chickens. There must be village,' Yadav said. But one of the passengers we had picked up en route explained that they were undomesticated forest fowl.

Seventeen hundred metres above Rishikesh, we reached Neel Kanth Mahadev. For five rupees we received large red tilaks and an orange. A steep climb to a small white temple was rewarded with a second tilak.

'Now you can say our visit is complete. Chalo, yaar.' Yadav had had enough.

'Yadav, I'd just like to see the Maharishi Mahesh Yogi's ashram. So many people from my country came to see him. Have you heard of the Beatles? They went there.'

'Beetles? Of course I knows beetles. Do you believe they visit ashram? But you are my wife, and if you want to go I must take you.'

Rishikesh has many ashrams, but no one seemed to have heard of Maharishi Mahesh Yogi. We were wrongly directed to an extensive complex of saffron-coloured buildings, where saffron-clad sadhus wandered round in what appeared to be saffron dreams. Two semi-naked apparitions, their bodies painted in garish colours, pranced up to us and pawed at my clothes, swinging tails that hung between their legs. One brayed like a donkey. His companion poked me in the ribs and gave a pig-like grunt. I pulled at Yadav's hand.

'Please, let's go.'

'But yaar, they are only beggars and this is good place. I do not understand your different taste. Why you wants beetles and ashrams nobody knows?'

We found the maharishi's ashram deep in the forest. A portly sanyasi studied us from behind padlocked gates and shook his shaven head.

'He say Indians are allowed, but no Westerners. Ashram must be for everyone. Now we have found this place and chalo, yaar.'

'Please,' I said. 'Just ask about the maharishi.' The sanyasi told us that these days the maharishi lived in Holland. He visited only occasionally.

At Haridwar, door of the gods and gateway to Paradise, the British had divided the Ganges into two branches, canal and river, making the water race along its short course through the city. High on the hilltop, the white temple of the mother goddess guarded the narrow streets. Orange, yellow, blue and green cable cars swung up and down, carrying pilgrims to do puja and leave offerings.

The concrete riverbank was a twilight stage-set of candy-striped domes, temples and twinkling lights. Down by the ghats crowds were massing for the evening aarti. We crossed a bridge lined with emaciated beggars rattling their bowls, their heads bowed and arms outstretched. The crowds chattered and laughed. Treacly film music blared from loudspeakers, vying with the amplified temple chants. Bathers, braving the darkness that had fallen, played and splashed in the water below us. Police whistles screeched at us as we climbed a metal stairway to a lookout tower, high above the heads of the crowds. Yadav joined his hands to them in mock supplication.

'Now please you look. Aarti is beginning.' He pointed to the crowds milling round the temples on the further bank. One by one, bright flames flared, wavering up and down in ritual prayer. The crowds prayed, laughed, shouted, ate, talked and chattered. The air was electric with awe, reverence and fairground camaraderie. Peanut, pakora, and papad sellers pushed through the throng. Balloons floated on high. A million tiny dried-leaf saucers filled with rose petals, ghee and flickering wicks were launched on the river, to wobble downstream on the tide.

The aarti fires died. The crowd shifted towards the bridge. 'Did you enjoy?' Yadav asked me.

'Yes, and thank you for bringing me. Today is Easter Sunday, and it's been one of the nicest I can remember.'

'Is my pleasure. I too like it too much. But Easter – what is this?'

'It's a Christian festival. We celebrate it with chocolate eggs.'

'Very strange,' Yadav said, puzzled. 'First we must go ashram to find beetles. Now you wants chocolate eggs.'

In the morning, we returned to Haridwar and bought a coconut, some sweets and some bindis and flowers, all wrapped in a scarlet cloth and tied with gold tinsel. This was our offering to the mother goddess. Swinging uphill in the overcrowded cable car, Yadav kept his eyes shut, only opening them once for a quick glimpse of the Ganges far below us. We waited in a long line to present our gift to the priest. He undid the tinsel, extracted the flowers, returned them to us with a handful of sweets and chucked the remaining contents of our tinsel-tied parcel on to a pile of similar gifts to be transfered by a helper into black plastic rubbish bags.

Halfway down the hill, a black sequinned statue with a heavily made-up face held out its hand to me. 'Jai Mataji,' it mouthed from a gash of lipstick. I leapt back, almost knocking

Yadav over. 'Is only another beggar, yaar, dressed up as the mother. Please don't mind.'

On the man-made bank of the Ganges, Yadav stripped to his Marks & Spencer boxer shorts (the only present he ever allowed me to bring him from England) and leapt into the river. He caught one of the chains dangling from the side, treaded the swift-flowing current and looked up at me.

'Come, yaar.' He held up a hand invitingly.

'I'd like to to, but I can't face wearing dripping-wet clothes.' Women were going into the water fully clothed. Before I knew what was happening, Yadav had caught my ankles and pulled me down beside him. A roar of appreciation and laughter rose from the people on the bank. We swam across the river together, the current pulling us slightly downstream. I arrived at the other side breathless and frightened but triumphant. I had swum the Ganges.

Yadav would not tell me where we were going. 'Is your surprise,' he said. We gave lifts to gentle schoolteachers, pungent shepherds and a shy young bride of yesterday, still in her tinselled scarlet dress. On and on we drove, through pine woods and tall rhododendron trees that threw long-reaching shadows across our path. We passed terraced wheat fields and white-washed cottages clinging to hillside gardens of lemon and banana trees. Quaint gold haystacks had been assembled around tree trunks. The glacier came and went, dwarfing us as it drew closer in the crisp, clear air. We were 2,010 metres above sea level.

'Please stop here.' We had driven through a pair of stone gateposts, then through tea bushes and a garden bright with French marigolds, snapdragons and cornflowers. I stopped outside Chaukori's tourist bungalow, surely the simplest, loneliest hotel in all of north India. Before us rose the blue and purple hills, and behind them the peaked, frozen pinnacles of the glacier.

'Now we are very near mountain, and I hope you like too much?' said Yadav. 'And now, chalo. We will walk to village. I must have to buy cigarettes before the night, and maybe they have puppy.' They did. A huge black-and-tan bitch lay on the road, soaking up the last rays of the afternoon sun.

'She looks me very fierce. Is completely what we need on farm to chase the nilgai and frighten the peoples.' The dog looked part Rottweiler, a domestic animal unsuitable in every way to life on a Haryana farm. When we found the owner we also found Tommy, the dog's only remaining puppy. He was endearing and funny, with even larger paws than those of the puppy we had seen in Mussoorie.

'Eight hundred rupees,' the owner said, looking at me rather than Yadav.

'Too expensive,' Yadav said. But nothing my husband could say would make the man lower his price. We left.

Yadav drove very slowly, hugging the contour of the hill to stay as far as possible from the steep drop down the valley. I offered to take over, but he shook his head. 'I want to have my courage,' he said. He drove all the way to Nainital.

We were boating again, admiring the picture-postcard prettiness around us. This lakeshore village was so reminiscent of the Raj.

'HONEY. CHEDDAR CHEESE. BEST PORK SAUSAGES,' said a faded facade. The local bookshop and its owner, both ramshackle, seemed proud of their British flag. I read book spines through the dusty window – *Lorna Doone, The Thirty-Nine Steps, Selected Poems of Walter de la Mare*. In the background, between snow-covered mountains, cable cars rocked perilously backwards and forwards on sagging wires. Hotels both grand and humble lined the lakeside. The near hills were dotted with Edwardian villas and castellated houses from a bygone age, crumbling reminders of chintzy interiors and chhota pegs on the veranda. Today middle-class Indian holiday-makers took constitutionals and swarmed round the shops and cafés, much as the ladies of the Raj, now safely ensconced in Cheltenham Spa, might have done sixty years ago. It was a miniature Switzerland with very English overtones.

Greedy geese trailed us across the water. Yadav talked to the boatman, a boy of fourteen. I could not understand what they were saying, but I knew what he was asking about.

'He say there is dog farm only sixteen kilometres away. He wants to leave this place and come with us. He ask if we need servant.' I could not help smiling. The idea of a servant on the farm was even more incongruous than that of a Rottweiler.

We took a taxi to the dog farm, and the driver walked with us down the rough track towards a group of buildings. A woman came out of the first house, followed by an auburn cocker spaniel. She seemed to be waiting for us. She was Indian, but she presented herself more as a middle-aged British woman. Her figure was loose and thick where her waist had once been; her bosom sagged beneath a crumpled jersey.

I told her we were looking for a dog farm. Her voice was hoarse and very English. 'Oh, my mistake,' she said. 'I'm waiting for English friends who I haven't seen for some years. The dog farm is up there.' She waved her hand uphill towards a wire-netted enclosure divided into four cages. Loud barking announced the presence of four Alsatians and a Doberman, all tethered on short chains. At our approach, the bark turned into a howl. The owner, who came from Haryana, wanted fifteen thousand rupees per dog. Yadav shook his head.

At Ranikhet we found a shawl factory. Soldiers were playing cricket in the barracks next door. Yadav wanted to buy shawls.

'But we already bought one in Almora.'

'We will buy four more. One for Shanti. She will not keep it for herself, she will give straight away to Meenakshi, but idea, it is nice. One for Nirmula, one for Banarsi, the daughter of Boss Brother, and even one for my sister.'

He was right about Shanti; she never kept anything for herself. She was always very kind to us, and she had always looked after Yadav's children and grandchildren. But I had only met Banarsi once.

'Yadav, maybe it's mean of me, but I don't want to buy shawls for people I don't know. I have my own children in England to buy presents for – I can't afford to give presents to your whole family.'

'All right, we will buy only two.'

Two girls came down the street carrying a rabbit, which Yadav promptly took from them. Fur flew as the animal wriggled and twisted, trying to escape his grasp.

'They say they has puppy at their home. Chalo.' My heart sank. Another unsuitable dog?

The puppy was a poor, mangy little creature. Yadav tried to pick it up by the ears. It yelped pitifully.

'What in heaven's name are you doing?' I shouted. 'Don't you know that's very cruel?'

'It is not. Ramesh told me, is good way to discover it is pure breed. If it is, it will not scream.'

'That's complete rubbish and if you ever do it again, I'll... I'll take your ears and pull them off.'

'I do not want this dog. Come, we will look again. I am sure we will buy puppy today,' Yadav said matter-of-factly.

In a small village, he stopped to buy a giant lemon for Shanti and to ask the fruit seller if he knew of any dogs for sale. The man pointed to a shop across the street which sold tinned food and dusty packs of biscuits. A child ran upstairs and returned a few minutes later cradling a black ball of fluff with a perky face, black-currant eyes and an ebony nose. We put it on the floor of the jeep. It was male and full of curiosity. It slipped and slid across the metal surface, sniffing and smelling our luggage in eager excitement.

Yadav reached to pick it up by its ears. I grabbed his and twisted hard. 'Ouch!' he yelled. The villagers, who had gathered round us, laughed.

I picked up the puppy and held its dusty little body in my arms. The fur under one of its front legs was matted and dirty. 'They say is tar from road.' The shopkeeper's wife cut away the fur with a pair of blunt scissors. Yadav paid her 380 rupees and took the puppy. He settled down on my lap, shut his sad brown eyes and went to sleep.

'Now we have a dog. Are you glad?' I asked Yadav.

'Yaar, I am, but he is not pure breed. I did want proper mountain dog.'

Two goatherds came up the steep hill towards us, one with a sack over his shoulder. A dog with a thick coat and pug nose gambolled amongst the goats.

'You see, like that one.' Yadav pointed, and then slammed his foot on the brake with a shout. 'Yaar, did you see? One man, he have puppy in sack.' He leapt out and ran to catch up with the disappearing men. He came back, triumphant, clutching a brown-and-black puppy. The men were close behind him. They wanted their money. Yadav pushed the puppy into my arms, jumped into the driving seat and started the engine. The man with the sack positioned himself in front of the jeep. The other put his face close to Yadav's and his hand on the steering wheel.

My heart pounded against my chest. The bus incident flickered into my mind.

'Yadav, have you paid them for the puppy?'

Yadav felt in his pocket and drew out a few small notes. He handed them over. The man pushed the money away.

'He ask too much. Is not right price,' said Yadav. He added another hundred rupees. At last the arguing and shouting stopped: the older man pocketed the money and, grumbling, he and his companion started back up the hill. Yadav put the jeep back in gear.

'Very good. Only 380 rupees for black one and five hundred for Moti. He is completely pure. Look, he has brown and black fur and a ruffle round his neck, and his tail does curl. In Hindi is called Bhuratya.'

'Why did you call him Moti?' I asked.

'Is same name as dog I had before. Is lovely name meaning 'little fat one'. Last one, he ran away. I liked him too much. He was my friend.'

My allegiance was to the black puppy. He was tougher and brighter, and he might stand more of a chance of survival in the summer heat of the plain.

'I want to call this one Charlie,' I said. The little black ball's sad, trusting eyes made me think of Charlie Chaplin. I held him closer.

'Yaar, I know you think Moti is not good dog for farm, but I did have to get him. I will shave off his fur. It will be all right. I will keep him cool in house of animals. I will put fan on table.'

I could not imagine Boss Brother allowing the puppies an electric fan, or even enough food to eat. We needed electricity just to make the tube wells irrigate the fields. The resulting yield provided meagre enough rations for the family itself. But it was too late; we had bought the puppies. I dreaded their fate.

At the base of the hills we came to a big sign.

Corbett National Park

QUALITY INN

'Is very good place. Once I bring my Indian tourist here. I think management, they will accept to have puppies.'

Not only did the management accept Charlie and Moti, but they adored them. We were the star attraction. The puppies were given saucers of milk, all the best scraps from the kitchen and constant attention. They raced round the lawns, playing with each other, with the beautiful half-wolf, half-Alsatian house dog and with the guests' children. They learnt to swim with us, in the hidden pools amongst the boulders and rocks in the river that flowed through the forested valley. We washed their fur with the last of my Daniel Galvin shampoo and conditioner, and mixed my precious vitamin pills with their food. Bored with the dark of night, they made mincemeat of Yadav's boxer shorts.

Still, Yadav was besotted with them. Moti felt the same about him – he never left his heel, waddling behind him wherever he went. Charlie was more adventurous, and kept disappearing to the bin behind the kitchen where the cook plucked and dismembered chickens. Yadav brought him back three times that afternoon, his mouth full of white feathers.

'He is too fond of feathers. This time I give him slap. He must have to learn not to run away. After slap I give him love. Now is all right.' Charlie yelped from the slap, then licked Yadav's face.

I forgot my fears for the puppies' future and enjoyed, with Yadav, our new-found family.

It was now April, and even in the Kumaon foothills it was already hot. Down on the plains it would be stifling. Yadav rinsed sacks in cold water, wrung them out and lined the back of the jeep with them. He bought thin chains in Ramnagar and tied the puppies up. 'Like this they will keep cool and not fall out.' I wished we could buy them nice leather collars and leashes. 'No, yaar, in village, the peoples they would steal. Is not suitable.' With Yadav's words reality returned to me; at Corbett I had been living in a fool's paradise.

How much of a fool's paradise I only realised when we got to Delhi. We took the puppies to the vet for inoculations against rabies and distemper, and there the vet's assistant chopped unsuccessfully at the beautiful black and brown fur with a pair of nail scissors. The real shave would come back at the farm, at the hands of Hari Ram and his razor blade.

On the outskirts of Delhi, Yadav stopped at a market selling fans and coolers. We sat beside the road in front of a new metal box. Yadav insisted that the shopkeeper fill it with water and turn on the electricity.

'But how can it work in the open air?' I protested.

'It can and it does,' said Yadav. He was right. Sitting immediately in front of it, we did feel a cold blast of air on our faces. 'But is very expensive. We will not take.' We drove away, leaving the shopkeeper with a torn cardboard box, a cooler full of water and a bewildered expression on his face. 'I did tell him we will come back tomorrow.'

Shaven, Charlie and Moti looked like a pair of little rats. Hari Ram had even taken the fur off their tails. I thought of the two pretty puppies we had bought in the mountains and my hackles rose. It was hard to look at them now, tied by their chains to the leg of a charpoy with only the dust to lie in.

But they were getting enough to eat. Chenamunia and her cousins, though they had always been taught to be wary of dogs and give them a quick kick when the opportunity arose, now played with Charlie and Moti quite gently under Yadav's guidance.

My last night had come round again. Yadav's Brahmin aunt sat with Ma, singing bhajans. Shanti fried puris and special biscuits for tomorrow's festival. Yadav and I washed and cut bhindi and shelled peas. The singing stopped.

'I must have to take my aunt in village. I will be back soon,' Yadav said, disappearing into the darkness.

Two hours later, caught between worry about what had happened to him and fury that he had left me on our last night together, I went to bed. Soon Yadav came back in a cheerful mood.

'Have you eaten? Good.' He began telling me about his evening.

'I don't want to know. You've been drinking, and I haven't even had a glass of beer because I wanted to help you stop.' I regretted what I was saying. I had not meant to start quarrelling. Yadav brought his food into the room and sat on a charpoy, eating noisily. He sliced raw beetroot, put salt and lemon juice on it and fed me a slice with his fingers.

Shanti and Boss Brother's wife were cutting mustard out in the fields. I gave Shanti some money for Boss Brother's daughter's marriage, and bent to give Ma's ankle a parting massage.

'She say she will not see you again. In six months she will be dead.' Ma always said the same thing. Hari Ram was hovering near the jeep with a puppy under each arm.

'Please look after them,' I told him.

'Yes, yes. You do not worry.' He smiled.

Rama and the children climbed into the back of the jeep and rode with us to the corner of the first field. We lifted them down. Their small, determined figures plodded away towards the farm buildings.

I was still angry about Yadav's drinking. Halfway to Delhi he pulled up outside a chai stall, turned off the engine and looked at me.

'Go on, go on. Be angry. But be careful. If you leave for your country like this, for six months you will think same and I will think same. We will build great wall between us. Soon or late it will separate us completely, even if we may live together.'

He was right. Tomorrow I would be in London. We would not see each other for six months. It was important to remember that life is never a long, rosy dream. We had to find a way to live with our differences and misunderstandings. We needed to start our separation with good feelings if we were to pick up our lives together again in October. It would be only too easy to sink into anger and resentment, and never find each other again.

'And now, my sweetheart.' Yadav's grave warning was forgotten. 'I want to tell you nice surprise I have thought for your last night. Can you guess where we will have our dinner this evening?'

'Claridges?' I had always wanted to dine there, at least in the coffee shop.

'You are right. How did you know it?'

At the hotel's entrance, Yadav asked the doorman to park the jeep.

He looked at it and at us with disdain. 'I do not park jeeps.' He pointed the way to the car park

My overweight suitcase rolled away and out of sight. Yadav, not allowed into the airport, waited outside. 'It's all right. You needn't take anything back – they've accepted it!' I had to shout. 'You will write...?' But he had turned away, and was lost in the crowd.

Six months later, when I returned from England to the farm, I found that Moti had died. No one was sure exactly why. He was lucky; Charlie lived on, lanky and sad. When not barking in despair on the end of a short chain, he scratched his mange-covered body till it bled. His daily ration of one old chapati was thrown at him through the kitchen door. Occasionally, freed from the chain for a few hours, he made forays to the village, fought with the local army of curs over evil-smelling garbage dumps and, faithful in spite of everything, returned to the farm. I could not bear to look at him.

'Couldn't you ask the animal doctor to put him to sleep?' I asked. 'It would be kinder.'

'What do you mean?'

'Kill him.'

'Of course we cannot. We do not kill life.' Charlie lived on in misery and degradation.

I took Yadav to the doctor in Delhi. They had not met for six months.

'So you had to wait for your wife to return before coming to see me?' Dr Prakash looked sideways at Yadav. He turned to me. 'How do you find him?' I said I thought he seemed better, despite his continued mixing of whisky and medication.

'I have told you before,' he said to Yadav, 'my treatment is not to be taken with alcohol. Please choose. Either you drink or you take my pills.'

'I'm sorry, Sir, Dr Prakash,' Yadav said. 'I could not succeed to stop, and sometimes I do have very bad headache.'

'Stop the drink and you will be fine. I have told you.'

'Yes, Dr Sahib. I will.'

I still felt it was my fault that Yadav was jobless, because of what had happened when we had gone to Gujarat. Our efforts to find intrepid tourists looking for alternative travel by jeep had yielded few customers. Yadav's lack of occupation worried me more than it did him. He seemed perfectly happy to spend most of his life on a charpoy, with little or no need to go anywhere or do anything.

Dr Prakash shifted in his chair. 'Libido?' he asked in a deadpan voice. He is a dry, cynical and most likeable man.

'What? Um, well, fine.' His question surprised and embarrassed me.

'Beat him,' advised the doctor jovially. 'Someone should have done so long ago. Do you know what is said, Mr Yadav? The one who lies on the charpoy all day wears the bangles.'

'What he means?' asked Yadav, when we had said goodbye.

'Nothing much.' He wasn't really interested.

Rama had sided with Raja Singh over a violent family dispute and had built a fine new hut by the second well, next to his cousin's house. Every day he drove his buffaloes down to our well for a scrub and a bucket bath. Neither he nor his family spoke to us.

'But already the two wives are quarrelling,' Yadav said with some satisfaction.

Chenamunia, just five, had returned to her parents' village to attend her local school. 'It is too bad here without childrens to play with,' said Yadav. He drove over to Meenakshi's farm to bring back Chenamunia's younger sister, Lalita, another great-niece for Shanti to look after.

Soon the farm would have babies of its own. Marriages had been arranged between Yadav's son Ashok, his cousin Hanuman and two sisters from a village thirty kilometres away. One of my first duties on my return to the farm was to meet my prospective stepdaughter-in-law, Anjali.

Anjali and her sister Usha lived behind massive wooden doors in a house built round a courtyard, on a street that was narrower and more treacherous, full of ruts and ditches, than any in our own village. I was seated at a low table and offered chai, halwa and namkin. Veiled and nervous, the girls presented me with a sari, and I gestured that I would like to try it on. They led me into a small dark room and, giggling, wrapped and tucked the sari round me. I did not see them again until months later, when they married the boys in the courtyard of their family home.

18

It was midnight. We stood in the crowd outside Delhi's international airport waiting for Caroline, my eldest daughter. Yadav was, if possible, more excited than I was. An hour passed. I was beginning to give up hope – and then I saw her.

'She's there! She's there!' I shouted. Yadav pushed past the policeman, rushed up to Caroline and swept her off her feet.

'Hi, Mum,' she said, as if we saw each other every day at one o'clock in the morning in the steamy night air of one of the most polluted cities in the world. 'Hello, Yadav. I'm really glad to meet you.'

Overcome with emotion, Yadav began massaging Caroline's head, calling her alternately his dearest stepdaughter and his sweetest niece.

For the first time in twenty years I was holidaying with one of my children, and it was happening in India – the land I had longed to share with all of them since I had arrived six years before. Free from the worries, preoccupations and doubts that had beset me and often upset our relationships in London, I lived in a state of unimagined bliss, enjoying every moment of our time together. We stayed in Delhi for two days. Caroline was unsure whether she was on her head or her feet, or had, by chance, arrived in an original brand of heaven or hell. Yadav whisked her from the narrowest street in Old Delhi to the Qutab Minar. We dined, in sharp contrast to our high-rise hotel, which bore strong resemblances to a prison, with our English friends in their spacious flat in a quiet, leafy part of New Delhi. We drove out of town, past the immense walls of

Tughluqabad, to the craft fair at Suraj Kund, where we shopped for chess sets, appliqué umbrellas, rugs and wall hangings at extremely low prices. On our way to Rajasthan – where we shopped again, went sightseeing, rode camels and shopped some more – we stopped briefly at the farm so that Caroline could meet Yadav's family.

'I hope you will not mind, my sweet niece, if I can ask you to borrow salwar-kamiz from your mum. My family, they does not know about Western clothes and legs of womans.'

Caroline did not mind at all, but asked him in return if he could stop massaging her head. 'You see, Yadav, in my country we don't do that, and it makes me feel rather embarrassed. I hope you don't mind my saying so.'

He contented himself with hugging her every so often and calling her his dearest stepdaughter. They both liked joking and horseplay, arts at which I have always been worse than useless.

Halfway through our travels in Rajasthan, Yadav had to return to the farm to receive his son's and nephew's new family, who were coming to present the dowries. A truck would bring all the male in-laws, squeezed uncomfortably between the marriage gifts: two refrigerators, two TVs, two coolers, two huge metal wardrobes, two dressing tables, two wooden box beds and a giant tin trunk full of saris, bath towels, wedding clothes and shiny, brown plastic brogues for the grooms and their brothers.

When Caroline and I arrived a few days later, Ramesh, my brother-in-law, took us on a tour of inspection. Everything was piled into a windowless, earthen-floored room, the appliances still encased in cardboard boxes – where, apart from one TV, they have remained ever since, worse than useless on our power-cut farm.

'Very best,' Ramesh beamed, patting a cardboarded fridge box. He opened the trunk to reveal tinsel and towels, shut it and stroked an over-elaborate headboard.

Perhaps of all my children, only Caroline could have coped with Indian life in the raw. We spent five days at the farm, celebrating Ashok's and Hanuman's weddings. She has been dining out ever since on stories of green chillis for breakfast, creaking charpoys and nights shared with farting buffaloes.

The farm was crowded; more than fifty relatives had come to stay. The strain on the charpoys and sleeping arrangements was considerable. Two nights before the bridegrooms' party for our village, the caterers arrived. They dug a deep hole in the floor of one room and filled it with red-hot coals. All night long Caroline and I sat with the women, rolling out discs from a mountain of dough. With a professional flick of the wrist, the master chef tossed our discs in and out of a vast pot of boiling oil, rapidly filling basket after basket with golden-fried puris, part of the requisite fare at every self-respecting Haryana marriage feast.

When the dough was gone and our arms ached from kneading and rolling, the chef and his minions turned their attention to a huge cauldron of subzi. The rest of us plunged our tired hands into a giant bowl of sticky laddu mixture and began shaping it into a thousand small, round balls.

Night turned into morning. When the sweets had been piled into big brass dishes, Caroline and I left the women and caterers to their work and went to bed for what remained of the dawn. Our room was filled with elderly farmers, doubled and tripled up on sagging charpoys. Thoughtfully, they had left one for us. The smell of raw garlic, painstakingly chopped and mixed into massive quantities of raita and eaten with gusto by the family and guests, hung heavy on the air. Loud snores, fruity farts and foul breath made sleep impossible. By sunrise, we were convulsed in helpless giggles.

'What is wrong?' asked Yadav.

'Better to laugh than cry,' we explained, our eyes streaming from garlic gas.

'I cannot understand your British joke. Did you sleep very well?'

'Not really.'

'Then I'm sorry,' he said. 'Now is time to wake up. Village will come to farm very quickly and we must have to be ready.'

Soon a stream of villagers began to arrive. They sat cross-legged in two long rows on either side of the strips of sacking laid out on the ground. Each stayed long enough to devour a helping of subzi, served on a dried-leaf plate, with a leathery puri. Rounding off their lunches with two or three laddus each, they ambled back to the village. By evening at least five hundred people had come to wish the family well and eat their food.

It was another difficult night. Yadav, drunk on a quarter bottle of Royal Challenge, insisted on giving us priority treatment. Puja, nine months pregnant with her second child, was turned off a small charpoy in Shanti's room to bed down wherever she could find space. Caroline and I, feeling guilty and awkward but unable to argue with the men, slept head to toe with Shanti, a grown-up niece and five children, all sharing the only other charpoy.

The morning was bright with spring sunshine. The mustard cast scented shadows across the track, along which two scraggy nags clopped in front of us – each with a bridegroom on its back. Continual beatings kept the pair in motion. The boys were garlanded with five-rupee notes, crowned with bath towels and tinsel, and identically dressed in shiny grey trousers, floral shirts and gleaming brogues. Mounted with their small brothers, Bubli and Ravi, whose clothes were miniature copies of the elder boys', they lolloped along. The jeep followed, carrying Boss Brother, Ramesh, Yadav, Caroline and me; behind us trailed the women and children. Charlie, ever faithful, ran beside the cavalcade. 'I can't bear to look at his sweet, conquered face,' said Caroline.

At the temple, where the two boys went through a short ceremony to pray for an auspicious life, the horses were abandoned for the jeep. After a brief argument with the driver of a tractor-load of hay, who sat obstinately immobile in the middle of the track, the women walked back to the farm and we started our journey to the brides' village.

The wedding band, dressed in scarlet jackets and white trousers, was waiting at the edge of the village to accompany us on our ceremonial entry.

'Now you will drive,' Yadav said. I drove painfully slowly behind the procession down the narrowest of streets, stopping every few minutes while the band played and the men, including a reluctant Yadav, got out and did a wild dance. At the dharamsala, I was released while the bridegrooms and band went ahead. Caroline and I sat on the ground to await our summons. Unaccustomed to sitting cross-legged for so long, I shifted my position. With a snap and a sigh, my petticoat string broke.

'What was that, Mum?'

'My sari's falling down,' I whispered, wishing Yadav had not persuaded me to wear it.

I was ushered along the street by one of Yadav's uncles, clutching my collapsed sari about me like a deflated parachute. Arriving at the brides' house, I was led across the courtyard into a small, dark room where the brides were having the finishing touches put to their forehead makeup with tiny dabs of Colgate toothpaste. Their mother pinned and strung me together again. Covered from head to toe in tinselled red dresses and veils, the girls were led away to be married in the courtyard to two boys they had never seen before and would still not meet until late that night, when they would confront their new husbands on hard, wooden dowry beds. We watched as, weeping bucketfuls of tears ('It is our custom,' Yadav said), the teenage brides were carried out of their house one by one, slung over the shoulder of their uncle like sacks of potatoes, and helped blindly into our jeep for the ride to the farm.

By the time we returned, darkness had fallen. Under the searing light produced by a rented generator, the new brides were made to complete an obstacle course in which they stooped to pick up thalis full of dough and heavy, clay water pots that had been set out in two crooked rows on the ground. Meenakshi, usually so quiet and gentle, was organising everything and revelling for one evening in her powerful role of elder sister-in-law.

That task over, a worse ordeal awaited the girls. Still veiled, they were seated on chairs under a spotlight while the women of our family queued to lift their veils, one by one, and squint curiously at their tear-stained faces.

Then, suddenly, it was all over. The brides and grooms had disappeared, all four shut away for the night in a windowless, earthen-floored room. When I asked Yadav about the wedding night, he became angry. 'We should not talk about our childrens like that,' he said.

'Thank God I was born in England,' Caroline remarked later on. I began to protest. 'No, honestly, Mum. Even you can't say it would be fun to be tied up in red tinsel with chains round your ankles and set to make chapatis for the rest of your life.'

'I'm sure it's not quite that grim. Anyway, the village wives I've met seem happier than many married Western women.'

'That's because they don't know anything else. If they did, it would be different.'

We stood outside the airport. Instead of the warm, excited anticipation of a month ago, we were chilled with a sad sense of loss. Caroline, dressed in two Rajasthani skirts, three sweaters and a jacket covered in pink and blue elephants and camels to avoid overweight luggage, mixed with the crowd and disappeared.

'She is really very nice girl,' Yadav said. 'I like her. And Ashok, my god, he love his stepsister too much. Now chalo, yaar. Chaloji.'

A plane thudded on to the tarmac, flushing all thoughts from our heads with an unearthly raging roar.

19

'Ek, do, teen, char, panch...' Bubli gave me a playful punch on the arm and burst into uncontrollable laughter. Caroline, having quickly learnt to count to five in Hindi, had taught him this game. Unaware of the pun between *panch* and 'punch', he continued to find it amusing, even though my daughter had gone back to England long ago.

She was still remembered fondly by everyone. 'How is my stepsister? Please you tell her I miss her. She must come back soon to India,' said Ashok.

'Caroline will be getting her proper food again,' said Rama. He and Nirmula had cooked for us, flavouring the food mainly with green chillis. Caroline had found it difficult to eat large amounts.

'My very naughty niece, she say she write me many letters, but even one has not arrived,' said Yadav with affection.

We now wanted to build a house of our own, but British banks and building societies were reluctant to lend money to a fifty-eight-year-old woman with a small income. Eventually, one mortgage company agreed to lend me twenty-five thousand pounds against my house in Pimlico.

As soon as the money arrived, we began our search. Every morning we left the farm and every evening we returned, having seen nothing feasible. We were looking for two acres, the minimum allowed in a farmland purchase. We wanted to be halfway between Yadav's farm and Delhi, where we would not be too far from the family but where the telephones worked and we could keep in contact with urban life and our urban friends. But everything we saw had major snags. One farmer offered us an acre on either side of the road; another had ten acres to sell and was unwilling to part with two at a time; another sent us on a wild goose chase to look at land he didn't want to sell after all; one plot was next door to the village cremation ground; one was too low, so it would flood during the monsoon; one was in a village with a bad reputation; one had brackish water; one was studded with electricity pylons, and so on.

Land prices had soared in recent years, leaving us and our twenty-five thousand pounds behind. We could no longer afford to buy and build. We decided to sell the jeep, buy an Ambassador and rent a flat in Delhi.

For a long time, Yadav had been yearning to fly to England in an aeroplane. I, too, was looking forward to introducing him to all my friends and, of course, showing him the country I had come from. We tried to get him a tourist visa and failed.

'You two are married!' everyone said. 'Surely...?' But the man at the visa department of the British High Commission did not think that way.

'You want to settle in England, I suspect,' he said. 'What proof can you give me that you will return to India?' His real thoughts – 'Too many of you bastards have slipped through our fingers and are sitting back in my country, enjoying the benefits of our superior welfare state' – were written all over his humourless face. He waited for Yadav to speak.

'Why should I settle in England?' Yadav said. 'My wife, she wants to settle in India. Now she is trying to borrow money to buy land. We will build our own house in Haryana State.' The man tightened his lips and disappeared behind a frosted glass door. The visa was refused.

I protested, and in response I received the most condescending letter I have ever opened.

As you appear to be having difficulty in borrowing the money for your Indian building works, I suggest that you put the money you would have spent on your husband's airfares towards your project in this country. I am sorry to have to inform you that, as stated on the form, we cannot grant Mr Yadav a tourist visa.

Yours, etc. etc.

Finally, the following year, we were granted the visa.

I have never really known how Yadav felt about his first visit to England. When Indians ask him, he tells them about the magic money machines outside banks, the soft seats on buses and trains, the huge variety of cars, the cleanliness of Tesco supermarkets and the terrible cost of living. My friends were extremely hospitable, curious to meet my Indian husband. Our social round, in and out of London, took us to a mixture of town and country houses. But English villages were not villages to Yadav.

'Where is farmers, yaar? Houses, they are all of rich peoples. This is not village.' His favourite house was just outside Farnham, where we had home-grown tomatoes and salad for lunch. 'See, yaar, there are peoples in street. House, it is very pretty and they even grows their own food. Is good.'

A stately home in Hereford was his least favourite. 'Is like prison. Why they should want so much space? They has no childrens.'

Our last stop was my cousin's house in Oxford. Yadav drank half a bottle of their Laphroig before we went out to dinner in a rather 'Anglo' Indian restaurant. In Hindi, he shouted at the Cockney Indian waiter to bring him the juice of ten lemons, left his food untouched and retired to the car to sleep off the whisky. The strain of our visit on both of us was considerable. With September greyer than usual, Yadav often lay shivering in a blanket at night. The chapatis were different; the milk was not from a buffalo. His affection for Westerners diminished. He spent much of his time chatting up busy Gujarati newsagents and buying lottery tickets from Pakistani grocers.

The following summer he came with me again, this time for my daughter Mary Jane's wedding. She was full of reservations about her Indian stepfather.

'He'll be bored, Mum. And you won't be able to look after him; you'll have other things to do.'

Distinguished in a Moss Brothers morning suit, Yadav behaved in an impeccably British way, taking photographs and meeting for the second time, with pleasure on both sides, all the friends who had been strangers a year ago. He stayed on for a month, coming with me as I guided the Sunday Bath, Salisbury and Stonehenge and the Wednesday Windsor. I stayed for another two months after he left, guiding between London and Inverness to earn our winter money.

For the first time ever, Yadav was not at the airport to meet me when I got back to Delhi. My stomach became a mincing machine, grinding up my nerves like a pound of New Zealand lamb. Everything was slipping out of my control. There was nowhere and no one to telephone. Was Yadav dead or alive? Had he had enough of life with his 'stupid British wife', as he often says in jest? No, it could not be that. Marriage for Yadav was for life, good or bad. He must be ill; he was drunk and had got into a fight; he was in prison. I turned back into the building to order a pre-paid taxi, and then I saw him waiting in the crowd.

'Why did you come too early, yaar?' he greeted me.

'I'm not early. You're late.' My worry turned to anger. 'And you're not even sorry.'

'Well, I am sorry, yaar. But how could I know plane would come so quickly?'

I got into our new Ambassador for the first time – Yadav had insisted on buying it just after I had left for England. Tired and jet-lagged, I felt cross that I had never smelt the newness of my own new car. It was already six months old.

'Are we going to look for a flat?' Suddenly the thought of the wet mustard and all that went with it was too much, at least as a permanent way of life.

'First we must have to be at farm. As I wrote in my letter, Usha, your daughter-in-law, she have birth our grandson. We must have two parties – one for village, one for Usha's relations. Later we will come in Delhi again and look for flat.'

When we arrived at the farm the next day, Usha was suckling her two-week-old baby on a charpoy in Shanti's dark little room. Her young brothers-in-law crowded round their new nephew, kissing and petting him as he fed. The farm was overflowing with people. Puja, Yadav's youngest daughter, had come to act as nurse-in-chief to her brother's wife, and she whisked in and out in a take-charge manner. Ramesh, on leave from Assam, was acting as chief cook. Yadav's two sisters had come to keep Shanti company. The moment we had taken my luggage from the car, Yadav drove off, returning later with three elderly farmers. They settled down on charpoys in our room, and Puja brought in a hookah. The men passed it round and stared at my half-unpacked clothes.

Outside, on the veranda, a video player hired from the village was showing a film of Ashok and Usha's wedding. Something had gone wrong: magnified heads of the couple, alternating with a bunch of overblown roses and a sign saying 'Wish you a happy life', flashed on and off the screen accompanied by the song 'Aaj mere yaar ki shaadi hai', set on the same repeat button. The guests sat mesmerised.

Yadav and I had a surreptitious glass of Scotch from a bottle I had bought on the plane. We need not have bothered to hide, however; groups of men sat in dark corners, emptying bottles of Indian whisky as if it were mineral water. Sitting on the ground, we ate fiery subzi and oily puris. I was not hungry. Yadav, who had already progressed from Scotch to Royal Challenge, asked me ten times whether I liked the food and was enjoying myself.

'About as much as you liked English food, which you never even tried, and about as much as you liked English parties, which you never stayed at for more than one hour.' I was ashamed of my bad temper, but why should I pretend to be enjoying myself when I wasn't?

'We want Rama will come to party. I am going to fetch him.' Yadav got unsteadily to his feet.

'Please don't go. You'll get into a fight again.'

'Then you will come with me. We will go in car.' I persuaded him to walk the quarter kilometre across the ploughed furrows to Rama's new hut, and went with him.

Anu and Vini sat on a charpoy, using their fingers to eat tidily from a shared bowl. Their mother was raking the yard. At the sight of the family who had once been such friends but who had refused to speak to us for the last two years, my overstretched nerves snapped. I burst into tears. I kissed Nirmula, hugged the children and begged Rama to come back with us. He refused. We walked back across the ploughed furrows alone.

'I think musicians will play very soon. Is getting late. We will go to our bed.' Yadav ordered the dozen or so men who were relaxing on our charpoys out of the room. I found my nightdress and sleeping bag and undressed quickly. The video was still blasting away. 'You want to clean your teeth?'

I did not want to walk through the sea of men packed together outside the door. There was a knock. Shiv, a Dalit builder, joined his hands in greeting. He was the most understanding and sympathetic of Yadav's friends. Our next visitor was Boss Brother, whose looks were eloquent enough to explain his sentiments. He ordered his friends back into the room. Yadav started to argue.

'Please, Yadav. I don't mind. Let them come.'

'No. You will not share room,' he said, and began shouting at his brother again. 'Chalo,' he said suddenly. I picked up my sleeping bag and, keeping my eyes on the ground, walked beside him in my nightdress through the crowd of men and musicians to a small, windowless storeroom. All I wanted was peace and some small space for myself. I laid out my sleeping bag. Yadav lay down and immediately began to snore.

The musicians had positioned themselves outside the storeroom. Their heavy rhythm thumped in tune to my bursting bladder, which felt like an overfilled set of bagpipes. I crossed my legs and arms and tried to think about something else. Yadav, reawakened, left the room in search of another Royal Challenge. I lay in an agony of discomfort, unable to make myself walk across the yard to the mustard fields through that crowd of singing, dancing men. Yadav came back, followed by Ashok and Raja Ram. The boys stood in front of me, pulling their ears and looking sheepish.

'Very sorry, Mum, very sorry,' Ashok said.

'Aunt. I too am truly sorry. Now my father-in-law he has drunk whole bottle of whisky.' Both boys started weeping. Yadav staggered and collapsed on to the other charpoy. Boss Brother looked in. Seeing Raja Ram he tugged at his sleeve, trying to pull him out of the room. Yadav slid off the charpoy and lunged at his brother's legs. A hard punch from Boss Brother sent him reeling back on to the plaited strings.

'Don't! Please don't start a fight.' Terror drove my physical needs from my mind.

My brother-in-law swivelled, leaning towards me across the charpoy. His eyes burned into mine. He spat out his words, spraying my face with cold spittle. For the second time that night I burst into tears. The boys looked on, helpless to interfere with their elders.

'Mum, please...' They leant their heads on my shoulder for a moment before turning to follow Boss Brother out of the room.

'Come on, yaar. All village they ask we enjoy party with them. Come on.' Yadav tried to pull me off the charpoy. Unable to move me, he lost interest and left the room again, shutting the door carefully behind him.

The party broke up at dawn. By the time we crossed the yard to our room all the guests had gone, taking with them our camera and my watch.

How could I stay? I wanted to get up and walk away, to be lonely and to prove to the world that I could be alone, as I had proved after the bankruptcy and the end of my first marriage. Boss Brother's face had shown how much a member of the family I really was. But where could I go? Town? Delhi? London? My need to pee overcame my other worries.

Yadav came back. 'Coffee?' he asked. 'Shall we change charpoy? This is wider one. Yaar, you must eat. I haven't seen you have your dinner.'

'We ate together. Don't you remember? Now please shut up.' But he was already asleep, snoring, grinding his teeth and having conversations in his own unique mixture of Hindi and English. I lay utterly alone in the darkness. Something white caught my eye, and I sat up. It was a large, empty, plastic jar. The relief was overwhelming.

20

I did not leave. I was still thinking of it, but when it came to packing my things and saying goodbye, I could not make myself.

By some quirk of fate, Yadav and I had found our mirror images. Husband and wife, lover and loved, father and mother, brother and sister, son and daughter, friend and foe – we were interchangeable components of the same machine. As such, we loved and hated, enjoyed and despaired, laughed and cried, parted and, like mercury, fused again in a single streak of quick silver.

For a long time after that party, I did not look at or speak to my brother-in-law; but Yadav convinced me that the venom had been meant for him, not for me, and time softens memory. Now Boss Brother and I speak and smile as often as we ever did. Communication between us has always been limited anyway.

Yadav's drinking habits seemed to be at the root of all of our problems. He used to drink so little, and never before evening, but things had changed. A drop on his tongue now relieved him of his senses and sent him reeling. I hated, with a white-hot hatred, the quarter bottles of Royal Challenge that had taken my place as the love of his life. Sometimes, imagining that I could turn it all into a cosy social event, I suggested we have a drink together, but more often the little bottles were hidden, cunningly concealed and swallowed in solitude.

We went back to Delhi and began looking for a flat. Yadav sat in the telephone office opposite our high-rise hotel, making a hundred calls to landowners. Six were possibilities. 'I will go myself, yaar. If I see good one, we will go together.'

A young estate agent showed him the perfect flat. 'I do not know, but I thinks you will like too much,' said Yadav. The house was in a quiet, tree-lined road in south Delhi, behind its own gates and courtyard. Up a flight of stairs, the flat had three rooms, a kitchen and two bathrooms with geysers. A terrace ran along the front, and the telephone was already installed. It was spotlessly clean, as if the friendly owners who lived next door had painted it just for us. There was not a stick of furniture. We took the flat, bought two mattresses, and moved in. The fridge, the cooker and the furniture – teak bedsteads, a dining table and chairs made for us in Munirka market – came later. The carpets are dhurries; the chairs and sofa, cane. Buying cushions, curtains and pictures was a time-consuming pleasure. Our sixteen pots full of flowers stand like sentries guarding the terrace. In one corner is a forest of what would be indoor plants in England, but grow quickly into giant outdoor trees in India.

Wanting, wanting, wanting. We had everything we had wanted: the court case was over, Yadav had been found not guilty, and we had a flat in Delhi, a car with a taxi licence plate and customers for our travel agency.

But we still had one problem: the quarter bottles of Royal Challenge. Seven years and our marriage were slipping away into the amorphous black oblivion of past time.

We went to see Dr Prakash. I asked him if he had heard of Alcoholics Anonymous and whether he thought it would help. 'Yes, we do have AA in Delhi,' he said, and he reeled off a list of days, times and addresses for the meetings. 'And Yadav' – his steady eyes met Yadav's – 'you will go to one meeting every day, and at the end of two weeks you will come and tell me that you have.'

'Yes, Dr Sahib. I will, Dr Sahib.'

'And you, Jill – go with him.'

We followed his advice, and for the moment the quarter bottles have disappeared from our lives. But, as Yadav says, no one can tell about the future. We can only hope.

Ma hobbled over to her estate behind the well – a guava and a lemon tree, a pomegranate tree with pink flowers, a banana tree with no bananas and three papaya trees standing sentry-straight in a patch of overgrown cabbages that Hari Ram had planted and forgotten to pick.

That day, on top of the petticoats she often carried on her head for fear of thieves, Ma was overloaded with swatches of blouse material that her relations had given her when she had visited her maternal village for a nephew's marriage. She took a swipe at a papaya with her stick. It landed with a soft thud, and lay like one of the overworked breasts hidden inside her blouse – an elongated oval on the brown earth. Ma stooped with difficulty, clawing at the fruit till she held it, then clutched it tightly against her body. Balancing everything – petticoats, swatches and papaya – she advanced slowly to where we stood by the car, waiting to leave.

'Ma, Ram Ram.' I bent to touch her feet.

'Ah, meri beti,' she said, pushing the papaya at me. It was my mother-in-law's parting gift, a present from her land, her domain. Tears pricked my eyes like needles.

In the car, I sat back in my seat. My driver, my love, was at the wheel, risking our lives at every turn and traffic light. It didn't matter; he was not the real driver, and I was not the guide. We were passengers on a universal train to an unknown city in the state of Eternity. We did not know the length of our journey, and it didn't matter. Fate and time, our fellow travellers, were in the next compartment.

'Yadav!'

'What is wrong, yaar?'

'I've forgotten something important, my Daniel Galvin vegetable hair colour.'

'Well, I've forgotten the tawa. I shall not be able to cook my chapatis.' His expression became that of a naughty child, his I'm-the-youngest-brother-and-I-can-do-what-I-like look. 'But I haven't forgotten this.' He held up a quarter bottle of Royal Challenge, and the smile fell from my face.

'Don't worry, yaar, it is bottle you fill with cold tea.' He smiled. I remembered the night I had found the bottle under the dhurrie in the spare room. I had emptied the contents down the loo and refilled it with Darjeeling tea made from a tea bag.

'I'm sorry,' I said, apologising for my suspicion.

'Koi bat nahin. I have more.' He smiled again, a secret smile. I didn't know whether to believe him or not.

He looked down at the papaya on my lap. 'Is not ready, yaar. Please throw away. We doesn't need it.' He stopped the car, took the papaya, got out and threw it with all his strength towards the giant red blob of ketchup-coloured sun. Swallowed up by dripping golden rays, the sun fell, lost in the pink and silver light of the dying day. Camels turned black against the fading fields. Farm lights twinkled. Sailing on a darkening sea, the white moon turned primrose, deep daffodil and finally sunflower as it swam, sure and serene, across its indigo sky.

'But Ma gave it to me. It was special,' I protested.

'No, yaar. Kuchha papaya, it is not special. Is rubbish. Now please, I am feeling to kiss you.' He leant across and kissed my cheek.

I did not argue with him about the fruit, as I might once have done. He was right; the unripe papaya was rubbish. But Ma's thought was not. It stayed, a universal thought, a particle of a particle that made up uncountable worlds far beyond our small lives and our human understanding.

Epilogue

In the beginning of this story, I tried to explain the enduring effects that my first husband's bankruptcy and the disintegration of my marriage had on me and my family. They took away forever my sense of security, leaving me unsure of – yet unsurprised by – whatever each day, or indeed each moment, could bring. Any feelings of 'divine right' that I might once of had, of belonging to the stratum of society into which I had been born, were wiped out. I was stripped of most, though of course not all, of the prejudices and inhibitions that had been instilled in me from birth. I was left with a pair of hands, a somewhat warped mind and five distraught children to provide for. To defend myself against my new self, I encased my feelings in an almost impregnable suit of armour.

But there were chinks. I retained a certain amount of pride in helping myself, and a belief in my friends. With their help and the support of the convent we were able, albeit with wobbly legs, to stand on our own feet again. I longed for peace of mind and freedom from worry. Twenty years later, through Yadav and India, I somehow found both.

After the break-up of my world as I had known it, I suppose I could have learnt to live a mediocre life, seeking government grants, social welfare, state education for my children and a council flat on the wrong side of the Thames. Perhaps that would have been better than the struggle for existence that I imposed on all six of us. But my pride stood in the way. Mediocrity has never appealed to me, nor, I believe, to my family, who in the face of adversity all became high achievers. Black and white were the only colours in my book – Fortnum & Mason or fish and chips, Chelsea or a crofter's cottage, oysters or winkles and welks, grand opera or slapstick comedy. I could not bring myself to become part of the grey middle slice of life. If I could not be rich and famous, I would be poor and eccentric.

It would be difficult to find a greater contrast to the London life I had lost than the life I eventually adopted, that of a peasant farmer's wife deep in the north Indian mustard fields.

You might call my life on the farm escapism. I am sure that, in part, it is an escape – an escape from the ever-present need to explain myself, my situation and my lack of enough time or wherewithal for normal emotions and the niceties of life. But most of all, it is an escape from loneliness, the aching loneliness of unshared problems, the loneliness of unsatisfactory relationships, the loneliness of not quite belonging anywhere.

Yadav's family accept me without question as an integral part of their lives. When I am at the farm, what is theirs is mine, and what is mine is theirs – both physically and emotionally, together with all the advantages, frustrations and misunderstandings that go with such generosity. I thank and honour them for this.

Yadav? He has faults. Don't we all?

Our marriage? It's not perfect. Whose is?

And the whisky? In a strange way, Yadav's drinking has cemented us together more securely. For each night that I have gone to sleep thinking alcohol has made it our last, I have awakened the next morning stronger in the certainty that, together, we will somehow conquer our most unconquerable problem.

Born and brought up in a certain world, it is impossible for me not to react critically at times to Yadav's behaviour, both towards me and in public. I often have to step back and remind myself that he is only behaving as an Indian farmer behaves. He is fond of telling me that Yadavs are 'rough and tough'. It is hard to imagine how difficult it must be for him to deal with a British wife and British ideals and judgements. He is a proud man – proud of his country, proud of his caste and proud of his family. In order to retain his self-assurance in the face of upper-class Indian and Western society, he sometimes acts more like a 'village Indian' than he really is. But he tries. 'Did I behave very well?' he asks anxiously upon leaving a dinner party or other social occasion utterly foreign to his previous experience.

I have chosen to live with Yadav because I love him and, most of the time, our life together in India. I ask myself only one question: 'What would I have in life if I did not have Yadav?'

The answer is: 'Nothing that I want.'

Together we have almost everything.

Afterword

Yadav was published in India in January 2003 to great critical and commercial acclaim.

Indian reviewers, who for very good reason are not taken with over-romanticised accounts of their country by wide-eyed foreigners, greatly admired Jill's honesty, her 'cool objectivity', her humour and her ability to convey her extraordinary passion both for Yadav and India – without the slightest sentimentality or gush. *The Times of India* called it 'a very real story, very realistically written', while *Today* admired the way that, without ever being in the least bit corny, it succeeded in 'emphasising the insurmountable power of love'. *India Today* agreed: 'Lowe is not a professional writer, but her sparse style gives this very personal journey of discovery a life and poignancy of its own.' Manjula Padmanabhan, the reviewer in Kipling's old paper *The Pioneer* was equally moved:

'Ultimately the book is about the man for whom it is named: Yadav. While the rest of the world around him – his own fellow Indians – dismiss him as a "mere taxi driver", as if that were a caste of people whose function is to be invisible, Jill, the foreigner, the outsider, looks at him and sees a warm, loving and lovable man. Like the best kind of documentary film, it opens doors inside the walls of our own minds and hearts, showing us what we could all find if only we bothered to look.'

Aided by amazingly wide and enthusiastic press coverage across the Indian media, *Yadav* quickly shot up the Indian bestseller lists, and Jill and Yadav suddenly found themselves unlikely celebrities on the Delhi literary circuit.

No one was more surprised about all this than Jill. Her book had not had an easy birth. Indeed it had one of the longest and most painful gestations imaginable: there were over ten years and many hundreds of drafts and rejections and rewrites – the despair of several literary agents – before the manuscript was finally accepted by Penguin India. Only a woman of Jill's astonishing persistence and passion would have seen her project through to a happy conclusion, just as with her affair with Yadav.

I first met Jill, and read an early draft of her story, in the spring of 1995. Jill had come down to Sheepwash in Devon to a writing course I was giving in an old and remote farmhouse tucked away in a valley in the wilds of Exmoor. All the other students were about half her age – young backpackers fresh from some adventure in Central Asia or the Sahara – and almost all of them had a far better grasp of how to get their stories into print than Jill.

Jill had come down to Sheepwash armed with a box full of old notebooks and some huge, badly typed bundles of manuscripts covered with Tippex correction fluid and yellow Post-it notes, and herring-boned with frantic crossings out. The drafts she showed me then were more or less unpublishable, as she was all too aware; but it was immediately clear that she had an amazing story, as well as the iron will-power and determination necessary to see the project through. I helped her as best I could, and over the following years we exchanged postcards and emails as the drafts followed each other. Her mood oscillated from excitement to depression and excitement again as successive literary agents took her up only to drop her again.

The breakthrough came in early 2002 when Penguin finally accepted the book. Jill's manuscript was given to Christine Cipriani – an American living in Delhi, who, like Jill, had fallen in love with India – and together, over a period of months, Christine and Jill thrashed out the book you are holding. When I read the final proof Christine sent me I could hardly believe it: Jill's writing had taken wing, and all the faults of the early drafts had simply dropped away. In several sections I found it difficult to read the book without tears coming to my eyes: she had succeeded completely in pinning to the page the strange tale of her difficult and passionate love affair. Her refusal to over-romanticise her story, or to gloss over the difficulties of her life – such as Yadav's fondness for his whisky – gave the book a rare veracity and integrity. It was funny, frank, candid and frequently very moving. No wonder it quickly became a bestseller.

I saw quite a bit of Jill and Yadav in Delhi around the time the book was published in the January of 2003, and was able to congratulate Jill on her success. She was a little bemused by her sudden celebrity, but was clearly enormously enjoying it. Only Yadav looked a little disappointed, remarking how he had hoped, after all the effort Jill had put into the book, that they might be able to earn enough to buy some land, but in the event the royalties had so far not proved enough 'even to buy a Qualis' – an SUV. But whatever their financial difficulties or disappointments, they visibly were as happy together as a pair of teenagers on their first date.

I then headed back to England and did not see either of them for a year. When we met again, it was by chance. One foggy winter evening we bumped into each other near the Qu'tb Minar, in the company of two American tourists whom she and Yadav were showing around. They were all smiles – and it seemed only as an afterthought that she pulled me aside just as we parting to whisper that she had been diagnosed with cancer.

Jill seemed so totally unconcerned by her illness that I presumed it was some particularly unthreatening form of the disease. In fact it was the very opposite: an especially malignant strain that had attacked both her bones and her lungs, and which was now in an advanced state. Shortly afterwards I saw her and Yadav at the Haryana farm of her best friends, Annie and Martin Howard. Again, Jill brushed off all attempts to commiserate with her, saying how incredibly lucky she was to have met Yadav and to have seen her book in print, and that she had no complaints. It was only as I was leaving that I discovered that the following day she was due to begin a massive course of emergency chemotherapy.

The treatment did not go well. The cancer was already too far advanced and had been diagnosed too late. By early April 2004, Jill had lost all her hair, was in severe pain and having to make daily trips to the Apollo hospital for further treatment. This was especially painful, and the fluid had to be fed into her neck through a 'port' that the hospital had attached there. Worse still, her body reacted strongly against the treatment and she suffered a whole litany of unintended side-effects and infections. On top of all this, Jill was also having to support Yadav, who had lost his first wife to cancer and was now in despair about the increasing likelihood of losing his second the same way. The trips to the English Wine Shop near their flat became more frequent.

In these circumstances, most people would have buckled, but Jill remained almost superhumanly cheerful. Every day after leaving hospital she would cover up her baldness with a red headscarf and continue taking her tourists around Delhi, all of whom remained blissfully unaware of what she was going through. But by the end of the month it was clear that the treatment was too little too late, and Jill took the decision to simply stop it. She had had enough, she said, and she was going to let fate take its own course.

Admirable as this decision was from a philosophical point of view, it meant that the cancer now quickly raced through her, and soon the pain became utterly insupportable. In May, Jill's son Nick came out to Delhi to see how she was getting on. He was horrified by what he saw and immediately took the decision to bring her back to the London Clinic in order to keep the pain, if not the cancer, under control.

Jill's final three months were spent in London; first at the Clinic, then at a nursing home in Clapham, and finally at the Trinity Hospice. Month by month, she got progressively weaker, and in July suffered badly from a severe infection in her leg; but she continued to receive an amazing stream of visitors, and to remain as stoically uncomplaining as she had ever been, right up until the final days. Despair and self-pity were both utterly foreign to her.

The end, when it came, was mercifully quick. Yadav was there, as was Nick and Jill's four daughters. In her last days a proof of this, the first English edition of her book, arrived at her bedside and she spent her final hours reading through it and admiring the cover. She died, on 21 August 2004, cradled in Yadav's arms.

Jill asked that her ashes be split in two: one half were scattered in England, while Yadav took the other half to the Ganges, where he immersed them in the great Indian river. He gave up the Delhi flat and the taxi business, and has now retreated to his old life with the buffaloes and the mustard crop in his Haryana village. He lives there now, still utterly devastated from his loss; but surrounded by his people, his children and his grandchildren.

Jill's was the strangest of strange journeys, a story not of the clash but of the clasp of civilisations: a baronet's granddaughter who had been presented at court, ending her days in an Indian village as the devoted and loving wife of a penniless Haryanavi peasant farmer. But Jill knew that she was lucky; that for all that she was going without, she had found in Yadav the man she really loved. She knew instinctively what she had found when she first met Yadav, and defying class, caste, race, religion and geography she had no hesitation in giving up everything she had to be with him. She knew how much he loved her, and she never let him forget how intensely she reciprocated that love. As she wrote, with typically moving simplicity at the end of her book:

'I ask myself only one question: "What would I have in life if I did not have Yadav?" The answer is: "Nothing that I want." Together we have almost everything.'

William Dalrymple